SAMUEL EDWARD DOLE SHORTT was born in London, Ontario, in 1947 and educated at McGill, Carleton, and Queen's universities, and the University of Western Ontario. He holds a doctorate in history and has been a sessional lecturer at Queen's and a visiting assistant professor at McGill. His current academic interest is medicine.

Within the context of the debate between idealism and empiricism, this book studies the ideas of six representative Canadian intellectuals of the late Victorian era. These six were chosen primarily because of their ideas on contemporary social questions – views which may cast disconcerting light on certain aspects of present-day Canadian society. All were academics, and shared a common recognition of social issues and a similar self-image, yet they were hardly a homogeneous group: they were individuals who expressed their own unique attitudes rather than a collective viewpoint.

Sir Andrew Macphail, professor of the history of medicine at McGill, was fascinated by the social implications of evolutionary naturalism. For Archibald MacMechan, professor of English at Dalhousie, British authors of the nineteenth century provided a romantic idealism that accurately defined man's place in the universe. Another professor of English, James Cappon of Queen's, built much of his thought, whether on imperialism or on literature, around a concept of culture similar to that of Matthew Arnold. Plato tempered with Christianity appeared to be a reliable philosophical guide to Maurice Hutton, professor of classics at the University of Toronto. Political economist Adam Shortt of Queen's University found much to admire in the ideas of John Stuart Mill; his counterpart at Toronto, James Mavor, borrowed many of his attitudes from British and French positivism.

Each man is the subject of a chapter consisting of three parts: a biographical section, a consideration of the essential core of his belief – his view of man, God, and the universe – and an examination of how his background and philosophy found expression in his ideas about culture and society. No attempt is made to document the influence of the ideas of these academics for, as they themselves asserted, they were essentially moralists, not men of action.

S.E.D. SHORTT

The Search for an Ideal:
Six Canadian intellectuals
and their convictions
in an age of transition
1890-1930

UNIVERSITY OF TORONTO PRESS
TORONTO AND BUFFALO

© University of Toronto Press 1976
Toronto and Buffalo
Printed in Canada

Library of Congress Cataloging in Publication Data

Shortt, Samuel Edward Dole, 1947 —
  Six Canadian intellectuals and their convictions in an age of transition,
  1890-1930.

  Bibliography: p.
  Includes index.
  1. Canada – Intellectual life. 2. Intellectuals – Canada. I. Title.
  F1021.S47   971.05   76-26507
  ISBN 0-8020-5350-5
  ISBN 0-8020-6285-7 pbk.

Contents

Preface

This book is the product of many concurrent influences, not the least of which is the relatively underdeveloped state of Canadian intellectual history. A notable exception is Carl Berger's *The Sense of Power,* which, together with Richard Hofstader's *The Age of Reform,* Walter Houghton's *The Victorian Frame of Mind,* and Robert Wiebe's *The Search for Order,* convinced me of the availability of the sources and methods necessary for a foray into uncharted historiographic regions. This conviction grew as isolated aspects of the Canadian intellectual heritage were revealed by several excellent teachers, notable Michael Oliver, S.F. Wise, and George Rawlyk. Such has been the genesis of my interest in intellectual history; the result is the present volume.

The research for this book was expedited by thoughtful assistance from Mr Ian Wilson of the Queen's University Archives, Dr Charles Armour of the Dalhousie University Archives, and Miss Sandra Guillaume, formerly of the McGill University Archives. The staff of the Public Archives of Canada and of the University of Toronto Archives extended similar efficient service.

I am particularly indebted to a number of individuals who shared with me their memories of the figures with whom this study is concerned. Mrs Dorothy Lindsay generously allowed me to examine the personal papers of her father, Sir Andrew Macphail, in the comfort of her Montreal home. Mrs Edith Dobson and Mrs Jean Willets provided a hospitable introduction to the Halifax of Archibald MacMechan, their father, and contributed valuable insights into his character. Mrs Muriel Clarke, a daughter of Adam Shortt, has at various times, through books and conversations, added to my appreciation of her father. Maurice Hutton's daughter, the late Mrs Joyce Wrong, graciously answered a number of written queries. Finally, my appreciation must also extend to the late Frank Underhill, who discussed with me James Mavor and Maurice Hutton, and to A.R.M. Lower for sharing his reminiscences of Adam Shortt in Ottawa.

During the organization and writing of this study I have, as well, imposed upon many persons. The manuscript was originally prepared as a doctoral dissertation at Queen's University under the patient and discerning eye of Professor W.R. Graham. Subsequent drafts have been read by Professor G.A. Rawlyk of Queen's University, Professor Ramsay Cook of York University, and Professor Carl Berger of the University of Toronto. In addition, both family and friends have provided encouragement and advice for which I am grateful.

Funds for research were obtained under a Canada Council Doctoral Award, while publication was made possible with the help of a grant from the Humanities Research Council of Canada, using funds provided by the Canada Council, and a grant to the University of Toronto Press from the Andrew W. Mellon Foundation. The editorial staff of the University of Toronto Press, particularly M. Jean Houston and Jean Wilson, have made publication an efficient and orderly process.

It is my hope that the scholars, archivists, and others who have contributed to this study will not be disappointed by errors or inaccuracies which, despite their efforts, remain in the text. Rather, my objective will be achieved if they and other readers feel this study sheds new light on some darker areas of Canadian history.

S.E.D. SHORTT

Abbreviations

THE SEARCH FOR AN IDEAL

1

Introduction:
'A Search for an Ideal'

In 1904, Arnold Haultain, for many years secretary to Goldwin Smith and an author in his own right, published a short article in the *Canadian Magazine*. Despite its brevity, his essay was a perceptive exposition of the intellectual quandry which faced an articulate Victorian at the turn of the century. He wrote:

The nineteenth century seems to have brought us to the edge of a precipice, and to have left us there gazing wistfully into outer space. That rather smug era led us to believe that we stood on *terra firma* whence ... we might bridge any chasm that presented. It was a scientific century, and − so it seems to us now − rather a myopic one ... given a collection of atoms and a law of evolution: and it constructed you a cosmos ... But things have changed ... [This is] an age that finds no anchorage in materialism, yet is afraid to drift; an age that feels that the nineteenth century solution of the world problem was inadequate, yet that ... is too far removed from the solutions offered by the eighteenth century to derive much comfort from them; an age which sees that it must find a solution for itself, but has no data for the task, and as yet can do little more than stand shivering timorously at the brink.[1]

Many Victorians joined Haultain on this awesome intellectual precipice and, staring into the abyss of what they considered social and moral chaos, recoiled in terror. The result was a frantic search for an ideal, a new world view which would explain the nature of man and his place in the universe.

Haultain's vision of intellectual turmoil cannot easily be dismissed. As Goldwin Smith's companion for two decades he occupied an unusually excellent position from which to assess the temper of the English-speaking world. Smith was well acquainted with most of the thinkers of his day in Britain − John

Stuart Mill, Matthew Arnold, John Morley — and continued until his death in 1910 to correspond with many other English intellectuals, among them E.A. Freeman, Benjamin Jowett, and Frederic Harrison.[2] In the erudite atmosphere of the Grange, Haultain, musing on the cultural turbulence in Britain, must have known that he was hardly alone in considering his time 'an age of transition.' Throughout the nineteenth century Englishmen had searched for 'a spiritual absolute,' attempting to replace the confident reason of the proceding century with a patchwork of philosophies as antithetical as Benthamite utilitarianism and Carlylean transcendentalism. Matthew Arnold expressed this attitude in his *Culture and Anarchy* when he demanded adherence to fixed 'standards of perfection that are real,' while John Stuart Mill looked forward to a time when 'right' opinions would be 'unanimously adopted.' Yet this characteristic will to believe was itself shadowed by deeper feelings of insecurity and fear. The 'seeds of radical doubt' were planted by 1870; a dozen years later even the eminent Victorian John Ruskin was forced to admit that a great 'storm cloud' blotted out the old 'harmony' of English culture.[3] Darwinian sociology, higher criticism, and literary decadence were but a few of the new modes of thought which challenged the often mechanical and usually Christian assumptions of the age.[4] For a time 'old and new ideas dwelt uneasily together' but the great storm of 1914 savagely swept away the last traces of Victorianism from a startled England. [5]

Haultain might have turned, as did Goldwin Smith, to the United States for intellectual solace. Certainly, Smith had many notable American friends. He was close to Charles Eliot Norton of Harvard and E.L. Godkin of *The Nation* and numbered among his more casual acquaintances Ralph Waldo Emerson, George Bancroft, and James Russell Lowell.[6] Yet it is unlikely that these academics and writers could have given much reassurance to Haultain: for the United States, as for Britain, it was a time of questioning. In 1890 an American intellectual credo existed which affirmed that eternal moral principles were known, that history was a chronicle of progress, however gradual, and that an inquiring mind might discern absolute standards of culture. By 1912 this complex of beliefs was shattered under the combined impact of the aestheticism of writers such as Oscar Wilde or Friedrich Nietzsche, literary naturalism, and the mystical vitalism of Henri Bergson.[7] A formalist approach to social theory was replaced, in the works of John Dewey, Oliver Wendell Holmes, and Thorstein Veblen, by an attempt to view society as an evolving organism quite unsuited to traditional static descriptions.[8] In this period of shifting values many older intellectuals such as Brooks and Henry Adams found themselves beset by a profound sense of personal alienation. It was their conviction that a cataclysmic 'holocaust would result from rejecting tradition.' Indeed, from their unpleasant isolation, it seemed that a world divorced from its past was a world not worth preserving.[9]

From his own observations and, vicariously, through Smith's contacts and correspondents, Haultain was forced to conclude that the foundations of nineteenth-century British and American thought were rapidly disintegrating. At the same time, however, he found himself in a comparatively obscure colonial city which, for all its pretensions, may well have remained untouched by the intellectual turmoil sweeping the outside world. Is it possible that at the weekly dinners of Smith's Round Table Club, men such as James Mavor, Maurice Hutton, John S. Willison, and Haultain himself sat secure in the knowledge that little changed in their provincial environment? This, certainly, is the conclusion Canadian historians seem to have reached. Preoccupied with the 'age of affluence'[10] or with 'fulminating against imperialism or continentalism,'[11] Canadian intellectuals, it is held, were 'a rather conservative and unchallenging lot.'[12] Yet fragmentary observations by literary scholars[13] and recent perceptive research[14] suggests that such judgements are not entirely fair. Perhaps Canadian intellectuals did, in fact, join their British and American counterparts in, as Haultain phrased it, the 'search for an ideal.'

Most intellectuals in late Victorian Canada were to be found in the rather inconspicuous academic community. While diminutive, however, the universities verged on a period of rapid expansion. In 1887 Queen's University had an enrolment of 419 and the University of Toronto claimed 891 students; by 1900 these figures would double and do so again, as at McGill, by 1910. Part of this increase was explained by the presence of women students, who were admitted to the University of Toronto in 1884. A much larger portion of the growth was related to the acquisition of new faculties such as education, commerce, and engineering, which often had previously existed as independent institutions.[15] The number of teaching staff grew as well, though less rapidly than the student body.[16] Yearly, principals Gordon of Queen's, Falconer of Toronto, and Peterson of McGill undertook recruiting trips to Britain searching for an ideal type: a Scottish university graduate suitably finished at Oxford.[17] Whatever its academic merit, there was a disingenuous pragmatism behind this policy: British scholars would generally accept lower salaries than Americans and were apparently dismissed with greater ease.[18] Except at the professional level, academic salaries remained largely static from 1890 to 1910 though general wage and price levels rose almost twenty per cent.[19] Perhaps the only economic benefit gained by faculty in this period was the introduction of the Carnegie Foundation pension scheme. After 1909 professors at the University of Toronto were able to retire at 65 with a moderate annual subsidy. However, until Queen's severed its formal ties with the Presbyterian Church her staff received no aid and Principal Peterson of McGill tended to view the Carnegie Foundation with vague suspicion.[20] Underpaid, often overworked, and few in number, Canadian academics might well have questioned their significance in the evolving university at the turn of the century.

Intellectuals were not only concerned with their status in the universities; as well, they were forced to consider their function in a rapidly changing society. Stephen Leacock's satirical comment on the popular image of the professor – his 'angular overcoat, his missing buttons, and his faded hat' revealing a mind 'defective and damaged by education' – was a description bitterly familiar to many academics. The 'professor more than the ordinary person,' Leacock continued, 'finds himself shut out ... the strenuous men of activity and success have felt an instinctive scorn of the academic class, which they have been at no pains to conceal.'[21] In many respects, this sense of exclusion was a reflection of the academics' own behaviour. As they recoiled from 'commercialism' or petty 'maple-leaf politics,' they tended to place themselves, in practical terms, outside Canadian society. Rather than actively participating in politics, they preferred to confine themselves to critical observations in academic journals or membership in quasi-clandestine organizations, a tradition beginning with the Canada Firsters, carried on by the Round Table Groups, and culminating in the League for Social Reconstruction.[22] A few intellectuals were willing to enter the public service, while others existed on the periphery of 'respectable' reform causes, but in general their type remained aloof. It was thus no accident that Goldwin Smith referred to himself as the 'Bystander' or that B.K. Sandwell, for many years editor of *Saturday Night,* said of society: 'I follow it at a respectable distance ... far enough away to make it clear that I do not belong to it.'[23] Yet this sense of personal alienation on the part of the intellectuals was, ironically, precisely that attitude which allowed them to make a contribution to society. As essentially disinterested observers, the intellectuals took the opportunity to criticize and advise on any issue of cultural or political significance. It was this important attitude which explained the self-fulfilment evident behind Andrew Macphail's assertion: 'A bystander sees most of the game; it is only a bystander who can direct a game or win a battle.'[24] The image, then, of the turn-of-the-century academics painted by Leacock may explain why history has ignored them, but the suggestive remark by Macphail certainly indicates that these intellectuals merit serious investigation.

Of greater significance to the academic community than these changes in social and economic status, however, was a controversy which appeared at first as a debate on the essential nature of education. During the late nineteenth century the assumption behind academic activity was that 'by knowledge was meant more than intellectual truth; it included an intuitive appreciation of spiritual ideals.'[25] From this epistemological assertion it followed that the professor was essentially a moral tutor while the student attended university to develop 'character' rather than accumulate facts. This vision of higher education was closely related to the standard subjects of instruction: philosophy, literature, and the classics. But, as Principal Falconer later recalled, by the end of the century this curriculum had changed: 'Steadily the supremacy of the traditional classical studies was challenged not only by the modern languages, but even more by history [and] the political and social sciences...' Academics trained in the older tradition objected that the newer disciplines represented an attack on 'classical humanities' by 'modern scientific ideals and methods.'[26] Their opponents not only defended the new subjects with their empirical focus, but began, as well, to attack what they referred to as 'the older theological line of education.'[27] The traditionalists, in fact, fought a losing battle, as the appearance of departments of political studies at Toronto and Queen's in 1889 suggested. Professors in this new discipline often acted as ad hoc government advisers, producing lengthy reports and, in the process, frequently attracting considerable public attention. By 1912 the interest in political economy was sufficiently strong to permit the formation of the Canadian Political Science Association. Though it lapsed during the war, the organization's appearance signified that the invasion of the universities by the social scientists had achieved marked success. The larger controversy, however, was hardly settled. The difference in intellectual orientation between the humanities and the social sciences soon extended far beyond the university: in a broader sense, it was a fundamental theme in Canadian thought from 1880 to 1920.

This conflict, in fact, reflected the two basic reactions by Canadian intellectuals to 'the age of transition.' The first, the idealist response, held as its central postulate the belief that the world was a part of a larger spiritual reality of which man could become aware only through intuitive perception. Though the original source of this type of thought was German, it was viewed through the very British filter of Carlyle, Ruskin, and, especially, Edward Caird. Its adherents tended to view political democracy with suspicion, industrialism with distaste, and the new education with outright revulsion. In marked contrast stood a second world view, empiricism, which drew heavily on the work of British utilitarians and Continental positivists. It was premised on the belief that metaphysical speculation was of little value in dealing with the material world; the only secure foundation for knowledge and, consequently, social policy, was the empirical observation of reality. Its exponents seldom issued sweeping judgements on social problems and still less frequently wrote of religion or aesthetics. They preferred to consider the technical aspects of specific problems with a view to isolating practical and efficient solutions. In many respects their thought focused on methodology and, as a result, lacked a metaphysical core. Armed with a faith in the empirical approach to social problems, they represented the emergence of the modern social scientist in Canadian academic circles.

Set within the context of this debate between idealism and empiricism, the present study is comprised of six biographical essays. The choice of biographical rather than thematic organization assumes that this method imposes a less artificial structure on the thought of the men considered by permitting each individual to speak for himself on those matters which he considered most vital. In this fashion, differences become distinct while any consensus which emerges is of special significance. Further, this approach concentrates not on what these men thought about a particular issue but, simply, on what they thought about and, more particularly, on how they conceived of the thinking process itself. The purpose of such methodology is to examine what may be termed 'conviction,' a loose amalgam of ideas and emotion, perhaps confused and contradictory, which formed the core of personal belief structures.[28] In this regard it is important to caution against judging late nineteenth-century academics by present standards of, for example, social awareness or culture tolerance. Seen from a later perspective, many of their debates may initially appear naïve or superficial. But this is not, surely, reason for ignoring or deriding their ideas; rather, it suggests a failure on the part of the historian to understand properly the context in which these earnest Victorians formulated their fundamental assumptions. The thought of the pioneer academics deserves to be considered seriously and, whenever possible, within their own terms of reference.[29] In so doing, not only will the nineteenth-century intellectuals receive an equitable hearing, but as well, their views may cast a disconcerting light on certain aspects of contemporary Canadian society.

In choosing individuals for study the problem is less one of selection than of exclusion. Henry Marshall Tory and Nathanial Dupuis, as prominent representatives of science, surely deserve a voice. John Watson was clearly the foremost philosopher in Canada for half a century and pre-eminent among his generation of academics. Administrators such as Sir Robert Falconer or Daniel Gordon certainly played central roles in the shaping of Canadian universities, as did scholars such as George Wrong or Pelham Edgar. There are, unfortunately, few if any guideposts in the existing literature to suggest which individuals are of greatest significance to Canadian cultural history. It may well be argued that it is precisely those figures previously ignored who most deserve close consideration. Influence upon contemporaries is a poor criterion for selection as it is both difficult to document and not always a reliable guide to the quality of an individual's thought. Choice must take into account, as well, the accessibility of personal papers and the number of published works available. Further, it is desirable to include representatives from a variety of disciplines with varied intellectual interests. Finally, by studying too few or too many individuals the study may lose, respectively, its applicability or its precision. Ultimately, then, the selection process becomes highly arbitrary. The individuals included in this study were chosen primarily because the ideas which they articulated on contemporary social questions, when stripped to their essence, were considered to be of inherent interest.

The following articulate Victorians are the major characters of subsequent chapters. Andrew Macphail, a professor of the history of medicine at McGill, was fascinated by the social implications of evolutionary naturalism. For Archibald MacMechan, professor of English at Dalhousie, British authors of the nineteenth century provided a romantic idealism which accurately defined man's place in the universe. James Cappon of Queen's, also a professor of English, built much of his thought, whether on imperialism or literature, around a concept of culture similar to that advanced by Matthew Arnold. To Maurice Hutton, professor of classics at the University of Toronto, Plato tempered with Christianity appeared a reliable philosophical guide. A political economist at Queen's, Adam Shortt, found much to admire in the ideas of John Stuart Mill. His counterpart at Toronto, James Mavor, borrowed many of his attitudes from British and French positivism. While hardly forming a homogeneous group, these individuals were all thoughtful commentators on the temper of their age.

Though their intellectual interests differed widely, these men did share three important characteristics. First, they experienced, both as students and later as teachers, a similar academic environment. All attended university in Canada or Great Britain during the late 1870s and frequently studied under the same professors. Three of them, for example, had studied philosophy at Glasgow University while the remaining three studied the subjects with disciples of the Glasgow viewpoint. In marked contrast, only one individual had any contact with an American university. Occasional references to Emerson, Josiah Royce, or Mark Twain sprinkle the writing of these Canadian academics, but the American influence was at best peripheral. Similarly, European thinkers such as Weber, Durkheim, or Marx were ignored in preference to mid-nineteenth-century British authors. Most of them started their Canadian teaching careers by the beginning of the age of intellectual transition, 1890, and were acutely aware of changes in social thought which challenged the values they had absorbed over the preceding thirty years. Indeed, their similar response to what contemporaries referred to as 'the Social Crisis' constitutes the second shared characteristic. A constant flow of articles, books, and speeches, none devoted to scholarly interests but rather to topics such as imperialism, feminism, education, or religion, suggests that the academics tended to isolate similar issues as crucial to their time. Finally, these activities were a reflection of a common conception of the academic's role in Canadian society. As university teachers they believed that they influenced the intellectual and moral development of the nation's future leaders, while as impartial commentators on national affairs they felt it their duty to offer advice to populace and politicians alike. Such pursuits continued until the early twenties, at which time social concerns gave way to scholarly research or slightly melancholy reminiscences. Sharing, then, the university environment, a common recognition of social issues, and a similar self-image, these individuals nevertheless expressed their own unique attitudes rather than a collective viewpoint.

Each of the following chapters, excluding the conclusion, is divided into three sections. The first is biographical, dealing with the formative influences in the subject's life and the details of his subsequent career. Space and balance set certain limits to the amount of information presented about each person. It might be of interest, for example, to know more details concerning James Mavor and the Doukhobor migrations or James Cappon and the severing of church ties at Queen's. But such considerations belong properly to full biographies; in the present context they would add little to an understanding of the man's convictions. The second section of each chapter considers the essential core of the individual's beliefs – his view of man, God, and the universe. By concentrating on emotions as well as ideas and recognizing that none of the men considered was a systematic philosopher (except, perhaps, Andrew Macphail), the problem of tracing in detail the intellectual antecedents of each man's thought is in part circumvented. Influences do, of course, receive considerable emphasis, but minor connections are avoided. Finally, the third section attempts to illustrate how the subject's background and philosophy found expression in his ideas about culture and society. No attempt is made to document the 'influence' of these ideas on Canadian society for, as the intellectuals themselves asserted, they were essentially moralists rather than 'men of action.' It is impossible to follow accurately the flow of their ideas for none of them held beliefs sufficiently distinct to be traced by their originality nor did acquaintances often recall falling under their intellectual sway. But the question of influence becomes irrelevant if one accepts the view that the deepest convictions of any individual have an inherent interest. This assumption is often considered the distinguishing feature of 'internal' intellectual history.[30] Yet by the study of such beliefs we come, as well, to a larger appreciation of that individual's time in history. In effect, what becomes of interest is not influence but congruence, that is, the degree to which a man seems to accord with his society and its values.

By considering the ideas of half a dozen intellectuals a suggestion is made that late Victorian Canada was beset by a profound debate between idealism and empiricism. It must be stressed, however, that the present work does not purport to describe all of the inhabitants of academic Canada,[31] let alone all Canadians.

But if Canadian historiography is to include the history of ideas, beginnings must be made in relatively limited areas. To borrow a final passage from Arnold Haultain:

Were no investigations to be undertaken, no theories formed, save for some definite and preconceived purpose, it may be that no new path would be found, no more distant goal discerned.[32]

ANDREW MACPHAIL
Proceedings and Transactions of the Royal Society of Canada 1938
Photo courtesy Royal Society of Canada

2

ANDREW MACPHAIL

The Ideal in Nature

The Victorian mind, despite its enthusiasm for the intricacies of a Dickens plot or the excesses of neo-Gothic architecture, held an innate predilection for the straightforward and familiar. Increased size or technical complexity gave rise to instant suspicion, for as complexity mounted correspondence with the natural declined. Certainly, many examples of unprecedented magnitude and startling innovation were marshalled to support the optimistic rhetoric of progress. But as each step forward represented a further departure from nature, and, by implication, God's design, certain sensitive Victorians paused to doubt the wisdom of continuing in that perilous direction.[1] Many Canadian intellectuals of the late nineteenth century found themselves, by temperament or training, among the pessimists, and none more so than Andrew Macphail. For half a century, using not only the conventional essay but classical sonnets and plays as well, Macphail issued to Canadian society stormy jeremiads on topics ranging from medicine to higher criticism. Throughout his work, and indeed, in the writing of many of his contemporaries, runs the firm conviction that man and society succeed only as they conform to the dictates of nature.

I

John Andrew Macphail was born on the family farm at Orwell, Prince Edward Island, in 1864. His Scottish ancestors arrived in America in the early nineteenth century when his paternal grandfather, a schoolmaster, had been shipwrecked on the Island, rescuing only his Bible and a copy of Homer. William Macphail, his father, had also been a teacher and later both an inspector of schools and superintendent of the hospital for the insane in Charlottetown. He was a Tory in politics, an ardent student of the Bible, and a devoted temperance man. Macphail described 'the master' as a perfect 'Christian gentleman,' and recalled with an appreciation born of maturity the discipline with which the family of ten children was 'kept under strict control.' Yet his real affection was reserved for his mother. Never emotional, she possessed an 'intense human sympathy' and a practical, inquiring mind. To her children 'the master's wife' taught two enduring lessons. She imparted 'a healthy scepticism,' an attitude of intellectual curiosity which refused to accept any belief without comprehending its value. Of more immediate significance was her view of education. In Macphail's words his mother impressed upon him that 'the school was the open door of escape for those who would enter it.'

Macphail learned the benefits of education at an early age, but not before he had become inextricably a part of his Orwell environment. The farm was 'a world in miniature' where he experienced the rigours of manual toil and absorbed the virtue of thrift ever present in the Gaelic household. His early religious training made an equally permanent impression. At the local Church of Scotland 'a discipline was developed comparable in miniature with the practice of the European Church in the time of Gregory.' The Shorter Catechism was recited in unison at home and his father rigidly enforced observance of the Sabbath. Beside religion and the work of the farm, education came as a welcome relief. At home Macphail devoured works by Macaulay, Dean Ramsay, Swift, and Shakespeare. Formal education followed, but of a type soon destined to vanish. The schoolmasters never taught: they 'felt that their whole business was done when they kept order, so that those who desired to learn were left free in silence,' while the dullards simply left. Macphail was one of those who remained and by 1880 won an entrance scholarship to Prince of Wales College. His Orwell days were formally concluded. But in the values and attitudes he absorbed he remained forever rooted in that time and place.[2]

Macphail spent two years at the small college of ninety-one students and three teachers. Under a rigid system of discipline students were expected to master classics, English, French, and mathematics, and to participate in 'infantry foot-drill' supervised by a veteran of the Indian Mutiny.[3] Completing this rigorous training, Macphail left to become a schoolmaster and the following two years were spent at the Fanning Grammar School in Malpeque where his father had taught before him. Feeling both underpaid and somewhat bored, Macphail conscientiously saved from his annual salary of $380 the funds necessary to continue his education. In 1885, having decided to become a physician rather than a minister, he entered McGill University, receiving a Bachelor of Arts in 1888 and a medical degree in 1891. It was a fortunate vocational choice for Macphail. He always considered medicine 'less a science than an art,' essentially an exercise in helping nature to heal the sick. As such, the emphasis on specialization and elaborate scientific preparation was largely superfluous: a sound knowledge of basic anatomy was the only learning required. But medicine did demand other attributes from its practitioners. Integrity, intelligence, and a desire to serve humanity were those listed by Macphail.[4]

During the years at McGill, Macphail confirmed his love of books. 'It was the library that destroyed me,' he recalled, 'Mathew Arnold, Ruskin, Walter Pater, Walter Bagehot, Renan, and Saint Beuve must bear chief blame.' Voluminous reading and a steady trickle of writing consigned him to 'the large middle average' in his university courses. But if his grades were unimpressive, Macphail's forays into journalism seemed more than adequate compensation. As a reporter for the Montreal *Gazette* he wrote many reviews and occasional articles on European politics or local events. By 1890 he was the accredited Chicago *Times* correspondent for Montreal[5] and earned from his various writings close to five times his previous salary as a teacher. By his graduating year at McGill he had accumulated savings of $1200 which, when combined with a reporting contract from an American newspaper syndicate, financed a trip around the world. Late in 1891 he arrived in London, England, where he resumed his medical studies.[6] In 1892, as a member of the Royal College of Surgeons and a licentiate of the Royal College of Physicians, Andrew Macphail returned to Canada.

For the following fifteen years Macphail led a relatively conventional and private life with little indication that he would later become what one friend described as 'the most eminent Canadian literary figure of his generation.'[7] A large man with a dominant red beard and a high, furrowed brow, topped by scanty hair, Macphail's countenance wore a perpetual expression of gloom. But behind the dour cast of his lengthy, tight-lipped mouth, sprawling nose, and penetrating eyes lay a personality marked by an enquiring intellect and dry Scottish humour. If he appeared opinionated, it was because he hated shallow pretension and, at the same time, possessed an unruly aptitude for the forceful epigram. His home in Montreal, where he lived with his wife and two children, 'had a distinctly Victorian atmosphere,' and was considered by his friends a place of excellent hospitality and stimulating conversation. An equally warm and congenial spirit was found at the Pen and Pencil Club, a small literary group to which Macphail, Stephen Leacock, John McCrae, and several other Montreal authors and artists had belonged since the 1890s. Dividing the majority of his time between extensive reading and his duties as a practising physician, consulting pathologist, and professor at Bishop's College Medical School, Macphail found time to edit the *Montreal Medical Journal* and was later instrumental in the founding and editing of the *Canadian Medical Association Journal.* But the fifteen years after 1892, marred by the untimely loss of his wife in 1902, were essentially a prelude to Macphail's subsequent rise to literary prominence.[8]

The decisive year was 1907. It was then that Macphail received his appointment to the professorship of medical history at McGill University, a chair he held until 1937. The position not only allowed him to continue in his chosen profession, but also permitted him to pursue as part of his academic duties the type of reading he had begun in Orwell and become obsessed with at university.

Related to the McGill appointment but of greater significance for Macphail's public career was the second major event of the year: his installation as editor of the newly formed *University Magazine,* under the direction of an editorial board representing the three universities by which it was sponsored, Toronto, Dalhousie, and McGill. In reality, the publication was the creation and personification of one man – Andrew Macphail.

The magazine appeared in 1907, proclaiming itself a forum for the discussion of 'questions immediately concerning Canada' as well as 'politics, industry, philosophy, science and art.' It was founded largely at Macphail's urging to replace the pallid *McGill University Magazine,* a journal analogous to the alumnae publications at Queen's and Toronto.[9] Originally McGill and Toronto agreed to provide one thousand subscriptions each, though Toronto paid a cash subsidy instead, a harbinger of fortune circulation difficulties.[10] Attracting contributors to the journal proved a less difficult problem, for Macphail initiated a policy of payment for acceptable articles. The topics dealt with ranged widely from patent law to city playgrounds and from militarism to the decay of spoken English. The types of contributor were equally diverse. The most prolific author was Macphail himself, and while most of the writing was done by other academics, especially those from Montreal,[11] pieces by men like Rudyard Kipling, Arthur Balfour, J.S. Woodsworth, or Sir George Foster found their way into the pages of the journal.

Macphail considered the appearance of the magazine an extremely important undertaking for it was his contention, and indeed, the firm belief of his academic associates, that Canadian society suffered from a dearth of intellectual leadership. Civilization, the editor once stated, owed its advance to the very professors it disparaged.[12] Academics 'merely stand and watch' but 'it is only a bystander who can direct a game or win a battle.'[13] With this premise in mind he appealed to his colleagues to 'descend from the pedestals which they have erected,'[14] while to the historian, George Wrong, he wrote: 'in the interests of the country ... detached persons like ourselves [must] endeavour to set forth principles for [politicians] ... to follow.'[15] While Macphail attempted on an individual basis to influence such political figures as Sir Wilfrid Laurier and Sir Robert Borden,[16] it was the *University Magazine* that provided the major source of influence for the editor and his academic friends.

Macphail's conception of his own role in the management of the journal was disarmingly simple. 'An editor,' he wrote, 'is merely a man who knows his right hand from his left, good from evil, having the honesty of a kitchen cook who will not spoil his confection by favour for a friend. Fear of a foe is not a temptation, since editors are too harmless to have any.'[17] He attempted to follow this humble philosophy of editorship[18] but the results, largely because of his forceful personality, were far from temperate. Despite the existence of a formal editorial board, in Stephen Leacock's words, 'After a meeting or two the magazine became and remained Andrew Macphail.'[19]

With his authority secure, the editor began to direct the views of the magazine on issues he considered important. He used his power of selection as a means to articulate his own views and, when necessary, refuted the opinions of others.[20] Of equal importance in his role as editor was the fashion in which Macphail often utilized his own essays to set the tone of an issue or clarify the journal's viewpoint. Most numbers contained at least one of his pieces and usually two. The force of his style was the natural corollary to his strongly held opinions. As one critic wrote: 'His prose glittered like the bayonets of an army on the march.'[21] The power of his argument lay less in inexorable logic or even in his extensive knowledge of history and contemporary affairs, than in his facility for the terse phrase.[22] Stephen Leacock caught the essence of this stylistic trait when he wrote that Macphail 'loved an epigram ... You couldn't tell whether Andrew really meant it, or just said it.' It was precisely that element of startled disbelief which remained with the reader that explained Macphail's success as an essayist.[23] When he combined this devastating power of his own articles with the freedom to select and edit other contributions, he was in an ideal position to mould the *University Magazine* in his own image.

For a dozen years the magazine provided a forum for Canadian intellectuals to express their views. But from the beginning there were problems beneath the surface which even a dynamic editor could not solve. The root of the dilemma lay in the journal's poor circulation figures. When Macphail remarked, 'The largest distributing agency in Canada ... takes eight copies of the *University Magazine* and sells them all,' the humour was tinged with bitterness. A high point in subscriptions was reached in 1912 with 5300. The following year the number dropped to 3300, and in 1918 there remained only 1400 subscribers.[24] With a decline in sales came a decrease of revenue. As early as 1909 Macphail contributed $1000 of his own money and McGill donated an additional $1500. By 1913 another $2000 of Macphail's money disappeared into the magazine but this time there appeared to be an explanation for its loss. The publisher who controlled the journal's distribution had simply 'taken what he felt proper for his services,' rather than the standard commission of 15 per cent. Indecisive legal proceedings followed, and despite decreased circulation during the war years, the journal operated with a favourable balance. Yet the old debt owing to Macphail remained. The University of Toronto refused to join McGill in liquidating the debt and attempts to raise an estimated $15,000 to recapitalize the quarterly were futile.[25] It was evident that the magazine was nearing the end by 1918. There were also, of course, non-financial reasons for the demise. Macphail had spent the war with the Medical Corps in Europe, leaving Principal Peterson and

Stephen Leacock in charge. Although their management increased revenues, it lacked the finesses of Macphail's editorship.[26] The lack of interest and participation by the University of Toronto was a constant handicap, especially when printing costs and technical details demanded increased attention.[27] Perhaps most significant was Macphail's claim that ill health forced him to allow the magazine to die.[28] Though he felt, in the turbulent years after the Great War, that the 'magazine was never needed more' the intransigence of Toronto and lack of funds were enough to discourage him.[29] More optimistic friends envisaged a revitalized journal under the editorship of Bernard Sandwell or Pelham Edgar,[30] but in Macphail's opinion the *Dalhousie Review* was the legitimate heir to the *University Magazine.*[31]

While its demise was regrettable, the journal had nevertheless served a purpose. For over a dozen years it provided an outlet for Canadian academic opinion and literary aspiration. Only the *Queen's Quarterly* offered a similar service to Canadians before 1920. The quality of articles was generally impressive and at least one literary career – that of Marjorie Pickthall – was launched by the magazine and its editor.[32] Macphail himself was proud of the publication, at times feeling it to be 'the equivalent of any Magazine which is published in the Empire.' Governor-General Lord Grey, though more moderate, echoed Macphail's tone when he wrote that the journal was 'the best periodical published in Canada.'[33] What other readers thought of the magazine, and indeed, who these readers were, is difficult to establish. On occasion, copies were distributed to every member of the Canadian Parliament, while Lord Grey personally sent issues to the Colonial Office, the Admiralty, the Prince of Wales, the King, and the *London Times.*[34] It seems that the journal's following included an assortment of readers as diverse in character and position as E.A. Partridge, the Canadian prairie radical, and John Strathey, editor of *The Spectator* in Great Britain.[35]

A further indication that the magazine was considered important by at least a small body of readers was the type of controversy it raised. Macphail found it necessary to disclaim in the journal's pages any anti-American sentiment and in private was severely chastised by the Montreal Local Council of Women for his unsympathetic article 'On Certain Aspects of Feminism.' To these sources of criticism he added several others in a letter to Archibald MacMechan. 'I am born to trouble,' Macphail wrote and listed his additional critics as Liberals, Conservatives, assorted professors, and the daily press.[36] A final indication that the views of the magazine reached a wider readership than subscription statistics suggest is the publicity it received in other publications. From Charlottetown, Montreal, Toronto, Boston, and London, England, came newspaper reviews of the more controversial articles.[37] It would appear, then, that the significance of the *University Magazine* lay in two factors. First, it provided a publication for Canadian intellectuals to express their opinions and literary talents. Secondly, it was read and appreciated by a small but diverse and influential group of academics and politicians in both Canada and Great Britain. The 1920s, despite the appearance of the *Dalhousie Review* and the *Canadian Forum,* seemed somehow less exciting without the trenchant voice of the familiar quarterly.

The demise of the journal represented the end to the most active stage in Andrew Macphail's career. He had once described himself as 'a journalist' and such he remained. But there were notable changes.[38] The old force and candour of his style continued, but the polemical element was often replaced by mature reflection or the reverie of an aging Victorian. His volume of publication actually increased after 1920, including four books as well as numerous essays and short plays.[39] Recognition, too, came his way. In 1918, as acknowledgement for his wartime service, he had been knighted and shortly after was awarded an honourary degree by his alma mater. The Quebec government prize for literature was presented to Macphail in 1928 and two years later he received the Lorne Pierce Medal of the Royal Society of Canada. But the pace of his public life, with the exception of a trip to Russia in 1935, gradually dwindled. In 1937 Macphail retired from his position on the Faculty of Medicine at McGill and, appropriately, spent most of his remaining days at Orwell.[40]

In these last twenty years of his life Macphail never felt at ease with the changes which followed the Great War. In 1926 he wrote to Archibald Mac-Mechan: 'the world does seem different.' In fact, as early as 1917 he commented that the 'complexity of this life gives me a sense of being lost' and suggested that tears for fallen soldiers were better reserved 'for ourselves and our children.' Viewing the society around him, he concluded 'that a great epoch has, as usual, ended in disaster'; no aspect of society remained intact.[41] The universities had become technical and Americanized, and as a result, the 'business of being a professor has fallen sadly.' In literature, Archibald MacMechan was 'the only one left who can write.' The old imperial vision was dying; it was only a matter of time until Macphail expected 'to hear the pillars and fabric of Empire come crashing into the abysm of chaos.' Democracy had proven itself devoid of political wisdom, while in economic thought he regretted that there was 'not a free-trader now left living in the world, not even in England.' With his values obsolete and his society rapidly changing, it is small wonder that Macphail concluded: 'The social fabric is falling. The old are left in gloomy isolation.'[42] Indeed, when Andrew Macphail died in Montreal in 1938 he left behind a very different world from the one he had entered at Orwell in 1864. But he had the ultimate satisfaction for a man of his temperament in knowing that he, at least, had remained immutable.

During his early years in Prince Edward Island, Macphail began to develop a profound respect for the type of society found there, a respect which grew with age. It was a closed community based on self-sufficient, agricultural families and governed by the religious precepts of the Church of Scotland and those legal and cultural conventions associated with the British heritage. These values were confirmed in Macphail's mind in subsequent years by his reading of such authors as Carlyle, Ruskin, and Walter Bagehot. Reverence for tradition and the moral dimension of life was coupled with hostility to the excesses of democracy and technological innovation. At the base of this system of thought lay the concept of nature: it was a manifestation of the divine, an obedience to which ensured not only temporal success but was, in fact, equated with morality. The social thought which Macphail built on this foundation was easily branded by the superficial observer as that of a simple Luddite or rustic physiocrat.[43] Indeed, because his philosophy refused to consider what was commonly labelled 'progress' as a forward movement, it was opposed to many of the changes which accompanied the twentieth century. To that degree, his thought remained attuned to the middle part of the preceding century, and was anachronistic. Yet it was deliberately so, for Macphail's philosophy was anything but unsophisticated. It was a synthesis of evolution and Christianity, augmented with prejudices from his personal experience, and adorned with varying doses of German Romanticism, late nineteenth-century British idealism, and American transcendentalism. Eclectic, at times abstruse, and always personal, the result was, nevertheless, a complete system of metaphysics.

Macphail's philosophy was born of 'the principal debate of the nineteenth century,' the confrontation between science and religion. 'Those alone who passed through the period,' he wrote, 'can understand the havoc wrought in the minds of men. The fabric of their dearest beliefs appeared to be dissolving....' By 1905, however, Macphail was convinced that both science and theology had been relegated to their separate and proper places, and men had realized 'that the conflict between them was merely a figment of the theological imagination.' The force behind this illumination was the writing of Hegel and the German idealists. The scientific concept of evolution had been in the process of devolving into a materialistic atheism. But the idealists rescued it with a belief in the operation of 'an external power by the unalterable method of natural law alone.' It was now possible for man to reconcile traditional Christian notions of God and morality with the idea of evolution.[44] By imputing a rational order to nature, the conflict between the Christian concept of design and Darwin's disturbing idea of random variation was removed. The gradual process of evolution could now be seen as the act of creation. Further, when the motivating force for evolution was considered divine, the process of natural selection was no longer equated with brutish struggles, but rather, represented the survival of the morally fit. Science tempered with religion became a system of ethics.

Macphail recognized that neither time nor space was absolute. Quoting Julian Huxley, the only material truth he affirmed was the existence in all created matter of a physical-spiritual substance which he referred to as 'world-stuff.' This was an important premise, for it meant that all matter and organisms were governed by the same 'external purpose.' This conviction, in turn, was the essence of Macphail's philosophy. As he phrased it:

Life is the final expression of the universal Will. That is the inner meaning of evolution ... Giraffes and men who tried to live without conformity to, or in transgression of, that Will have come to a bad end. ... By this universal formula of the emergence of the universal Will, every problem in biology is solved – the problem of good and evil, of ease and pain, of right and wrong, of sin and poverty, of necessity and freedom, of riches and poverty, of life and death.

In this synthesis of idealism and evolution, Macphail found the belief which pervaded his thought for half a century.[45]

The obvious difficulty suggested by a faith in the 'universal Will' was epistemological: how did an individual come to perceive the existence of the guiding spirit? Macphail's answer was simple and unequivocal: the methods of reason and science could never be applied to metaphysical problems. Recalling Kant, he asserted that all human belief and conduct 'has its roots in the emotions' and only then is 'moulded by the reason.' The intellect can deal only with 'the immobile and the dead,' as Henri Bergson suggested, while the instincts are equipped 'to comprehend life which is continuously mobile.'[46] For Macphail this process of discerning natural law was more than the mere acquisition of knowledge; it was the groundwork of all ethics. In this assumption he joined the modern anti-rationalist tradition dating from the English Puritan Revolution and buttressed by the New England revival of philosopher-theologian Jonathan Edwards, two movements with which he was thoroughly familiar.[47] 'The essence of religion,' he wrote, 'is the conscious adjustment of conduct to the divine will. The identification of that will with morality is the foundation of ethics.' By implication a rejection of the natural order was equated with immorality. This exact definition of morality was extremely important for a man who believed that 'all questions are moral questions' and that the ethical quality of an individual's mind could be inferred from his actions. In fact, taken together, these ideas provided the standard by which Macphail judged the worth of both men and societies. 'It is the mind that forces species on their upward evolutionary way,' he wrote, 'The superiority of man over the beast, and over the rudimentary beast that lies in each one ... is measured by the extent to which the mind is made to control the body compelling it to scorn delights and live laborious days.' In other words, the success of a species or individual depended upon the degree to which the mind, intuitively accepting the dictates of nature, controlled the actions. This, in turn, was simple morality.[48]

Macphail's mind, though inherently mystical and eclectic, was also tidy. He could with coherence weave together elements of Puritan theology and Kant's critique of reason, combine Emerson's 'Over-Soul' with Hegel's *Welt Geist,* and mix Ruskin's ideas on morality with Carlyle's interpretation of German idealism. Yet the resulting synthesis of faith and evolution, though personal, was not original. Many British intellectuals such as Thomas Arnold had, in the halcyon days before Darwin, equated natural law with Divine will. Evolutionary naturalism temporarily discredited nature in late nineteenth-century religious circles, but it was not long before men like William Henry Drummond in England or Henry Ward Beecher and Lyman Abbot in the United States incorporated the principles of evolution into their traditional faiths.[49] Andrew Macphail had, as a result, considerable precedent on which to base his Christian theism.

Though his views on God and nature were consistent from his earliest works, it appears that only in the 1920s did he attempt a synthetic statement of his metaphysics. His 'History of the Idea of Evolution,' which appeared in the *Dalhousie Review* in 1925, had begun as an address to the McGill Biological Society earlier that year. Four years later, an altered version was published as 'Evolution and Life' in the *Annals of Medical History.* Finally, in 1934, the Montreal *Herald* printed a synopsis of the argument under the heading, 'I Believe, This is My Credo, My Philosophy of Life.'[50] If his ideas remained, then, in unsystematic form until later life, it is nevertheless apparent that Macphail's belief in a natural moral ordering of the universe was the underlying hypothesis on which even his earliest writings were constructed. Society, politics, industry, and art fell under his seer-like scrutiny and, when found wanting, were judged accordingly.

III

The link between Andrew Macphail's metaphysics and his social thought lay in his conception of man, for as he stated, 'the unit of all organized society is the man himself.' He rejected the austere Calvinist view of human depravity, asserting instead that 'there is a moral principle in human nature, a desire to do right.' Yet some men were evil, dispelling the myth that all men were created equal. What made the difference was less environment or education than heredity, both racial and familial.[51] The good man was defined by his adherence to the natural conventions on which society was based and by his realization that the affairs of the world are 'so complicated that it is little influenced by what men can do.'

The great man was he who helped society evolve upward 'away from the beast' to which it was always in danger of regressing.[52] The average human found himself possessed of three basic drives: the need to propagate, the desire for food, and an innate, emotional propensity towards religion. The latter urge Macphail considered the key to man's ultimate purpose. The 'chief end of man' was to seek the kingdom of heaven, a sense of unity with the divine, through the improvement of his character. This purpose meant that man was 'merely a part of a whole which lies outside the region of knowledge' and that, as such, he could best achieve his end by an intuitive perception of the universal will.[53] The individual's 'state of inner discipline,' Macphail wrote,

arose from a systematic obedience to the laws imposed by nature, against which it was useless to contend by force. But the powers of nature could be subdued and directed to human needs by a continuous effort of the mind and will ... By obedience to these inevitable laws he acquired a morality; by developing the feeling of submission and dependence ... he acquired the rudiments of religion. Then he could profitably go to school and learn from the recorded experience of those who were wiser and older than himself.

With a scriptural reference, Macphail summarized his response to the question of man's purpose: 'The best answer I know of is that which was given by a Hebrew writer: that a man should rejoice in his labour and do good in his time.'[54]

At first glance, Macphail's view of man was deterministic, focusing on the importance of racial and familial heredity in the ability to accommodate to the order of the universe. There were, he felt, 'breeds of men' which 'have their own affinities and their own repulsions.' The highest rank on the evolutionary scale was 'whiteness,' best exemplified by the British, a mixture of Saxons, Celts, and several other superior northern European strains. The particular genius of the English was their reverence for order, truth, and precedent. They slowly evolved, as Bagehot suggested 'upon the experience of uncounted yesterdays,' an insight into the natural principles of law. Within the race 'a considerable number of families of pure blood' carried an hereditary superiority, for as Macphail asserted, 'belief arises from nature or type of character.' It was these families who ruled England.[55]

Yet this racial and hereditary determinism was qualified. In the first place, a 'species, when true to itself, however humble is admirable.' Therefore it was possible for the poor to live 'a life of virtue ... in the slums as easily as on the castellated heights.' In so doing, the common man reached an accord with nature to the best of his limited capacity. It was society's duty to help him reach this moral state by providing certain institutions to instruct him in basic ethics.

Secondly, it was equally possible for a person of lowly birth to rise by sheer force of character and intellect to a higher position on the scale of being. Again it was society's responsibility to provide the facilities for both the discovery and fostering of this capacity. Macphail's social thought, then, was not rigidly deterministic. Education, work, and religion existed as a testing ground for natural ability and as sources of ethical instruction for the less adept.[56]

The 'best system of education is worse than no system at all,' wrote Macphail, 'Education, like religion, is an inner experience,' an exercise in conforming to the universal order. In his view it was not designed to transform pupils into uniform, mediocre repositories of knowledge, but rather existed to develop 'character' and a 'philosophy of life.' Such objectives could never be 'taught'; they could only be learned by each student. A teacher, consequently, was primarily a disciplinary agent, an office which could never be filled by a woman and which could not function properly in the 'promiscuous' atmosphere of co-educational classes.[57] Clearly the source of Macphail's ideas on education was his own experience in Orwell. In the austere classroom pupils were confronted with the simple choice of learning or leaving. 'The law of natural selection would have free play, and from this sure ground, the boy would proceed according to his bent of mind ... to the task for which by nature he was designed.' For 'most persons education must come mainly from work done with the hands.' But such training was not at all morally inferior to more intellectual pursuits. All 'education is one': its value lies not in the subject matter but in the discipline of the process by which it is acquired. This procedure developed the character and capacities allotted by nature, however limited, and supplied the means by which society distributed the lower positions in its natural hierarchy.[58]

A privileged minority of students, however, discovered a natural facility for learning. For them, the only proper form of education was classical. It taught not only self-discipline, but also discouraged attempts to view education as something primarily utilitarian. Eventually, an awareness of the continuity of history, a fondness for literature, and a tolerance for other civilizations seeped into the student's mind. Such had always been the basis of English education, with the result that English schoolboys 'acquired a tincture of learning, a sense of fairness and of duty, a contempt for low conduct. They feared God, honoured the King, and loved their country. They had character.' The best among them rose 'and became leaders of men.' Based on the simple premise of natural selection, this was Macphail's thoery of education. He felt it 'is as near the town dweller may come to that which many a country boy has received to perfection ... brought up by ... godly parents with the assistance of a good schoolmaster armed with a short stick.' Whether one became an artisan or scholar in later life, the system would impart to him 'love of country, harden the habits into morality and develop the feelings of submission and dependence into good manners and religion.' Education, attuned to the natural order of the world, was essential to the formation of 'character' and the emergence in society of an élite based on aptitude.[59]

If education began the task of sorting individuals into their natural occupations and instilling certain values, work continued the process in later life. 'Work,' wrote Macphail, 'in itself is neither good nor bad.' What made it beneficial was the degree to which it corresponded to one's natural abilities, placing the individual in harmony with the universal order. From such a congruence many admirable characteristics would develop: initiative, self-reliance, thrift, stability, and, if the 'struggle' was difficult, an element of the 'heroic.' The individual, nevertheless, was wise to guard against the enervating temptations of ease; pride in his appointed calling was the only defence.[60]

This self-respect was essential in reconciling one to society, for 'it is foreordained from all eternity that the world shall be forever composed of classes of men rising one upon the other from the ploughman ... to professors.' On this basis Macphail echoed Carlyle in his assertion that equality was a 'fiction' and that a 'nation can not endure without an aristocracy of some kind.' Reflecting his own success, he asserted that certain 'noble natures,' to whom 'manual labour is servitude,' naturally rise to the top of the social hierarchy. To ensure the freedom of these superior individuals to develop, governments must 'maintain a state of affairs in which each person shall be as free as possible to manage his own affairs in his own way.' Attempts to change this natural order, whether by altering the material circumstances of the poor or mouthing the rhetoric of democratic equality, were futile.[61] Instead the individual must be taught that in doing his own work, at his own level, he adheres to nature's plan and thereby becomes a moral person. Macphail managed to capture the essence of his philosophy of work in a single paragraph'

A man who is a rail splitter or a tanner by nature will not split rails or tan hides well if to-morrow he expects to be called upon to preside over the councils of the nation. By this continual eruption of material from the lower strata our society is in a condition of surge and tumult and cannot clarify itself. We have been proclaiming that all men are free. If we were to declare that all men were slaves, we should solve our social problems and be stating the truth besides. If the labourer who digs in the street could but understand that the physician who drives by in his carriage, the rich man who strives to look unconscious in his motor-car, or the woman who passes by in all the pomp of the afternoon, are hedged about as strictly as himself, he would begin to do his work with content and end by doing it with joy. All work is the same. None is more menial than another.

In Macphail's conservative conception of society there were no 'classes,' but rather a hierarchy of individuals, called to their station as Calvin suggested and locked in 'organic unity.'[62] In this environment the individual, through diligence in his natural vocation, both improved himself and helped to create a stable, prosperous society.

In the end, neither education or work was as significant as religion in the process of acquainting the individual with his place in the universe and in imparting basic moral precepts. Much of Macphail's thought on religious topics was a product of his revolt, perhaps covertly encouraged by his mother, against the austerity and dogmatism of his early connection with the Church of Scotland. This rebellion was furthered by his familiarity with Scottish theological works, especially, it would appear, with the Hegelian-Christian synthesis of John and Edward Caird.[63]

According to Macphail, the attainment of perfection was man's basic end, and could only be accomplished by 'a union of the spirit of man with the spirit of God.' Contact with the divine had nothing to do with a man's social position or intellect, for the religious impetus lay in 'the human heart' rather than the brain. Theology, especially the 'New Theology,' by attempting intellectual explanations of God, contributed nothing to the real spirit of Christianity. The 'Social Gospel' was an equally misguided movement, for as the church moved into the world it departed from the spiritual realm. The true function of theology was to provide guidelines for 'those feeble and imperfectly developed natures, which constitute the bulk of humanity ... to lean upon.' Instead of becoming distracted by esoteric debates in higher criticism, it was the theologians' task to help men accommodate traditional beliefs to changing circumstances, that is, to prevent a cataclysmic disruption of faith. The precise content of religious dogma was irrelevant since all doctrine was merely a guess at the meaning of life, 'which at best has only some degree of probability in its favour.'[64] For any 'person born of white parentage' the conventional belief was Christianity.

But this doctrine ultimately paled before a more important function of the church, 'to provide an atmosphere where men can for a moment lose themselves in the Infinite.' The Roman Catholic church, with its music, ritual, and symbolism became 'a place of calm for the senses, a retreat from the world ... an incentive to worship.' Here man was not, as in most Protestant churches, asked to understand his doctrine, but was simply 'bidden to accept certain beliefs formulated by persons wiser than himself.' Free from the doubts which accompanied reason, and encouraged by his ethereal surroundings, his spirit found union with the divine. This holy nexus, according to Macphail, was beneficial in two respects. First, man gained insight, however small, into the meaning of the universe and his place in it. Secondly, religion provided both the ethical basis for individual conduct and a standard by which society as a whole could judge its members. Religion for Andrew Macphail, then, was the means by which his metaphysical system related to the individual and society. For that reason he was disturbed at the apparent decline of faith in the twentieth century and often wrote, with more hope than conviction, of an impending spiritual revival.[65]

Macphail considered the average man a well-meaning if somewhat simple being, governed largely by his heredity and striving for unity with the divine. One was helped to reach this accord with the natural order by education, work, and religious experience. But these experiences also helped the individual to live in society, which itself was essentially a group exercise in discerning the laws of nature. Civilization, a fragile human creation of Greek origin, had evolved 'by the slow labour ... of a few gifted men endowed with a desire for perfection ... for wisdom, and for general amenity of life.' The resulting structure was founded on conventions which in turn were 'based on the "law of kindness" ' between men. To destroy faith in these conventions, however peculiar or mythical, was a crime, for no superior system of regulated behaviour, based in abstract reason, could be devised. The result of each tampering would be 'disorder' which, wrote Macphail, 'in itself is bad.'[66] Yet circumstances change and conventions, to avoid social 'decay,' must adapt and evolve. Since those members of society 'who are well bred' best understand these matters, the hierarchical principle 'of God and the King is embedded in human society.' Such 'noble natures' are the natural leaders of society characterized by 'organic unity.' With the co-operation of the 'lower orders,' they direct society towards an accord with nature. Only in this fashion can the ultimate objective of 'security of life and property' be achieved.[67] For Macphail, then, society was governed by two natural principles: hierarchy and laissez-faire. On these concepts he founded his ideas about social structure, economic policy, and political organization.

According to Macphail, the family lay at the base of all advanced social structures. Though hardly an unusual view, this assumption was based primarily on his own experience together with what sociological studies he could find to support his position. His boyhood community in Prince Edward Island was small, rural, and compact. In 'the whole district of Orwell there were only a hundred families,' none of whom carried the stigma of poverty. His own family, like the Island itself, was 'a world in miniature.' Within its confines, one learned the value of thrift and received instruction in both religion and formal education. Equally important was the fact that 'the whole force of the family [was] directed towards a common end' such that 'children from the age of four were self-supporting.' Still later, while teaching at Malpeque, Macphail realized that the family was instrumental in reconciling the individual to his natural station in life. 'For the first time,' he wrote,

I learned, what I had always suspected, that humanity is not one, but a congeries of families each with a unity of tradition, a similarity of interest, an equality of education, an identity of thought, manners, and morals; a 'society' in which the upper members could of their own free will penetrate to the bottom; in which the lower members could only by sheer merit and incredible difficulty rise to the top.

It was this process of inculcating values and discerning the early capacities in the child which ultimately produced the nation's leaders. For Macphail this belief was substantiated by the example of Britain's most venerable families, who 'supplied the personnel of the army, the navy, the church and the diplomatic service.' The family, then, was simply nature's way of organizing society. As an institution it dated from the 'earliest tribal customs'; it was the government's duty to legislate for its continuance. Macphail concluded his thoughts on the family with the forceful assertion:

National life is merely the sum of family life. Wherefore, it is important to cherish our family life, to preserve intact, to strengthen those ties of affection which bind us together.[68]

The pivot upon which the family centred was the woman. In this belief Macphail again drew heavily on his own experience, as the record of his admiration for his mother in *The Master's Wife* suggests. Kind yet never excessively emotional, intelligent in a practical fashion, and religious without being dogmatic, she provided a paradigm for Macphail's view of the ideal woman.[69] He began with the assumption that nature had created men and women as distinct yet complementary beings. The woman agreed to accept the moral and intellectual values of the male, including the definition of a woman's role, while he, in turn, protected her and worshipped the image of virtue he had created. This virtue comprised a number of traits. Women were deeply conservative and religious, both characteristics of importance in ordering the household and raising children. Further, women were naturally gentle, refined, and modest. As such they completed man's rougher character. Their duty was, like the soldier's or the priest's, to 'live in subordination to their essential idea.' By reaching this accord with nature, these domestic pillars placed the family, and ultimately the entire social structure, in harmony with nature.[70]

Macphail's ideas on the nature of the family and the role of women corresponded with the reality of his mid-nineteenth-century childhood experience in Orwell. On such a basis, he wrote, 'we worked out a complete system of civilization.' But by 1912 something had happened. Macphail was forced to admit with disapproval, 'in my own lifetime I have seen all this pass away.' Women no longer understood their natural place. They demanded the franchise, despite the fact that they would simply vote as did their husbands. Failing to realize that a measure of poverty was a natural condition in all societies, they launched futile schemes for social amelioration. Finally, and perhaps most deplorable, women now left their homes to find jobs in offices and factories. Macphail was willing to accept to a degree the idea that as circumstances changed, the conventions determining certain facets of women's role must also evolve. For that reason he had no objections to women entering professions at which they excelled. But the idea of group rather than individual emancipation, extending to all aspects of social life, he found an anathema. Such agitation, he surmised, was the work of women bored by 'luxurious idleness alone' or a form of compensation on the part of 'the masculine type' who were 'deficient in their instinct for husband getting.' This senseless 'bawling in public places,' however, had a yet deeper meaning for Macphail: it reflected the disintegration of the family and, therefore, of society.[71] This conviction was the basis for his assertion that 'all the social evils which we suffer are due to the breaking down of the family.' It was his belief that the institution could not survive in the frenzied complexity of the city. Nor could it withstand the impact of industrialization, a process which dragged women from their natural function in the home.[72] Urban industrialization, then, was the disease which destroyed the family and gradually weakened that larger family, the nation. Despite his gloomy diagnosis, however, Dr Macphail was only too willing to prescribe a tonic.

The solution to the problems besetting modern society, and the nexus between Macphail's ideas on social structure and economics, was his concept of the agrarian life. In this physiocratic doctrine, he joined early nineteenth-century tradition, in the United States best represented by Thomas Jefferson and in England dating from the 'rural rides' of William Cobbett.[73] It was both a product of his own background and of the type of reading to which he was drawn. For example, while translating Louis Hémon's bucolic French-Canadian romance, *Maria Chapdelaine,* in 1921, Macphail referred to it as 'the book that has interested me most in all my life.'[74] The underlying premise for this idyllic conception of socio-economic organization was that an agrarian, laissez-faire society was closest to nature's order and, therefore, morally superior to industrial society. Macphail openly admitted that for him the doctrines of Adam Smith contained an 'inevitableness' that was irrefutable, though he later confided that the work of John Maynard Keynes 'instills doubt.' He never abandoned his conviction that a government failed to conduct business more efficiently than an individual, and, in fact, fostered corruption, uniform mediocrity, and bureaucracy. But he did, in defence of his agrarian bias, eventually reach a 'Red Tory' position similar to that of English thinkers such as Carlyle and Disraeli. The order and the organic unity inherent in the doctrines of democratic socialists such as Ramsay Macdonald appealed to Macphail. 'The Conservatives have always contended that they were socialists,' he wrote, 'but if they were going to fire a gun they would draw the trigger slowly.' Russia provided an excellent example, in 1935, of the salubrious results one could expect from socialism. While he never condoned the revolution, Macphail admired the inexpensive public transportation, the educational and housing facilities provided for workers, the lack of strikes and unemployment, and especially the emphasis on ability as the determinant of vocational status. But Macphail's agrarian, laissez-faire bias remained immutable nonetheless; he approved of specific Russian institutions but would have preferred them to be the result of a sensible free enterprise system. Indicative of this essential consistency was the one facet of Soviet society he criticized: the futile attempt to collectivize farming. If Macphail, then, appeared a Red Tory, it was only because he felt that state action was essential to preserve a traditional way of life.[75]

In 'the contact of his fields and the companionship of his animals,' with 'his labour in the woods, by sea and stream,' the farmer found what Macphail described as 'the way back to the normal of living.' Such a man, 'who lives on his own land and owes no man anything, develops all the dignity inherent in his nature.' He represented the 'one free man in the world,' in total harmony with the eternal rhythm of the universe. As such, it was natural that society should rest upon his shoulders. Indeed, it was the Saxon peasant 'who in the last resort always saved England.' As well, Britain possessed what Canada lacked, 'country houses ... inhabited by important families, represented as such in the councils of the nation.' What made these farmers and squires indispensable was their superior morality born of proximity to the soil. The farmer was completely self-reliant, making no selfish demands on the government. Healthy, educated within the family, and avoiding excessive mechanization, the country dweller's life was self-contained. For that reason, farmers tended to be conservative in politics and a safe ground on which to found the fragile system of democracy, so easily corrupted by the false egalitarianism of the city.[76] But farmers were, for Macphail, more than the basis of politics: they were the key to all economic systems and especially important to the Canadian economy. 'We in Canada are not traders,' he wrote, 'We are farmers; at least 62 percent of us live on or near the soil.' The rich natural heritage God gave to the nation forever placed Canadians in the role of primary producers. The imperial connection was simply a logical extension of this function. Canada would supply food and raw materials for the British Empire, and in the process, help England 'rejuvenate herself ... by contact with the land.' To turn 'our faces away from an agricultural and pastoral order' was for Macphail a disastrous revolt against nature. Consequently, 'if we are to have any meaning to our history,' he advised, we must realize that 'Our life in Canada will always be rural. Wherefore let us aspire after rural joys.' This could only be done properly, as Macphail spent most of his life reiterating, by a return to the land.[77]

There were, however, certain sinister forces militating against the rural destiny of Canada; their pernicious influence Macphail set himself to expose. First among the offenders was the city itself. Sprawling towns were a blight on nature, a surly rebuke to God's creation. Quoting Matthew Arnold, he asked, ' "Who can see the green earth any more? When shall we drink of the quiet again?" '[78] The only conceivable justification for the existence of the city was 'as a centre of intellectual and moral stimulus; and who ever heard of any intelligence proceeding from Toronto or morality emanating from Montreal?' In fact, it was quite the reverse. The 'popular view of the city dweller as a fat man sitting in an easy chair, smoking a big cigar, and reading the newspaper' was regrettably a 'serious matter.' Divorced from nature, these social drones lacked all the virtues Macphail associated with a rugged rural existence. Worse still than the middle-class Babbitt was the factory worker, 'more miserable than a Macedonian shepherd and less efficient than a Chinese peasant,' who had gained political 'liberty and sacrificed inner freedom.' These alienated beings derived no satisfaction from their work and as a result never acquired the moral values accompanying a sense of accomplishment. If the cities continued as they were, disaster would strike the race for 'the white man will not contend in the sweat shop ... slum and ghetto he can not endure.' Attempts to improve urban life, whether by idle women or misguided clerics, were fruitless since moral improvement, by definition impossible in the city, alone could elevate man. Equally futile were schemes of public assistance which destroyed what little initiative the poor possessed. In this atmosphere of degeneration, existence became complex yet meaningless, 'so vast and intricate' that 'daily life is bound up with telephones, trams, [and] delivery services of all kinds.' The natural tranquility of the farm was gone, and with it went man's inner peace. It was small wonder that Macphail saw town and country separated by 'innate hostility.' Yet this habitual 'latent tension' was of considerable importance, for it was his conviction that the city as an institution was about to meet defeat. Nature would triumph and man would gladly return to 'rural joys.'[79]

The impending collapse of urban life was evident for Macphail in the decline of the industrial system, 'the twin sister of the slum.' In fact, from childhood he personally remained apart from what contemporaries termed mechanical 'progress.' At age ten he saw a telegraph line for the first time, but it was another five years before he set eyes on a railway train. The suits he wore, even in the 1920s, were cut from cloth once woven by his mother in Orwell. Radios and telephones he considered annoyances, while the cinema he dismissed as a passing craze.[80] But Macphail's hostility to mechanization was more than individual eccentricity: it was based on the conviction that such artificial innovations destroyed the natural order on which society was based. The decline began, he felt, when the industrialist invaded bucolic Canada with a new system of priorities. Recalling Orwell in the 1860s, he wrote: 'Into this community ... came the manufacturer with his machinery, and his love of money, and his theories about efficeincy, saving of labour, industrial development and progress.' This money ethic was 'the root of all evil.' The factory owners reduced their employees 'to a condition which [had] many of evils from which a system of frank slavery was free.' They lost a sense of moral honesty and became increasingly alienated from their products as human skills were replaced by machines. The finished goods were of inferior quality and proved, in the long run, more costly than handmade articles. The family was disrupted in its traditional division of labour, especially if the woman held a job, while the indiscriminate gratification of artificial desires was simple wastage. Finally, the race itself was gradually degraded and diminished in numbers by the degeneration of its young men removed from their rural homes. Paradoxically, however, Macphail discerned a gleam of hope in the relentless progress of mechanization. 'A machine or a system,' he wrote, 'in the end breaks down by the weight of its own complexity.' With each step away from the simple and, consequently, natural methods of production, industry came closer to collapse. In fact, it was Macphail's belief that a return to cottage industry was not far distant.[81]

Had the factory owners stuck to manufacturing alone, the industrial problem would have eventually solved itself. Goods would again 'be made not in the factories, but in the homes, not in the cities by machines but in the villages by hand.' But the industrialists were bent on perpetuating their unnatural system with the artificial support of the tariff. The result, according to Macphail, was that for years 'the government of Canada has been carried on by a politico-business alliance.' Obsessed with their factories, the businessmen 'lost all political principle and missed the very aim of life,' a moral harmony with nature. Their greed 'led to the corruption of public life and to misery, to the political lobby and the social slum.' If production under protection was faster or greater in volume, the price 'when moral issues were involved' was too high. Macphail's conclusion was that 'political life in Canada is a conspiracy inspired by business-men' whose energy and intellect, lacking a moral dimension, could never be relied on to lead the nation. The 'business spirit ... destroys what it touches, he wrote, 'religion, friendship, love, education, literature, art ... wither and die.'[82] This comprehensive hostility to commercialism, specifically when extended to government, was the nexus between his economic ideas and his political theory.

Macphail assumed, as the foundation for his political philosophy, that God had not created all men with equal capacities. To believe otherwise was to undermine society's goal of securing liberty and order. Yet this was precisely the fallacy upon which democratic theory was based. Democracy was originally a disorganized state of primitive savagery in which men had not yet comprehended the order of the universe. Its purest form found expression in modern history in the mob rule of Tammany Hall, the Russian Bolsheviks, and the Paris sans-culottes. The results were purely destructive, 'pulling down what our fathers found to be good and useful.' In place of these revered institutions grew a politics based on parties instead of principle, a corruption that pervaded all aspects of bureaucracy and judiciary, and a false egalitarianism rooted in a desire to escape work by stealing from society's most industrious members. The false faith in equality also explained democracy's propensity to foster futile schemes of social amelioration. A certain segment of any society was condemned to poverty by natural inability. Only through moral reform, that is, instruction in the moral verities of nature, could paupers be rescued from their plight. Yet 'idle and ignorant busybodies' destroyed self-reliance with social insurance plans, lessened the amount of food available by demanding pure food legislation, and undermined thrift through old age pension schemes. Founded on a false premise and destructive of the natural order, the political thoery of popular democracy was rejected by Macphail.[83]

A proper political philosophy accepted the hierarchical structure of society, beginning with God, and followed by the king and an élite of able individuals. 'Democracy has never succeeded, or a monarchy, either,' wrote Macphail, 'where the "best men" followed their own pleasure and allowed the worst men to seize the reins of government.' It was the 'well born' and 'well bred' who best under-stood the working of society. In Canada, lacking a hereditary aristocracy of superior families, businessmen had assumed the functions of leadership. But they 'have been tried and found wanting,' asserted Macphail. Their ethic was based on money rather than the concern for man necessary to political leaders. What government required was disinterested men such as Sir Wilfrid Laurier and Sir Robert Borden who would give service without thought of personal gain. Fur-ther, the nation's intellectuals could not be 'content to stand afar off proclaim-ing their own holiness, disdaining the labour and sweat of those who carry on the government of the country.' Rather, it was their duty to give politicians the benefit of their detached viewpoints.

In Macphail's case, by his own admission, this viewpoint was likely to be con-servative, a tendency which reflected the second inherent feature of politics: the natural division of men into either liberals or conservatives. He defined a conservative and in the process painted an intellectual self-portrait:

The Conservative is a being with a definite frame of mind. He is tolerant of the old, suspicious of the new. In his pristine state he honoured the king, feared God, and was friendly to religion so long as it did not meddle too much with his private life. The world to him was a vast and complicated concern which he did not create, did not understand. If it could be improved at all, the improvement would be slow, and those who strove for improvement were only striving for change. Experiment was dangerous, and theory half false. He would risk a check but not a change. His main desire was to leave bad enough alone lest worse might follow. He had no faith whatever in legislative enactments. Legislation was one of those evils which must be endured, but it was a dangerous weapon. To him the Liberal was a gad-fly which stirred him from repose, but he was careful not to move too fast.

Content to be ruled by the logic of nature, the Conservative was the mainstay of all stable political systems. If liberalism had a place in this scheme, it was only as a foil or moderating influence for the dominating conservatism.[84]

The model from which Macphail drew his political thought was the ancient British constitution. This venerable tradition, seen through the filter of such writers as Carlyle and Bagehot, represented for him the epitome of hierarchical conservatism. 'England never was a democracy, is not now, and never will be until England is no longer England,' he wrote. 'England carries on by reason of its old monarchical inertia.' Britain 'has always been conservative' by nature, for it was the 'genius of the race to which we belong to do nothing in advance of necessity.' Shunning adherence to abstract principles, the constitution grew, as Bagehot suggested, 'out of the life of the people.' It proclaimed the sovereignty of the King in parliament from which all else followed. For that reason Macphail considered parliamentary democracy 'the best system that has yet been devised.' But it was not the rancorous democracy of the United States or even that of Canada; it was essentially an early nineteenth-century Whig view of Parliament presided over by the élite of the nation. Under such a system men had been truly free since the lower ranks of society were guided by the upper in the performance of their natural functions. Like Carlyle, Macphail equated this congruence with nature with both freedom and morality. In contrast to Carlyle, he saw this natural state as a corollary to a general legislative policy of laissez-faire. Such a principle could exist only if the 'community' was 'represented as a whole, and not as composed of various classes.' If self-seeking interest groups were allowed to enter Parliament, the sacred British ideal of compromise would surely disappear. The English system of government, based on the twin principles of hierarchy and conservatism, exemplified for Macphail the natural form of political organization.[85]

This reverence for the English political tradition linked Macphail's political thought to his imperial conception of Canada's destiny. Indeed, imperialism was a belief which gave practical expression to most of his basic convictions. He was willing to admit that as a Maritimer he shared an historical attachment towards Great Britain based on comparative proximity and that for many central Canadians the loyalist heritage predetermined an imperial bias. But his own loyalty was predicated on a deep affection for the British tradition: he would remain 'loyal to England as long as England is loyal to herself.' His conception of imperialism, then, was basically cultural which, in turn, explained the amorphous, ill-defined form it adopted. Loyalty, he wrote, was 'an inner experience like religion.' The product of simple loyalty to the king, the emotion was embedded in the race. It was the proper fashion in which to honour the commitment made by Canada's forefathers to perpetuate British institutions, and bind together the Empire. Because the English mind was never logical, distrusting one 'who has a political formula, a doctrine, a device,' no practical scheme of imperialism had been devised. It was obvious to Macphail that the answer did not lie in preferential trade alone. Canada could best fulfil her role by doing what she did naturally: providing food for the Empire. This vicarious contact with the land would not only 'rejuvenate' England, but also, by providing a challenging place of settlement for Britian's poor, would 'purify the race.' In effect, Canada, 'by serving her own interests first ... serves the Empire best.' Through service she became Britain's equal, and therefore, through the imperial tie, became a free nation. There was no need, then, for Canadians to alter their behaviour. In being what we naturally are, agrarian and British in culture, Macphail wrote, 'we do not know what more to do.' For that reason, he never advanced any complex schemes of imperial organization and remained content with the perceptive assertion that 'imperialism is in reality a way of looking at things, a frame of mind, an affair of the spirit.'[86]

If Macphail saw a model for his social and political beliefs in Great Britain, he found their antithesis in the example of the United States. This was, he asserted, 'a nation from which we must differentiate ourselves.' Certain superficial similarities would appear simply because Canada and the United States were both North American nations. But beyond that, Canadians were advised to avoid contamination and learn from the United States' mistakes. The deterioration of the Anglo-Saxon race through 'inferior' immigrants, urban political corruption, and a materialistic creed were the faults against which Macphail directed his criticism. Much of the American problem could be traced, he felt, to an 'incorrect theory of society' based on the fallacy of equality. This was reflected in the American inability to decide where 'real sovereignty lies' between the people's representatives and the president. The resulting society was unstable and chaotic. These characteristics were the legacy of the emotional element in Puritanism and lawlessness of the Revolution. Equally, in Macphail's opinion, they were a form of divine retribution for 'the enslaving of their fellow man.' A nation disfavoured by God and wracked with internal disorder had little for Canada to admire and much to be abhorred. Yet Macphail never managed to abandon entirely an element of hope for the moral revival of the United States. This sympathy was based largely on the belief that the United States was Anglo-Saxon in origin and could one day rejoin the great British tradition. He especially admired the best of this original American type, that minority 'of educated man one meets in the universites, clubs, churches [and] offices.' These were the men who had led the progressive reform movement and the campaign against the tariff. Macphail felt the commission style of municipal government could provide a good lesson for Canadians and his own free trade bias led him to advocate reciprocity. Nevertheless, the assumption which lay beneath Macphail's general view of the United States remained constant: Canada was a nation naturally rooted in the British tradition and, as such, both superior to and separate from the Americans.[87]

Macphail's social thought was a unified whole, growing naturally out of his idealistic, evolutionary metaphysics. A moral being at heart, the individual's understanding of the world was never profound and usually circumscribed by his racial and family heritage. Through education, work, and religion he was assigned to a place in society commensurate with his natural capacities and made to realize that in his harmony with the universal order he had developed the morality inherent in his nature. Such individuals, organized in family units, were the basis of society. The resulting structure was fragile, based on slowly evolved conventions and dedicated to the preservation of order and liberty. These goals could best be attained by basing economic and political organization on those principles intuitively perceived in nature. This conviction suggested a rigid adherence to the idea of laissez-faire, the complement to which was an agrarian economy free from the unnatural blight of cities, factories, and machines. In political matters, the guiding concepts were ruled by a hierarchy of ability and a conservative outlook which accepted the immutability of natural laws and allowed society to evolve according to their direction. These principles were the genius of the English constitution and the missing element in the American system. For that reason Canada's future lay within the British Empire close to the tradition from which he had originated. A product of his temperament and early experience in Orwell, and later substantiated by the reading of Carlyle,

Ruskin, and Bagehot, these were the convictions which comprised Macphail's social thought. It was with profound regret that he realized, 'In all these things there is a record of a society which in forty years I have seen passing away.'[88]

Andrew Macphail's metaphysics and his social thought combined in a philosophy of history. He saw history as a cosmic drama in which good ultimately triumphed over evil in man's slow evolution 'away from the beast' towards union with 'the Infinite.' The guiding force in this movement was the desire for perfection on the part of certain 'gifted men' who saw most clearly the inner order of the universe. Consequently, Macphail asserted, the lives 'of great men' are 'strongly recommended as a subject of contemplation.' In this assumption that history was didactic he revealed what he considered his own purpose and that of historians in general. The historian's duty was to 'make the past to live' as a lesson for the present. At the same time, he was aware that history, like God, ultimately defied absolute or scientific description; the writer of history was a captive of his own environment and could seldom transcend its limitations. Nevertheless, the major outline of the world's course was clear. If history was progress, it did not move smoothly forward; rather, civilization advanced only to regress as man lost contact with nature. Periods of moral growth were inevitably followed by ages of moral decline, though never quite to the preceding level of degradation. History, in effect, moved in slowly ascending cycles. For Macphail there were essentially two variables involved in this process, one economic, the other political, and both related to the natural order. In political terms it was equality, the antithesis of natural hierarchy, which led to degeneration:

History is very simple and always the same. It is a record of the rise from democracy — for the original democrat was the savage in his lair — to an organized society; and of the descent into democracy again from which the slow laborious Sisyphus task had to be resumed once more.

Equally significant was the economic factor, for as man departed from the bucolic he left behind morality. Quoting Justus Von Liebig, the nineteenth-century German chemist, Macphail asserted:

Both the rise and decline of nations are governed by the same law of nature. The deprivation of the soil of the conditions of fruitfulness brings about their decline, while the maintenance of such conditions leads to their permanence, prosperity, and power. The nation is not fed by peace nor destroyed by war — these conditions exercise only a temporary influence on it. It is the soil on

which man builds his home that is instrumental in holding human society together or dispersing it, and in causing nations and empires to disappear or
become powerful.

The eighteenth century, with its rationalism and industrial revolution, was an age
of decline while the nineteenth, tempered with romantic idealism, saw man again
rise on the moral scale. It was Macphail's firm conviction that society in the
twentieth century was about to plunge once again into the depths of depravity.[89]
    This insight was, in fact, both Macphail's message and his accomplishment.
Looking backward to the tranquility of his childhood, a process in which he was
encouraged by his readings in British idealism, he also looked forward to mid-
century when the liberal faith in technological progress would be loudly challenged. He called himself 'the only Tory left in the world' and others referred to
him as Goldwin Smith's successor or 'the gloomy dean of Canada.' But in fact he
was best described by himself when he spoke of 'the spirit of prophecy which so
often comes upon me.' This was his role in Canadian society. In an obscure
sentence tucked in a book of history, he gave a fitting summation to both his
philosophy of the natural order of history and his own oracular career:

History is something more than record and something less than praise; it demands selection and judgement, judging events as if they were far in the past,
and men as if they were already dead; it implies censure as a warning, lest those
who read may be misled. History is for the guidance of that posterity which
follows and finds itself involved in historical circumstances, which always recur
in identical form; for history is the master to which we must go — history with
its pensive and melancholy face.[90]

ARCHIBALD MacMECHAN
Proceedings and Transactions of the Royal Society of Canada 1934
Photo courtesy Royal Society of Canada

3

ARCHIBALD MacMECHAN
Romantic Idealist

The quarter century preceding the Great War was a period of shifting values in literature, philosophy, and political theory. The sensitive odes of Tennyson faded into the wastelands of T.S. Eliot and the heroic adventures of Kipling paled beside the literary naturalism of Ibsen, De Maupassant, or Dostoevsky. The idealism which Edward Caird and Benjamin Jowett had popularized in Britain during the 1870s withered before the analytic philosophy of younger thinkers such as Bertrand Russell. Political philosophy underwent a similar change with the critical idealism of Ruskin and Carlyle attacked by both Fabians and liberals alike. Many older intellectuals, Archibald McKellar MacMechan among them, had formed their ideas on art and society in the relatively stable period before 1890; the changes of subsequent years they tended to view as ethical and cultural anarchy. In the face of relativism, MacMechan posited absolute values, while in contrast to liberal empiricism he proclaimed a Christian idealism. In the process, his writing became, by his own admission, a paradigm for Victorian concepts of morality and aesthetics.

I

For more than forty years Archibald MacMechan was a familiar figure at Dalhousie University. He was a man of solid build, somewhat under average height, and slightly disfigured by a limp, the legacy of childhood polio. Despite his handicap he created an impression of unruffled dignity and impeccable deportment. His high forehead was crowned by receding brown hair, while his chin was always concealed beneath a neatly trimmed, spade-like beard. Perhaps the most revealing feature of his large face was the expression in the eyes: kindness, sentimentalism, and a dash of shyness were a part of his gaze. But these indiscreet eyes were often preoccupied with reading, hidden beneath a pair of eyeglasses suspended on a black silk ribbon. The spectacles were the perfect complement to his fastidious, conservative manner of dress, in turn, an accurate reflection of the man within. For Archibald MacMechan, though an emotional romantic, was outwardly the epitome of moderation, balance, and restraint. At the time of his death in 1933 a boyhood friend captured his character in a single phrase: 'He was indeed the model Christian gentleman.'[1]

Though he spent the better part of his life in Nova Scotia and developed a profound attachment to the province, MacMechan always felt himself something of an outsider and retained a lasting affection for the Ontario of his boyhood. He was born at Kitchener in 1862, the son of the Reverend John MacMechan. His Irish Presbyterian father had arrived in Canada in 1857 and soon after married the eldest daughter of the Honourable Archibald McKellar. The family moved to Picton in 1866 where, MacMechan recalled, 'the existence led ... was simple, wholesome, and natural.' His family was not wealthy, yet these early years were marked by the comradeship of two brothers and youthful games made all the more exciting by the otherwise demanding 'background of school, church-going, and chores about the house.'[2] Many of his attitudes in later life originated in this very early period. He thrived in the outdoors, particularly while tramping a country road. His religious emotion, a spirit always close to the surface of his thought, was born in the manse where, he wrote, 'I was brought up on sermons.' This religious training was buttressed by reading, particularly *Tom Brown's School Days* and later, works by his early idol, John Ruskin. Even MacMechan's adult fascination with military history was rooted in his childhood experience. 'When I was a boy,' he wrote, 'there were two old men in my own little village who had served in the War of 1812 ... They performed the office of monuments to me ... These two veterans I remember better than any two men of those early years.' The Picton days, carefree yet formative, always remained among the happiest of MacMechan's memories.[3]

This idyllic period was brought to an abrupt end in 1870 by the death of his mother. What his attitude towards his father is difficult to assess for he described him as both heroic and an unambitious failure. But for the memory of his 'dear and beautiful young mother,' he had nothing but sorrowful affection. Half a century after her death he could not bring himself to attend church on Mother's Day, 'fearing what I should hear.'[4] Her departure meant more than the loss of a family member: it was the beginning of an entirely new life for MacMechan. He was sent to live with grandfather McKellar in Hamilton, where he remained throughout what he later considered a rather dull high school experience. Here he made the most important friendship of his early years. A cousin, Jessie McNab, seven years his senior, nursed and kept house for his grandfather until 1894. Their relationship he later described in one of his many semi-autobiographical fantasies:

It is not love I celebrate, but something rarer and almost as sweet, − a perfect friendship. On the one side, a shy, awkward, country-bred young scholar. He has been brought up among books, and he loves them ... He fancies the real world is peopled with such rare and beautiful forms ... he cannot pluck apart the real and the unreal, nor does he care to do so. What is there for such a dreamer but an inevitable, cruel awakening? ... Only one thing can save him. To learn life as it really is, slowly, under the tutorship of a noble woman. And for once the stars are kind; the impossible happens. For on the other side is a pure woman ... fitted to be his tutor.

Still a romantic but tempered by the practicality of the motherly Jessie, Mac-Mechan left Hamilton for the University of Toronto in 1880.[5]

At 'Varsity' MacMechan studied modern languages and, in the process, became a member of a small circle of student *literati*. He wrote, even after graduation, a column entitled 'Bohemian' for the college paper, a title which also described the innocent decadence cultivated by himself and his friends. In later life he recalled these immature attempts to ape the artistic lifestyle:

We hunted out German families in the city to board with, to improve our German; we spent our vacations in Quebec, to improve our French; we taught peanut vendors in the Italian Sunday School, to improve our Italian. We worried the authorities into bettering the courses. We cultivated literature on a little oatmeal; we published an anthology of our own immortal writings; we astonished the world with a new Protestantism. One oddity diverged from the regular prescriptions into heraldry and Russian. Our Shelley spent a winter in Paris, where he consorted with people called Anarchists, and returned a missionary of the gospel of Henry George. We went to England as cattle-men, that we might stand in the Abbey in Poet's Corner and see with our own eyes those sacred places which had belonged to the geography of Fairy-Land. We read 'Sartor' for the Blumine episode; we despised 'gig-men'; our greatest oath was, By Saint Thomas of Carlyle.

But for all the camaraderie of these naïve Bohemians, life at university had its lonely moments. It was this aspect which MacMechan fantasized in his 'Porter of Bagdad.' When the anonymity and drudgery of Varsity overwhelmed him, he found instant escape in literature. Through books and his own vivid imagination he could transcend time and place to find peace in the romance of other ages.[6]

Reality, however, intruded on 'the dreamer' in the form of financial difficulties. His grandfather had contributed to his education but he was forced to borrow funds to complete his course at Toronto. Like many other young college graduates of the day, he then entered the teaching profession. After a year in a Brockville high school, he moved to Galt where, though he enjoyed teaching, particularly languages, he was not happy. Religion provided a source of comfort but he was lonely and confused about the future. 'I seriously doubt my own identity,' he wrote to Jessie, 'when I consider how I have thought and acted for long periods ... I doubt often if I shall ever attain to maturity.' By late spring of 1886, however, MacMechan seemed to find a sense of purpose; that fall, with accumulated savings of $400, he left to begin a doctorate in modern languages at Johns Hopkins University. While he was still lonely and insecure in Baltimore, and given to morbid speculations on a romantic death, MacMechan seemed to approach the practical entente with life that had been lacking in his earlier years. Some of his tensions were resolved by writing brief descriptive articles for the *Week*. Religion, too, was a solace and he came to the conclusion 'that peace is better than happiness.' The concrete result of this attitude was 'that "carry on" feeling' which helped him complete his dissertation, 'The Relation of Hans Sachs to the Decameron,' in 1889. That same year he married Edith Cowan of Gananoque, whom he had courted for the previous half decade, and received his appointment to Dalhousie as George Munro Professor of English Language and Literature.[7]

In Halifax MacMechan at last found both a spiritual and physical home. 'Dolcefar' was the name he gave it in his writing 'because it has given me almost everything I ever wanted ... a quiet nook in a bustling, rushing continent.' To his journal he prophetically confided, 'Something tells me I shall live and die in Halifax ... It would not be a sorry fate. I love the place.' This affection for his city was in part explained by his home life; his marriage was exceptionally happy and the quiet house on Victoria Road was soon filled by the addition of three daughters.[8] Despite these many blessings, however, MacMechan never quite escaped a tendency, developed in earlier years, towards romantic pessimism. He constantly complained of debts hanging over him as they had over Thomas Carlyle, though his salary was sufficient to provide domestic help for the home and English boarding schools for his children. Introspection was a frequent preoccupation during which he accused himself, despite a constant flow of publications, of becoming 'idle and smug.' Linked to this obsession for work was a strong fear of death. In his journal he often wrote of the departed, particularly his parents, and concluded that his own end was at hand. He derived comfort from religion and made a practice of regular attendence at Fort Massey Presbyterian Church. Equally relaxing were his favourite recreations, boating, swimming, golf and, above all, walking. In fact, when he paused to reflect seriously on his remaining premonitions, doubt usually vanished before the reality of his good fortune. He often concluded his journal entries by admitting that he was 'almost frightened at the goodness of it all.'[9]

An important part of this 'goodness' was the satisfaction MacMechan derived from his post at Dalhousie. When he came to the university there were 10 professors and 150 students. He saw himself as 'a living link with the past,' joining the present to 'the last of the race' of academic giants who composed the faculty in 1889. Though enrolment increased and faces changed, he never abandoned his pledge to carry on this tradition. This commitment rested on his conception of the university: it was a place of absolutely pure 'moral atmosphere' where the leaders of the nation were trained. As such, the role of the professor was 'essentially a religious one.' On arriving in Halifax, MacMechan wrote of his new responsibilities: 'perhaps I can help ... the students who will come under my direction and look up to me for guidance.' After five years of teaching he managed to reduce his philosophy of education to two maxims: 'the teacher must be a *man*' and 'I want my men to be gentlemen.' He seldom missed an opportunity to put this theory into practice, whether at Dalhousie student gatherings, the Royal Canadian Naval College where he taught naval history, or in the large American universities at which he spent his summers. He was, according to former students and colleagues, an ideal synthesis of ethics and culture, a model from which his students learned of both literature and life. It was precisely this approbation that MacMechan, who always craved approval, found most rewarding. 'The usual prizes of life – wealth, fame, place – do not come the teacher's way,' he wrote, 'He knows he is scorned by the man of the world ... as an unpractical recluse.' But in the end the teacher finds his compensations, of which 'the chief is merely that he should not be forgotten by those he has taught.' Respected by his students at Dalhousie, MacMechan at last found the self-respect for which he had searched in earlier years.[10]

The confidence engendered by his success as a teacher found practical expression in a prolific volume of publication. His first books were either collections of romantic fantasy, 'autobiographic' and embodying 'the decency principle,' or scholarly introductions to editions of such great Victorian writers as Carlyle and Tennyson. Though he later published a survey of Canadian literature and an account of responsible government, his interest after 1914 shifted to descriptive and historical works on Nova Scotia. Many of his descriptive essays were privately published and sold as pamphlets in Halifax. Some of these 'chapbooks' were used as supplementary reading in schools, while most of them reappeared in *The Book of Ultima Thule*. His most popular works, however, were collections of sea stories, carefully researched and embroidered with romantic prose. When the first of these compilations appeared in 1923 MacMechan commented to a colleague, 'I think this is the most important work I have done, and the one for which I shall be remembered.'[11] Indeed, the book received glowing praise from friends, became a school text, and was partially reprinted in 1947. A prominent member of the Canadian Historical Association and the Nova Scotia Historical Society, MacMechan asserted that his literary interest had naturally led him to a consideration of history.[12]

If his work as a scholar had become primarily historical, his activities as a journalist continued to reflect his literary concern. In the late 1880s he contributed several small articles to *The Week* and subsequently became one of the journal's shareholders. Arriving in Nova Scotia he began 'The Reviewer' in the Halifax *Herald*, devoted to a survey of British periodical literature and assessments of the great Victorian authors. In 1906, through the efforts of a former Dalhousie student, Fred Yourston, MacMechan's first 'Book & Beaver' column appeared in the Montreal *Standard*. The following year the title was changed to 'The Dean's Window' and it remained a weekly feature for the next quarter century. A variety of social commentary and literature was reviewed by 'The Dean,' including works by Rudyard Kipling, Sidney Webb, Henrik Ibsen, James Mavor, and Andrew Macphail. By 1930 this tremendous volume of journalistic and scholarly publication had won him wide recognition. Honorary doctorates and both the presidency and Lorne Pierce Medal of the Royal Society of Canada were among his trophies. Through literature he at last managed to grasp that 'maturity' he had once considered so elusive.[13]

In his adult years MacMechan, though still introspective and often insecure, had a clear image of himself and his role in society. One of his honours students who knew him well recalled, 'Archie was proud of being and remaining a Victorian, and he was equipped with an armoury of definite reasons for his pride.' For MacMechan the essence of his Victorianism was an idealism best exemplified by Ruskin, Carlyle, and Tennyson. He realized, too, that in the twentieth century an adherence to this type of belief consigned him to a select group of older intellectuals. In his journal he described a dinner attended by a number of such individuals, including Maurice Hutton, Pelham Edgar, W.J. Alexander, and Sir Robert Falconer:

It was delightful to be treated as an equal by such men as Hutton. Edgar put his arm around my shoulder, called me a 'dear old conservative' and, addressing Hutton, 'a man after your own heart.' As I said at the time, he could not pay me a higher compliment.

MacMechan had clearly chosen his side in the great empiricist-idealist debate of the nineteenth century. Though he considered himself a 'bookworm' lost in the 'enchanted forest' of his library, he felt it his role in society to proclaim a high idealism. Like the thundering prose of his idol Carlyle, it was the purpose of his sea sagas, he confided to Lorne Pierce, to reveal the 'heroic' as 'inspiration and example' to 'Young Canada.' Concurring with his friend Andrew Macphail, he regretted that his fellow academics were not equally able to express their views 'to combat the various forms of popular madness which arise in the Commonwealth.'[14]

As he grew older, the task of proclaiming the ideal seemed increasingly difficult. Towards the turn of the century, with the death of the last great Victorian, Tennyson, MacMechan felt the 'world is darker than it was,' and asked, 'Who is there that we can reverence?' Though a time of anguish, the Great War initially appeared as a sign of reviving idealism. But events such as the Winnipeg General Strike forced him to conclude that the 'world is still in ferment.' A decade later he wrote in his journal: 'Leafing over January's *Harper's*, I am repelled or saddened by most I read. Behind the times. Old. But they do not seem very happy times.' What MacMechan actually meant when he referred to 1929 as unhappy was that it was vastly different from 1889, the year he had arrived at Dalhousie. His own thinking, based largely on British idealism, had congealed in the late Victorian period. In the twenties, he found many of his basic convictions ignored or disputed by an empirical, technological society. He captured his own dilemma in a simple, penetrating question: 'How can a generation fed on movies and bred on motors understand Wordsworth?' Within himself, Mac-Mechan knew the answer to his enquiry: Victorian idealism was a dying system of beliefs. But, with his friend Macphail, he refused to abandon the foundation on which his life had been constructed. One of the last entries in his journal before his death in 1933 reads like the 'Everlasting Yea' of Carlyle's Teufelsdroch. 'I am old,' he wrote, 'and not cynical.'[15]

II

Archibald MacMechan once wrote of himself, 'I am not and never could be a metaphysician.' By temperament he was too much the romantic dreamer ever to pursue with consistent logic a particular line of philosophical reasoning. Yet this same romanticism predisposed him to accept an idealist philosophy created for him by other minds. The men to whom he turned were Professor George Paxton Young of the University of Toronto, Thomas Carlyle, and in later life, G.K. Chesterton. A combination of temperament and training placed him firmly in the tradition of late nineteenth-century British idealism.

When he arrived at university, MacMechan already realized he was 'a dreamer of dreams' quite different from his more pragmatic brothers. This innate romantic bent had been fortified by the reading and religious instruction of his childhood, but it was the idealist philosophy taught by George Paxton Young which gave it coherence. He never managed to advance from an emotional appreciation of Young's idealism to an intellectual comprehension. In fact, he wrote, 'No member of our class will ... dispute my claim to being the worst metaphysician in it,' and his university notebook, largely filled with poems and scribbles, substantiated his claim. But Young, 'a survival of that extinct race of giants, the Edinburgh metaphysicians,' remained for him the paradigm upon which he attempted to pattern his thought and conduct. With Edward Caird and John Watson, Young based his objective idealism on the writing of Plato, Kant, and Hegel, standing in opposition to the materialism of Bentham and Mill. To his students, MacMechan among them, he taught that the material world was but a shadow of a reality which was essentially spiritual. A knowledge of this sublime truth was inherent in every individual, making each a small miracle in the larger miracle of creation. Such a philosophy, for one student at least, gave 'a new meaning' to life, confirmed 'the dignity of man,' and justified religious faith. Recalling these lessons years after, MacMechan wrote, 'I would not trade Young's course in metaphysics for all the others I took at Toronto.'[16]

While attending Young's lectures, MacMechan read a number of authors who substantiated his developing idealism. Like Macphail, he was conscious that he grew up in a period which attempted to reconcile the idea of evolution with traditional concepts of 'man, life, and the universe.' For him, Carlyle, Ruskin, and Tennyson 'helped to shape some sort of via media between science and religion.' Above all others it was 'Saint Thomas of Carlyle' who most influenced the young romantic and in later years he proudly described himself as a 'professed Carlylean.' The 'most remarkable man of his age,' Carlyle wrote with 'unerring truth' in an age of disintegrating belief. While Newman demanded a reactionary withdrawal into the church, according to MacMechan, Carlyle was essentially a radical, inspiring 'the young in heart' by his lonely crusade 'to get the conventional, Philistinian England of his day back to first principles.' The 'first principle' on which the 'ethical appeal' of his work rested was his belief in 'a moral order in the universe.' Though he faithfully championed the common man against the scourge of industrialism, Carlyle's ultimate praise was reserved for those men of natural ability whose superior insight discerned that 'Nature is a just Empire.' MacMechan, from his own study of German literature, especially appreciated the Goethian foundation of Carlyle's opposition to materialism. The essence of his message was found in *Sartor Resartus*, 'a modern Pilgrim's Progress,' in which he considered the dilemma of the mature man who finds inadequate his childhood beliefs. Only through losing sight of his own problems in the larger light of human suffering could one resolve to cope with life. By contemplating nature as the manifestation of the divine and in the determination to replace disillusioned inertia by action, man finds the meaning of existence. To MacMechan, Carlyle's message, when stripped of Goethe, was simple Christianity.[17]

Though he remained a devotee of Carlyle throughout his life, MacMechan felt that the age of Tennyson, Carlyle, and Ruskin came to an end with 'the death of the Good Queen in 1901.' In the arid philosophical wasteland of the twentieth century, he found but one man to follow: G.K. Chesterton. 'I admire Chesterton greatly,' he wrote, 'I was the first critic in Canada to review him at length; I keep his books always close at hand...' MacMechan considered him a 'Conservative Radical,' the successor to Carlyle in his 'protest against modern fatalism.' With a firm faith in individual worth, Chesterton was the champion of the little man. He eschewed both the uniform anonymity of socialism and the selfish individualism of capitalism in favour of common sense co-operation among men. This was to be achieved through redistribution of property to make the family unit once again the basis of society. Enervating 'commercialism' or the ravages of misguided feminism would have no place in this retreat to an older, more natural society; instead, the Christian religion would bind men together. These ideas, reflecting the values MacMechan had earlier absorbed from the great Victorians, won his immediate approval. Lacking a philosophical mind, he was not alienated by Chesterton's emotionalism or inconsistencies; if anything, he identified with the romantic, religious jeremiads of the British literary figure. Chesterton became for him the last prophet in a materialistic century.[18]

From his temperamental romanticism, Young's formal instruction in metaphysics, and the reading of Carlyle and Chesterton, MacMechan accumulated an arsenal of basic ocnvictions. Unlike Macphail, he never attempted a synthetic statement of his beliefs; they remained confused and sometimes contradictory. But the essence of his thought was clear: he conceived of the world in orthodox Christian terms. The central theme of existence was man's struggle to transcend his fallen state, to create for himself a home in a hostile environment. Each human was an individual miracle, an example of 'the universe compressed into a single inch,' who, if not intelligent, was romantic in spirit and potentially heroic. He experienced 'moments of intuition when the soul seems lifted above and out of itself and discerns truths higher than the cold processes of reason ever show.' Because truth was perceived by the emotions rather than the intellect, pure philosophy could never give man the satisfaction he derived from religion.[19] A union with the divine could be attained by an appreciation of God immanent in his creation, or by tranquil contemplation in religious surroundings. This union revealed the simple essence of Christianity: 'God is love. Love one another.' Yet here also was what MacMechan termed the 'paradox of the Christian religion.' As God's creatures, he wrote, 'Something within us responds to the superhuman ideal. That is the Law. That is Right.' At the same time, as mere mortals, 'we fail when we try to obey that law.' A being of high aspirations but limited accomplishment, man had been expelled from heaven to an earth with which he was constantly at odds. His life became a struggle against raw nature; his own morality determined his success in the battle to control and order creation. For MacMechan morality became 'co-extensive with life' in man's attempt to re-create paradise.[20]

This simple creed underlay most of MacMechan's thought. His romantic mind was readily susceptible to a spiritual interpretation of life, while he lacked the independence of thought necessary to reject beliefs absorbed in childhood. The sermons he had been raised on in the manse at Picton, substantiated by his interpretation of the philosophy of Young and Carlyle, remained the standard by which he judged others and regulated his own conduct. 'Work and Pray' were his constant guidelines, the latter supported by his regular attendance at both Wednesday prayer meetings and Sunday church services. He never accepted his friend Macphail's iconoclastic critique of theology, feeling instead that higher criticism was useful in clarifying certain historical aspects of the Bible. His concept of the church was strictly orthodox: a place of prayer, it was neither a social institution nor an instrument of social reform. Equally orthodox was his approach to doctrine. He considered Unitarianism unacceptable and sceptical treatment of the cosmogony of Genesis he branded as 'radical.' If he deviated at all from the 'stoical, fatalistic, Presbyterianism' of his youth, it was only to assert that man's good works were of more importance than most Protestants would admit.[21] His mind, in fact, was analogous to the Biblical paradox of which he himself was conscious. On the one side was his praise of force, of Kipling, of struggle against raw nature reminiscent of the retributive justice of the Old Testament. On the other side was his affection for beauty, for Wordsworth, for the divine in nature similar to the redemptive love of the New Testament. Just as the spirit of God united the two sections of the Bible, MacMechan's own roman-tic temper harmonized his two antithetical states of mind. The concept of love was the essential element in his thought: it was, he thought, the emotion which animated both the dreamer lost in a host of golden daffodils and the hero spanning the rivers of India with bridges of steel. The expression of the affection between man and his God, his fellow beings, and his environment was the force, according to MacMechan, which energized the world. This conviction, in turn, was the core of his philosophy.

III

From the crest of Bedford Basin, Archibald MacMechan described his view of 'Dolcefar':

On the high and distant rock rose one of Turner's mysterious cities, dwellings and walls and white airy towers soaring out of the unnameable gloom. I looked and looked and could not believe my eyes for there I knew were only squalid hovels of the very poor, a hospital, and a jail.

This passage was characteristic of his thought; as he had earlier written, he often found himself unable to 'pluck apart the real and the unreal' nor did he 'care to do so.' Though conscious of this congenital tendency to romanticize, he made little attempt to control it; without a secure foundation in reality, he was precluded from developing any practical social thought. Certainly he was aware of the more pressing issues of his day and his opinions on them usually concurred with those of his friend Andrew Macphail. Apolitical himself, he considered movements of political reform largely futile. Society was guided by leaders of natural ability whose duty it was to protect their weaker followers. This organic concept explained MacMechan's mild sympathy with socialism in his early years and his approval of Chesterton's redistribution scheme, though he modified his ideas in the aftermath of the Russian Revolution. Like Macphail, he personally recoiled from the business world and condemned 'the brutality of our modern mammon.' Commercialism was linked in his mind with political corruption, urban slums, and the mechanized drudgery of the sweatshop. Many of these evils he associated with the United States, the proximity of which he hoped to counter by a strong imperial tie.[22] Beyond these general attitudes, however, MacMechan's social thought was limited: the real focus of his attention, dictated by his own romanticism, was literary. Still, in the course of both his critical and creative writing he developed ideas on ethics and culture which were, in effect, an alternative to more pragmatic social theorizing. Literature, in his view, was the highest activity of civilization, an exercise in morality, supervised by the nation's rightful leader, the poet. For a society which produced great art and heeded its teaching, conventional social thought became largely superfluous.

MacMechan's conception of great literature was born of his idealism and substantiated by the aesthetic theories of the great Victorians, particularly his boyhood idol, John Ruskin. If the material world was but a shadow of a spiritual reality, as Young taught, then art, properly conceived, was an attempt to capture that elusive reality. It was, as Ruskin suggested, an attempt to arrive at certain principles of design inherent in God's universe and, as such, essentially an exercise in discerning morality. Tennyson, for example, succeeded where Whitman failed because, MacMechan wrote, 'he set himself humbly to obey eternal and unchanging law for the principle of beauty inheres as firmly in the universal as the law of gravitation.' Quoting Algernon Swinburne and Ruskin, MacMechan asserted that poetry, to be considered excellent, had to combine both this adherence to the principles of 'beauty and harmony' and an insight into reality, 'a criticism of life.' In contrast to the emotional beauty of poetry, he wrote, in 'prose we have a right to expect, first and foremost, intellectual qualities' since this form was basically didactic in intent. The model for good prose, that is, for 'clearness, force, and ease,' was the work of the eighteenth-century masters, Addison, Swift, and Goldsmith. Though all writers were the product of their time and place, by attaining to these classical principles of balance and refinement they transcended their temporal limitations and tapped 'the poetic Kingdom of God.' Because each human possessed an element of the divine, he possessed the capacity to respond to the morality inherent in great literature; in this sense, literature became the basis for social morality. Complete artistic freedom was opposed to the good of society as a whole, for it was based less on adherence to immutable principles than on individualistic eccentricity. Equally enervating was the literary realism of Ibsen or Zola. Because their interest was focused on the sordid material world, rather than on the principles of natural beauty, they were incapable of discerning moral truth. Finally, the idea of 'art for art's sake' was the harbinger of decadence for it lacked any commitment to form and, therefore, morality. True literature, according to MacMechan, followed nature's principles of balance which, in turn, enabled it to reveal to the mundane world the inner order of the universe.[23]

Great literature was the product of a superior mind. To both MacMechan and Ruskin this quality of superiority was simple morality, the product of the writer's proximity to nature. In the untainted wonder of creation, the poet was free to seek the divine and, like Tennyson, enter 'that small band of illuminated spirits to whom the universe reveals itself chiefly as wonder and beauty.' Equipped with this intuitive perception, the poet created a work which expressed his revelation only if he wrote of what he himself experienced and used both balance and restraint in form. Archibald Lampman was for MacMechan the Canadian who came closest to being the ideal poet. He wrote of Canada, focusing on the nature with which he was familiar, using both standard forms and ethically acceptable imagery. In sharp contrast was Charles G.D. Roberts. His early career paralleled Lampman's, but he eventually left his Canadian home to waste his talent on 'artistic experiment' with 'alarming ethical heterogeneity.' Like Matthew Arnold, MacMechan felt it was the duty of the critic to point out such distinctions between good and bad art 'for the multitude' because men 'turn to poets instinctively for guidance in matters of faith.' For a society so guided, less elevated discussions of social theory were largely irrelevant: the morality of art was the ultimate standard of social value. This condition had prevailed, MacMechan thought, in nineteenth-century England. In an age when authors from Scott to Tennyson were objects of popular acclaim, he wrote, 'men and women were sensitive to beauty in all its forms, possessed broad culture and thorough refinement, lived on moral uplands and envisaged with earnestness the tremendous riddles of life and destiny.' But with the passing of Carlyle, Ruskin, and Tennyson the world became a darker place; the twentieth century, devoid of literary leadership, lacked all the virtues absorbed from fine literature. In MacMechan's opinion a culture marked by the decadence of Oscar Wilde was manifestly inferior to one inspired by the heroic idealism of Rudyard Kipling.[24]

MacMechan's literary career was the practical extension of his theory of aesthetics: through creative writing he attempted to explain his concept of morality in the universe. Just as his philosophy had two distinct strains, the violent and the pastoral, his creative writing fell into two separate categories, one reflecting what he was, the other what he would have liked to be. The first type was romantic or descriptive fantasy, the product of the 'effiminacy' he felt was inherent in most writers. It was focused on the present, dealt with the beneficence of God in nature, and stressed the need for harmony between man and his environment. Historical romance was his second type of writing, reflecting the author as a 'man of action.' These stories described the brutal conflict among men and between man and nature, conflict carried on under the surveillance of a vengeful though equitable God. The contrast between these two approaches towards man and existence was particularly obvious in MacMechan's single volume of poetry, *Late Harvest*, which combined sensitive odes with rollicking ballads of adventure. It was equally evident in his personal life. He confided to his journal a 'sense of defeat' at 'not having converted' his students to Wordsworth, while at the same time he confessed his immense enjoyment of 'the ringside announcer's account of the Tunney-Dempsey fight over the radio.' What harmonized these two apparently contradictory attitudes was his belief that great literature was as illuminating to the reader as actual experience. The writer, therefore, became a mirror of life; it was his duty to portray both the pitfalls of evil and the moral precepts learned in the course of existence. The concept around which MacMechan's own message centred was Christian love. This emotion animated both the dreamer enraptured by the beauty of 'Dolcefar' and the sea captain struggling to save his ship and crew. Though neither a systematic thinker nor concerned with practical social problems, through his writing MacMechan revealed his most basic social and moral values.[25]

Romantic and descriptive fantasy was the first type of literature he wrote, beginning with columns in the University of Toronto *Varsity* and culminating in collections such as *The Porter of Bagdad* and *The Book of Ultima Thule*. Woven into these essays were two consistent themes, the product of his own experience and his familiarity with nineteenth-century romantic poetry. The first principle he affirmed was the validity of human intuition as a guide to a moral existence. All men, he asserted, possessed an innate idealism at birth which, for those few who managed to escape the cynicism of age, equipped them for a full comprehension of life. Their idealism had three essential facets. An 'innate, universal, underlying instinct of romance' prepared the superior few for the extraordinary life on which, as Carlyle suggested, the advance of civilization depended. Secondly, the idealist possessed 'affection,' initially for his fellows and then for all creation. Finally, the least cynical were likely to respond to the 'superhuman ideal' known as religion. The idealist with his romance, love, and piety was susceptible to an intuitive recognition of God immanent in creation and, by virtue of this, was well suited for a position of social leadership. The idealistic writer such as Charles Dodgson with his whimsical *Alice in Wonderland*, or MacMechan himself with his 'decency principle,' became part 'of the great and subtle forces working silently about us for good.' The social implications of this romantic belief in the intuitive insight of the idealist, though seldom overtly stated, were very evident in MacMechan's thought. Because all men possessed a capacity for idealism at birth, they were, in a sense, equally created. Yet certain individuals managed throughout life to retain this idealism and its concomitant insight into the universal order. The combination of egalitarian respect for the human soul and an élitist reverence for superior minds explained MacMechan's 'Red Tory' strain which endorsed the conservative radicalism of Chesterton. It also accounted for a portion of his self-image: as a writer sensitive to nature it was his duty to proclaim his idealism. Equally important, by equating the natural with the divine, he arrived at a standard for morality that was immutable and, therefore, inherently stable and conservative. Finally, in placing intuition above reason he rejected liberal empiricism and its attendant faith in technology and innovation. His romantic fantasy, then, affirmed an essentially conservative view of society.[26]

The second theme which pervaded his descriptive writing was closely related to the belief in intuition: just as the individual derived his moral strength from insight into creation, so society as a whole prospered as it remained close to nature. This ideal of harmony with the natural was similar to the physiocratic bias of Andrew Macphail, though it was less pragmatically expressed. The agrarian way of life symbolized to MacMechan man's final entente with his environment: man imposed order on untrammelled nature and, in turn, received his livelihood. This was the charm of England, the destiny of Canada, and the heritage which the United States rapidly abandoned. The countryside was calm, uncomplex, and regenerative in its effect on the soul. The home and family, to MacMechan the symbols of love, security, and self-reliance, were integrally re-lated to a rural existence: in the frenzied complexity of urban life they quickly disintegrated. Equally destructive of the bucolic ideal was the machine. He dis-missed the railway as 'a mere irrelevance in the landscape, a troubler of the peace' only slightly less detestable than the 'oil-reek' of the automobile. The evil force behind both urbanism and industrialization was the materialistic ethic of commercialism. Work lost its pleasure when it became a mere quest for affluence and, worse still, left no time for quiet communion with nature. Only through proximity to nature could a society foster the idealism inherent in each individual. This was the message of MacMechan's descriptive and romantic prose.[27]

If his romantic fantasy emphasized the harmony between man and nature through a knowledge of God, MacMechan's sea stories stressed the heroic struggle between man and a hostile environment. Canadians, he once wrote, were 'a prosaic people.' Yet 'deep down in the nation's heart' there existed 'a capacity for the ideal'; it was this latent idealism which he set himself to awaken. In his chronicles of the 'traffics and discoveries, the disasters and the heroic deeds of the seafaring provincials,' he saw himself as 'another Hakluyt' proclaiming 'the greater glory of Nova Scotia.' He modestly suggested that his work would merely 'serve some native Carlyle of the future as data in a study of heroes and the heroic in history.' But in fact he saw himself in the Carlylean role, for he wrote to a friend:

You have perceived the main intent, not consciously followed, perhaps, but always there — the revelation of the heroic. These plain sailor men have in them the element of greatness. Their lives, their achievements, their records form one of our richest natural assets ... My real point is that young Canada does not need to look outside our own borders for inspiration and example.

The specific lessons he hoped to impart were 'pride of race and admiration for mere human courage and devotion to duty.' This goal was best achieved through an accurate presentation of the past, for true adventure was both more inspiring and spectacular than fiction. MacMechan scoffed at Thomas Chandler Haliburton's historical account of Nova Scotia because of 'his naïve conception of history as dealing only with matters remote and romantic,' while of his own work he wrote, 'My aim is plain truth; "romance" I avoid and abjure.' If his stories appeared romantic it was only because he saw the heroic element inherent in man's struggle against the untamed aspect of nature. By celebrating this conflict MacMechan hoped to raise Canada above the pedestrian confines of daily life and relate her existence to the eternal course of history.[28]

In his three collections of sea stories and adventure, published between 1923 and 1928, he established certain common themes. The plots centred on a struggle between the forces of evil, whether human or an element of raw nature, and a particularly good individual who ultimately vanquished his foe. Often staged in the eighteenth century, 'the heroic age of Canada,' the adventures traced the exploits of Nova Scotian privateers, merchants, shipbuilders, or simple sailors, against a background of violent seas or raging war. The adversaries of these maritime heroes were men marred by a tragic flaw of character or members of a 'lower race,' often Greeks or American Indians. Always religious, the heroes were dedicated to a higher cause such as loyalty, yet modestly disclaimed their valour as mere duty. In a time of crisis the natural leader emerged at the head of a tightly disciplined crew and, through quick wits and hard muscles, averted potential doom. Always in the background was Providence, using the elements to punish the evil and reward the just. Though embroidered with romantic settings and heroic characters, MacMechan's sea stories were, in fact, simple lessons in Christian morality designed to inspire, in 'Young Canada' at least, admiration and, it was to be hoped, emulation.[29]

In these historical adventures MacMechan revealed certain of his basic assumptions about man and existence. The stories were built around the Carlylean assumption that superior men appear in a time of need. The captain of his ships was always 'the man of resources, the natural leader who emerges in a crisis,' for at such times 'the grand distinction between man and man is developed, and the full ascendancy of a powerful and well-regulated mind makes itself felt.' Yet beside the faith in superior minds went his perennial concern for the common man. Quoting Montaigne, he wrote that 'a man may show as much courage in dislodging a musketeer from a hen-roost as in slaying a champion in the sight of two armies.' The valour he chronicled was 'typical of our Nova Scotian sea-faring men,' a resource shared by all the inhabitants, however humble, of the province. Part of the explanation for the communal heroism lay in the bracing effect of proximity to the sea, in MacMechan's opinion God's most spectacular creation. A 'race living by the ocean,' struggling for survival, 'must of necessity have a stronger soul, a wider outlook on life' than inland people. Equally important was the racial heritage of Nova Scotia. The 'stubborn will, the indomitable energy' of the British people was evident 'wherever a ship could sail.'[30] This English superiority was constantly juxtaposed in MacMechan's stories with 'savage blood-thirst' of American Indians or 'the caved and treacherous foreigners' ever on the verge of mutiny. The same supremacy evident in the eighteenth-century wars with France was transferred to the twentieth-century conflict with Germany. MacMechan still saw war as a gallant game with the foes of Britain as the ruthless, chauvinistic aggressors. Halifax again assumed her historic role of 'Warden of the North' during which her people were literally tried by the fires of the Great Explosion in 1917. But as always the hand of Providence intervened on the side of the altruistic, disciplined Nova Scotians who united to salvage their city.[31] Past and present mingled, as usual, in MacMechan's mind, but beneath all his writing ran the conviction that God helped man combat the evils of his fallen state according to his measure of morality. Nova Scotians, by their continuing struggle with the sea, achieved a degree of morality which received divine recognition in the form of victory over both human and natural foes. A people chosen of God, they were a fitting object of emulation for 'Young Canada.'

By his own admission Archibald MacMechan was too much the romantic to concern himself with conventional social thought. Instead his ideas on society emerged as a by-product of his major interest in literature. Echoing John Ruskin, it was his conviction that great literature was an exercise in morality, for both ethics and the principles of beauty were inherent in God's universe. As a writer, it was his function to discern the ethical precepts in nature and express them in his writings. His romantic fantasy stressed the attainment of morality through harmony with nature, a recreation in effect, of the initial garden. On an individual basis this harmony was best achieved through an intuitive perception of God's will in creation, while society as a whole would prosper only as it remained close to nature. In his historical romances, MacMechan stressed the ultimate triumph of the moral individual against the inherent evil of the environment to which his fallen state consigned him. The heroic deeds of the past, woven with the themes of Anglo-Saxon superiority, the glory of war, and Carlyle's theory of great men, were presented as a model for emulation by a modern but mundane age. Underlying both his romantic and heroic prose was one unifying concept: Christian duty. By discerning God's will through nature and by struggling against the evil of the world, man ultimately transcended his fallen state. This, whether presented in the manner of Keats or Kipling, was MacMechan's message. He remained to the end a 'professed Carlylean.'

JAMES CAPPON
Proceedings and Transactions of the Royal Society of Canada 1940
Photo courtesy Royal Society of Canada

4

JAMES CAPPON
The Ideal in Culture

James Cappon, by temperament and education, felt a profound affinity with the diverse strains of idealism current in the late nineteenth-century English-speaking world. German romanticism, American transcendentalism, and British idealism provided the basis upon which he formulated his basic conceptions of man, society, and God. Human nature he conceived of in spiritual terms, suggesting that man possessed an intuitive awareness of the World Spirit. This Spirit, in turn, was a reservoir of absolute principles, including those which governed both aesthetics and ethics. Man, therefore, had an innate appreciation of literature, for great prose and poetry, as Matthew Arnold established, combined perfection of form with elevated moral content. Literature, or in a wider sense culture, became the key not only to individual but also to social morality: it provided the criteria by which a particular nation was defined and evaluated. Culture became Cappon's basic concept, the idea which connected his views of history and art with his attitudes to politics and imperialism. It was a term rooted in the metaphysical abstractions and transcendental assumptions of the nineteenth century. These roots, in fact, were the source of its demise, for as Victorian idealism withered in the twentieth century, the idea of culture built on that branch of philosophy was left without an anchor. In 1930 Cappon and his convictions, by his own sad admission, were no longer relevant to a materialistic world.

I

James Cappon was born in 1854, the son of a Scottish shipowner from the tiny village of Broughton Ferry. Though in later life he seldom wrote of these early years, his high school days in Dundee he recalled with particular vividness. Like Andrew Macphail he considered his schooling a formative experience, writing with affection of the 'old Scotch dominie of forty years ago teaching his classical "selections" and reading Addison and Cowper to his pupils, training them in the sound traditions of industry, prudence, reverence, and intellectual discipline.' It was with such a background that he entered university in 1874, including in his studies classics, modern literature, history, and philosophy. In these years, Carlyle made a marked imprint on his thinking, as did Tennyson and Matthew Arnold, but the most important influence was his mentor and friend, Edward Caird. To a mind familiar with Carlyle's pessimistic view of nineteenth-century society and his painful investigation into the problem of personal faith, Caird's synthesis of German and Platonic idealism with traditional Christianity provided a welcome check to doubt and despair. Though Cappon ultimately chose a career in languages rather than philosophy, traces of this idealism were evident in most of his later writing and teaching.[1]

In 1879 he received his degree from Glasgow. Academic appointments in Scottish universities were difficult to obtain since 'the Arts curriculum hardly required more than nine or ten professors generally attaining longevity,' while 'the few assistants employed occupied only a temporary or hopelessly inferior position.' For half a dozen years Cappon remained at the university as a tutor, supplementing his meagre income by reading for publishing houses and contributing articles to *Blackies' Encyclopaedia*. In 1885 he left his 'inferior position' in Scotland for a post at an English school in Genoa where he remained for three years. On the strong recommendation of both Edward Caird and John Watson, and in preference to such competitors as Archibald MacMechan, he was appointed to the Chair of English at Queen's University. This position he filled for thirty-one years.[2]

On a stormy October evening in 1888 Cappon arrived at Queen's. He was then thirty-four years old and already possessed the rather awesome dignity captured in a later portrait by F.H. Varley. His hair was thick, cropped at the sides and, like his prominent eyebrows and bushy moustache, of a reddish-brown hue. The structure of his face was angular, his cheekbones and finely etched nose in perfect harmony with a firmly set jaw. His narrow mouth, when not distracted by a pipe, and his penetrating eyes combined in an expression of serious scholarly aloofness. The clothes which draped his tall frame were always of excellent quality and conservative cut. As a friend wrote, 'He may not have had *many* things – for example, he never owned a car – but he had the best of everything – the best hotels, the best whiskey, the best society.' At the same time, however, Cappon was modest and retiring, enjoying the privacy of his large house on Macdonald Park where he lived with his wife, Alice, or the quiet of his cottage at Métis Beach. In the seclusion of his library, 'generally encumbered with books and memoranda,' as well as an aged dog and cat, he spent his happiest hours. Quoting Goethe, he asserted, perhaps in reference to his own experience, 'A talent ripens best in the quiet.'[3]

Despite his penchant for solitary study, Cappon had an extremely active career at Queen's. He considered himself a 'born teacher' largely because, as he phrased it, 'I loved my subject.' It was the nineteenth-century British writers, Wordsworth, Browning, Ruskin, and Arnold who won his special affection in preference to the later Russian novelists, the French symbolists, or the Celtic school. Perhaps because of his respect for these writers and also due to the exacting standard of his own scholarship, he often appeared vigorously dogmatic in the class room. If this tendency discouraged the creative element in students, it nevertheless developed their critical capacity to a high level. This, in fact, was Cappon's ultimate goal. He considered literature 'an interpretation of life,' the study of which was, therefore, a training for existence.

This view of the function of a literary education was similar to that of Archibald MacMechan, as was the attendant role assigned to academics. Scholars were 'a mediating class between the Government and the people,' interpreting one to the other, and bringing 'rational freedom and progress' in the process. The professor, conceived of in this idealistic light, transcended the classroom and assumed the heroic stature which Carlyle accorded the Man of Letters. In practice, however, Cappon was willing to concede that the rewards of teaching were often slight. Like MacMechan, he craved only appreciation from his students, as he explained in a letter to his friend William Lawson Grant:

There is one good thing in our not over highly rated or remunerated profession of teaching, that whatever we have been able to do is bound up with the pleasant and always tender memories of student days for hundreds of old pupils.[4]

Yet Cappon's role at Queen's consisted of many duties in addition to his teaching. From 1906 to his retirement in 1919 he was, as Dean of Arts, deeply involved in the administrative affairs of the university. Here, as in his classes, he often appeared authoritarian. Recalled a friend, 'No motion failed that he strongly supported, no motion passed that he strongly opposed.' If opinionated, however, he was always fair. A theology professor who found himself in opposition to Cappon on at least one occasion wrote: 'In public matters he was decided but not bigoted. "I will fight," I remember him saying, "but I will not quarrel".' No matter how obscure an issue was, he seemed to take a lively interest. For example, when a cornerstone inscription was devised for Grant Hall, he wrote numerous letters to Sir Sandford Fleming, his friend and chancellor of Queen's, insisting that any legend ought 'to have a certain noble simplicity and gravity' before it was approved.

Of greater significance to his career at Queen's was Cappon's active stand in the controversy over the separation of the university from the Presbyterian

Church. His argument was stated with customary logic and lucidity. Only the faculties of arts and theology were under direct church control which meant that, unlike the faculties of engineering, medicine, and education, they did not receive provincial grants and their professors were ineligible for Carnegie Foundation pensions. It was Cappon's conviction that the three affiliated faculties would break away from the university and Queen's would survive, if at all, 'as a feeble appendage to a Technical Institution.' Such a result was bitterly ironic for for the simple reason that church control existed only in theory: whatever the constitution of Queen's proclaimed, the church did not interfere in the affairs of the university. Except in the case of the theological college, its real influence was extra-constitutional, based on a spirit of loyal affection and mutual support. Why, demanded Cappon, retain a constitution which was largely irrelevant when to change it would promote the growth and prosperity of Queen's?[5]

The struggle to separate from the Church, which began at the turn of the century, was finally carried to a successful conclusion in 1911. Though much of Cappon's energy was devoted to this debate, he managed as well to undertake a large share of the editorial and administrative work connected with the *Queen's Quarterly*. The journal was founded at a meeting of 'alumni and friends of Queen's University' in 1893. Capitalized with $500, the magazine's assets dwindled to a deficit by 1898. Like the *University Magazine*, the quarterly confronted various problems – insufficient advertising, poor business management, a hostile publisher – but the basic weakness was the paucity of subscriptions. In 1893 the readership was centred largely in Ontario, composed of clerics and professors, some students, a few politicians, and several institutions such as the Parliamentary Library. The total number of subscribers in the first year amounted to only 476, while sales in bookstores were described as 'practically nil.' After a dozen years of publication the journal issued 3000 copies per quarter, including in its subscription list 46 libraries and 265 schools in eastern Ontario. Nevertheless a deficit amounting to at least $1200 remained. Throughout these early years Cappon was a mainstay in the quarterly's organization. He was initially appointed editor for literature and art, but soon became general revisions editor and was often responsible for the publication of an entire issue. In addition, he regularly contributed, from 1894 until his retirement in 1919, to the 'Current Events' section of the journal and frequently wrote articles on literary and social topics. Perhaps the key to his devoted service to the quarterly lay in his conception of the role of the academic. In all nations, but especially in an intellectually immature country such as Canada, it was the duty of the man of letters to express detached opinions for the guidance of both politicians and the public.[6]

Cappon's association with the *Queen's Quarterly*, combined with his teaching and duties as dean of arts, left him little time for other activities. By 1910, in fact, the strain became apparent in two areas: his administration of the English department and his literary scholarship. When he arrived at Queen's in 1888 there were 400 students in attendance; by 1911, 563 students took English courses alone. In 1909 Cappon described the dilemma of increased enrolment to Principal Daniel Gordon:

For many years all my classes (except two Honours Classes of about 70 each) were 100 or over. Having to teach such classes twice a day and keep their interest active all the time, not only ruined my individual and exercise work, but has had, I think, a good deal to do with that peculiar nerve exhaustion from which I now suffer.

Though he was given a year's leave in 1910, the department continued to operate under a strain. In 1915, for example, the five English instructors, Dean Cappon included, were forced to share a single office. This type of tension must have influenced his literary work. Prior to 1905 he had published three major books, dealing with such diverse topics as the work of Victor Hugo, the British presence in South Africa, and the poetry of Charles G.D. Roberts, but it was another twenty-five years before his last work, a study of Bliss Carman, reached the press. Similarly, of his articles in the *Queen's Quarterly*, only two after 1899 were devoted to literary topics. Though he found himself able to undertake extensive research and, in some cases, as his unpublished study of Wordsworth suggested, prepare a first draft, final revisions were often beyond him. It was, consequently, with a measure of relief that he viewed his retirement. To his friend Sir John S. Willison he wrote:

It is something of a wrench for me to leave the old ship, and I shall feel too, the limitations of my income, but I shall be glad to have the six or seven years of working life that may remain to me free for a kind of work for which I have been preparing all my life.[7]

Though he lived for another two decades, Cappon in fact had already accomplished the work for which he would be remembered. In recognition of his contribution to Queen's he was made Professor Emeritus of English and also received not only membership in the Royal Society of Canada but two honorary doctorates as well. Despite these tributes, however, like both Andrew Macphail and Archibald MacMechan he felt increasingly isolated in the nineteen-twenties. With an element of melancholy he described, in 1917, the social changes of the preceding generation:

In most places the old pier or hotel you loved in the nineties disappeared by the end of the century and its place is taken by the newest and biggest brand of that thing which the architectural imagination can conceive. The shop in which you used to linger, perhaps unconscionably, over old prints or buy the rarer sorts of books in is gone in a few years, and the spacious emporium with many departments that occupies its place hardly keeps anything that does not sell at the rate of a hundred in the season.

In political and cultural affairs as well his conservative and idealist views, he felt, were no longer appreciated by a materialistic, egalitarian society. After the Great War he confided his fears to his friend W.L. Grant:

I don't know how you feel about the present condition of things, but I have at times to fight against a tendency to depression. We seem to have reached the decadent days of that great middle-class mercantile civilization that was so proud of itself ... even twenty years ago ... Quite a half of the legislation and movements we think progress ... are merely the movements of a sick man tossing on his bed ... The other half represents the gradual advance towards a Labour civilization, in which, for a time at least, the higher elements will suffer deterioration.

From the vantage point of 1927, his early days at Queen's assumed a rosy hue. 'I know that to you I am part of a past which is sacred in your memory,' he again wrote to Grant, 'and indeed, it now appears in a kind of ideal light to myself when a band of really fine workers and teachers were grouped around your father.' With his values and accomplishments lost in the past, Cappon died in 1939. His friend and colleague, W.E. McNeill, wrote a fitting conclusion to his career:

He was buried on a gray September day. Some yellow leaves, too early sere, brightened the ground. Only half a dozen old friends stood by the grave for he had outlived his generation.[8]

II

James Cappon belonged to the philosophic tradition of nineteenth-century idealism. Unlike Archibald MacMechan, whose idealism was born of a romantic temperament, his own ideas rested on an intellectual appreciation of a variety of transcendental thinkers. Exposed to European thought at an early age, he later recalled, 'I have been a student of German literature all my life and in my High School days "Deutschland uber Alles" used to be sung and played by us at home about as often as "Annie Laurie".' This initial acquaintance through German with the 'transcendental mode of thought' and 'its power of reconciling all the diverse historical manifestations of the human spirit' was developed fully at the University of Glasgow. In these years the 'great stimulating forces ... were Tennyson and Carlyle,' the latter especially, with his 'idealistic treatment of life and fundamental questioning of the whole social fabric,' becoming 'one of the cults of the studious youth.' Of greater importance for Cappon personally, however, was his exposure to Edward Caird. Arriving at Glasgow in 1866, Caird was 'to all academic Scotland the apostle of a new philosophic Idealism, which sought to vitalize old forms of belief by restating them in terms of reason.' His firm belief in a 'higher unity,' a spiritual absolute, was asserted in opposition to the 'common sense' school of Sir William Hamilton and the scepticism of Hume. Like T.H. Green at Oxford, he defended the tradition of Kant and Hegel, supplementing this synthesis with his own profound Christianity. To this grounding in German and British idealism Cappon added American transcendentalism, with which he became familiar, especially during his study of Bliss Carman's poetry. Emerson, he felt, proclaimed a 'spiritual optimism which permitted itself no doubt of the benevolent wisdom in nature, or the rule of the Oversoul in the world process.' While he 'laid perhaps a dangerous stress on the soul as a source of truth apart from understanding,' his position was 'carefully guarded at all points for the scholar and poet by insistence on adequate preparation [and] adequate knowledge.' These ideas had a beneficial liberating influence, making all men equally capable of communication with God, and freeing writers from 'the excessive reliance of New England Puritanism and the academic culture of the day on the authority of the past.' From the transcendental traditions of Germany, Britain, and America, then, Cappon fashioned his idealist philosophy.[9]

It was his basic conviction that the 'law of humanity is eternal.' This concept did not refer to the 'sentimental Humanitarianism' which gave rise to various movements of benevolent social reform. Rather, it meant that the moral individual intuitively perceived the ethical principles inherent in the universe and then forced his reason to govern his actions accordingly. It was this innate and enigmatic 'spirit of man' which the 'pure rationalists' such as Mill and Spencer were guilty of ignoring. Plato, the 'greatest among the great,' had begun the idealist tradition but it was left to other men to build upon his foundation. Kant, for example, had shown 'that the existence of a moral will' in man 'involves *the idea* at least of God and immortality,' though Cappon felt 'the stringent reasoner' might not 'formally' accept his logic. The man whose system he fully endorsed was Hegel. His reasons for this acceptance were twofold: first, Hegel's system was all-inclusive, explaining the course of history with faithful adherence to the realities of existence; secondly, he had a 'vital' conception of the Absolute, humanity, and the relationship between them. By, in effect, reuniting the realms of reason and metaphysical speculation previously separated by Rousseau, Hume, and Kant, Hegel had achieved the synthesis for which the Western mind had searched for centuries. For Cappon the essential addition to his system was made by Caird: the Absolute was identified with the Christian God.[10]

This Hegelian idealism provided the underpinning for most of Cappon's personal convictions. But its implications extended beyond his own thought, for it was his belief that the ethical integrity of any nation depended on the degree to which it collectively subscribed to an idealist philosophy. One source from which such values could be derived was religious faith, the basis on which 'the fabric of society' was constructed. The Bible he considered 'the supreme expression of that faith,' making necessary its preservation 'as a vital element in modern life and thought.' This was precisely the task undertaken by higher criticism, 'mediating between the reason of modern man and the capacity for faith which exists in him.' Closely allied to religion in the work of inculcating idealism in society was education, a process which Cappon always considered in a spiritual light. To a large degree this conviction reflected his conception of the professor as the mean between the rulers and the ruled, the detached observer capable of advancing an objective and ethically sound opinion. It also reflected his attachment to his own particular discipline for it was from the study of literature, he felt, that society acquired high ideals. In fact, he wrote:

The average man's knowledge of what is going on in the world around him ... is derived from literature ... It is really literature which binds men together in a spiritual world and gives such solidarity of moral consciousness to society as it has attained ... the profoundly systematized thought of Fichte with its austere logical form appears in a later stage of development in Carlyle ... In this way the latest and most concrete form of Kants, Rousseaus, Hegels, Lamarks, and Savignys may be ultimately found in the poetry of Schiller and Wordsworth and Browning, or in the novels of Tolstoi and Bourget.

A society in Cappon's view, acquainted with religion and great literature, the latter defined as works which embodied ethical principles, would necessarily subscribe to a higher idealism.[11]

His faith in Hegel's philosophy of history and his familiarity with Carlyle's idealism determined as well the nature of his personal political philosophy. He considered himself 'a Conservative in politics' and, indeed, felt the entire 'University culture is conservative ... a kind of rational counterpoise to the exaggerations of the passing day and the narrowness of spirit that is hardly alive to anything beyond its local horizon.' Yet he realized, like Hegel, that liberalism had once been a necessary and beneficial stage in the development of civilization. Nineteenth-century liberalism, with its 'watchwords of humanity, progress [and] freedom of speech,' was dedicated to 'the removal of abuses ... inherited from a past state of society.' Emphasizing individual freedom and free trade, condemning positive government and imperialism, it 'was an inspiring creed as long as that particular class of constitutional abuses existed which a parliamentary statute can reform.' By the twentieth century, however, such beliefs had become obsolete. The freedom of liberalism degenerated into the crass materialism of utilitarianism, and society, 'a huge, ugly, uniform structure founded largely on systematized greed and extortion,' lost all contact with cultural or humanitarian ideals. This situation, in Cappon's opinion, demonstrated 'the necessity of finding the right line between the unwise restriction of freedom and the suppression of abuses.' Such was the message of Carlyle, Froude, and Ruskin, and such, he believed, was the ambition of Joseph Chamberlain's 'new conservatism.' A 'wise conservatism,' he felt, would 'never oppose itself blindly and impulsively to reform and reconstruction' but would 'assist in every readjustment needed to accommodate them to the growth of democratic forces.' By viewing liberalism and conservativism locked in the dialectical process, Cappon arrived at a political philosophy not unlike the 'Red Toryism' of Carlyle.[12]

From the Hegelian concept of inevitable dialectic Cappon derived his view of history, while from his belief in the spiritual unity between man and the Absolute he found the basis for his literary judgements. These ideas on the course of civilization and the elements of aesthetics combined to make him a conservative idealist. All men were organically related to each other and their environment through contact with the Absolute; nations, in turn, rose or fell according to the degree to which their national culture approximated to the truth inherent in the World Spirit. First encountered during his early years in Scotland, these ideas developed into the basis for most of his thought in later life. Indeed, as in the case of Andrew Macphail, they explained the pessimism he felt at the conclusion of the Great War. In one of his last 'Current Events' columns for the *Queen's Quarterly*, he sadly wrote of the chaotic materialism which had grown up in the society around him:

This disease to which our middle-class civilization is so peculiarly susceptible was long ago diagnosed as a deadly one by thinkers such as Carlyle, Froude, and Ruskin ... Ruskin's views formulate exactly the questions which have become the most urgent problems of civilization to-day while Mill's fundamental principles have become as clearly useless as the steam machinery of his time.

Cappon remained to the end a nineteenth-century idealist.[13]

III

Cappon's conservative idealism was, as with Ruskin and Carlyle, the matrix from which his social thought developed. He conceived of society itself in a Hobbesian fashion, for he wrote: 'There can be no free condition of man previous to society with rights to surrender which are rationally or morally superior to those of society even under the worst forms of despotism.' Society rested on neither convenience nor coercion, but rather, on the individual's recognition that the community was a fragile creation founded on mutual co-operation. 'Respect for the principles on which society is based is the only thing which can hold a free society together,' he asserted, 'When that respect begins to fail, the chaotic flood of Revolution is not far off.' Organized collective existence, in other words, was the conscious formulation of man's mind, depending on his belief in the 'law of humanity' for its success. It was an exercise in 'harmonizing the freedom and the unity of the diverse elements,' an attempt to define 'the rights of the individual as against the claims of the state.' Only if men were motivated by a Christian idealism absorbed from literature and religion could such a harmony be achieved. The further a civilization advanced, wrote Cappon,

the more does society require not only mechanical and social organization by means of science and law but also the purely intellectual or spiritual organization which gives all the rest harmony. A moral consent which is profoundly aesthetic in its character is the necessary cement of a highly constituted society.

The assumption underlying this statement was Hegelian in origin and profoundly important for Cappon's thought. It not only demonstrated his belief that a nation was defined primarily in terms of its culture, but also revealed his tendency to rank a particular society in a hierarchy of civilization according to what he inferred as its ethical standard. Society was an organic blend of varied elements, helping each to achieve freedom through co-operation with the whole. As each individual attained a higher degree of morality, the collectivity advanced. This, ultimately, was the dynamic of all human history.[14]

Cappon's political thought followed naturally from his conception of society and was centred largely on the problem of reconciling individual freedom and equality with both social unity and high cultural standards. 'When the people cry out there is always a real grievance,' he wrote, 'but the remedy they ask for is not necessarily the right one.' Quoting Hegel, he asserted, 'those who know govern, not the ignorant.' Such was the case in Britain where, in contrast to Germany, an aristocracy 'trained to work with democracy' guided the nation. Since the United States was a commercial society and needed the supervision of experts in that field, the potential for leadership existed among 'the ablest, the least tainted' businessmen, Morgan, Harriman, and Hill. Under the enlightened guidance of an élite, the modern democracy would avoid the pitfall of corrupt, unprincipled 'partyism' and instead realize that legitimate government derived its power from a slowly evolving constitution, from adherence to the rule of law rather than the rule of the people. The people, in effect, reached freedom through the careful, orderly supervision of their superiors.[15]

Before such a model state could be attained, however, democracy had to face the problem of combining a belief in equality with the maintenance of high cultural standards. 'The possibility of democracy maintaining itself at all,' Cappon wrote, 'depends on its capacity for education, that is, on its capacity for discerning honesty and truth.' The solution to the problem of preserving high ethical-cultural standards fell again to an élite, in this case composed of scholars and journalists. The intellectual mediated between the rulers and the ruled, advising the former and teaching certain standards of morality to the latter. The journalist, on the other hand, while participating in the educative task, existed primarily as a watchdog commenting upon the activities of government. Cappon's view of political society, then, was based on a conception of liberty which emphasized order, gradual change, and organic unity among all elements of society — rulers, intellectuals, and the people. The principles of conservatism and idealism combined to formulate Cappon's political philosophy; as a result, he joined his contemporaries, Macphail and MacMechan, in the 'Red Tory' tradition of Carlyle and Ruskin.[16]

This mixture of élitism and sympathy for the lower orders of society was equally explicit in Cappon's economic thought. Unlike Andrew Macphail, he harboured no delusions about a bucolic future for Canada. 'I have no wish to see conglomerations ... like Blackpool ... planted on the shores of the St Lawrence,' he wrote, 'but they are likely to come for all that...' And with urbanization would come industrialism. This process had been tolerable in the optimistic days of mid-nineteenth-century Britain when the businessman was a 'well-bred gentleman.' But by 1900, especially in the United States, such men no longer existed: their successors were crass materialists emphasizing the new rather than the best and corrupting society with their false ethic. Unfortunately, when he examined American society, it was Cappon's conviction that 'the problems which are theirs today may be ours to-morrow'; consequently, he took a particularly favourable interest in the activities of Theodore Roosevelt and the progressive reformers. In 1880 he felt competition and trade practices had been self-regulating but inevitably larger corporations had emerged which could only be regulated by some form of government intervention. In Canada this type of control would combine with the new imperialism of Joseph Chamberlain and would include not only a higher tariff, but also federal subsidies for specific industries.[17]

Supervision of industry was not, however, the only aspect of the economy which required attention: a reconciliation between labour and capital was even more important. 'Nothing but respect for the honesty of the means by which the superior position is acquired can still the envy of the labouring millions,' wrote Cappon, 'or give the superior minority the moral power to defend and maintain that position as a rightful one...' If American business leaders insisted upon interpreting personal worth in monetary terms, they would ultimately breed revolutionary discontent among the 'working-man who will never have more than they need for bare existence.' It was time to leave behind the myth that anyone could become affluent, a relic of the optimistic days of laissez-faire, and devise a new creed suited to the age of giant corporations and a permanent working-class. What was needed was a 'true education' for the worker, devoid of materialism, which 'would place him in the matter of intellectual and aesthetic enjoyment of life on a level with the highest professional.' He concluded: 'I think such a gospel, combined with sufficient improvement in the working-man's condition, might be a practical one.' Based on the realization, then, that industrial development was inevitable, Cappon's economic thought stressed two major concepts: government supervision of industry and a conscious attempt to reconcile the worker to his station while at the same time improving that position. As in his political thought, he managed to combine both concern for the many with a firm belief in supervision by the few.[18]

Though he often wrote of political or economic affairs, it was evident that the major focus of Cappon's attention was with the idea of culture. In fact, his consideration of social problems was often simply a chance to express his attitudes towards aesthetic or ethical issues. The link between the two areas of thought, social and cultural, was his Hegelian definition of 'the State as embodying a cultural end which expresses the traditions, the instincts, and characteristics of the people.' This national value system, he asserted, 'does not come to any race quickly,' nor is it created by 'some exceptional individuals.' Rather, it required 'a collective ability to ... establish ... what is best in itself and maintain that as a moral order over all its individuals.' Once such standards had been discerned the 'state must do what it can reasonably do to make this life of the nation homogeneous and universal as an inspiring and supporting tradition for every one of its members.' The nation, in Cappon's view, was primarily a cultural entity, each citizen organically related to the whole by a set of traditional ethical and aesthetic assumptions. Like Matthew Arnold, he believed that the best means to preserve and develop this national culture was through education, specifically, the study of literature.[19]

The 'main line of education,' he contended, 'is ... a literary and philosophical interpretation of life...' It is an attempt to acquaint students with the 'spiritual life' of mankind, an exercise in showing the continuity between the present and all that has gone before. These assumptions explain Cappon's assertion that 'university work' is 'one of the main supports of civilization.' Both 'conservative in its standards' and the product of an aged, evolving tradition, the university was a 'rational counterpoise' to the transient whims of society. It was a place of idealism, divorced from utilitarian pursuits, where enlightened scholars taught of what was best in man's past.[20]

This view of the university suggested the general purpose which Cappon assigned to education: it was a process designed to cultivate certain socially acceptable standards of conduct and opinion. 'The old ideal of the educationalist was the scholar,' he wrote, 'the new ideal is the citizen, that is the successful tradesman, farmer or engineer.' A select minority in a country received a university education. Later, as the 'intellectual leaders of the nation' they would convey the idealism they had been taught to 'the mass through the press, the stage, the pulpit, the platform, through literature, and professional labour generally...' Unfortunately, education seemed to Cappon progressively less able to fulfill its function: it was increasingly regimented, geared to the mediocre student, and dominated by technical subject matter. In its proper place, he asserted, there was nothing wrong with technical education, but it should not intrude upon either the university or the high school. The only valid type of education for citizenship was literary:

For the man of to-day lives in a large mental area and in a complex social organism in which his general efficiency as a citizen depends more on his power of psychological analysis, his power of judging from speech and written accounts as to the nature of what is happening around him, than on his observations of the phenomena of nature. That is, it depends on a kind of power which we may call broadly the literary sense.

Both individual morality and the success of democracy appeared to Cappon as a function of education; and education, in turn, was based largely on literature.[21]

Two important questions were suggested by this theory of education: first, what constituted great literature?; secondly, when did it exert a beneficial influence on its readers? Cappon's answer to these inquiries was found in his definition of poetry and artistic form. Echoing Matthew Arnold, he wrote: 'The vision as interpretation of life is of course the first thing, the fundamental impulse in poetry and all higher art...' For this reason, it was profoundly important that the poet write from his own experience. Bliss Carman, for example, produced his best poetry when he chose bucolic Canada as his subject. Equally significant, as the French critic, Charles Augustin Sainte-Beuve, had shown, was the poet's own background. In Carman's case the high ethical tone of his poetry derived at least in part from his New England Puritan and Loyalist ancestry. Ideas, however, were not the sole component of poetry: form was of almost equal significance and in some cases actually gave inspiration to the subject matter. The principles of style were eternal: beauty, imagination, and reason, the essential ingredients, remained immutable and transcendent truths. A stylistic revolt against these varieties was, therefore, futile: true freedom of expression could come only from harmony with the absolute of beauty. It was on the basis of their aesthetic theory that Cappon formulated his critical judgements. With equal disdain he dismissed both the ethical instability of Oscar Wilde and his dictum of 'art for art's sake' and the formless aberrations of Walt Whitman. In his taste in literature he remained a follower of Arnold and Sainte-Beuve.[22]

Through his definition of poetry and the principles of art, Cappon hinted at the way in which he believed literature to exert a beneficial influence on society. Art, he felt, appealed directly to an innate characteristic of mankind:

The aesthetic sense of life ... is not the mere produce of direct contact with nature ... It has a nobler root in the sense men have of the passage of human life, of the relation of the present to the past, that humanizing, half-pitiful sense humanity has of its own movement onward...

The best authors appealed to this inherent 'aesthetic sense' by borrowing the formal ideas of the philosopher, embodying them in poetry or imaginative prose, and ultimately implanting them in the 'moral consciousness' of society. Of course, poetry could only 'express aspects of the truth in a fragmentary way,' never showing 'their place in a philosophical system.' But if the intellectual scope of poetry was limited, it had the advantage of poetic form to establish its message. By using the absolute principles of beauty the poet tapped the soul of the universe. As a result, wrote Cappon, he 'sees the true form of life admidst the confusing multiplicity of the phenomena and presents it with superior clearness of vision.' This characteristic was the great merit of modern French poetry with its 'intellectual austerity' and the great failure of materialistic, vulgar American verse and prose. Literature, in effect, not only mirrored the culture and character of a nation, but was instrumental in its formation. Beside the transcendent importance of literature and education, politics and economics seemed to fade into obscurity.[23]

The idea of culture, then, considered in literary rather than political terms such as Hegel employed, became the distinguishing feature of the nation. For Cappon, this conception of the state provided a reasonably objective criterion by which to allocate positions in the hierarchy of civilization. Since culture was a reflection of morality and morality, in turn, was an attempt to reach harmony with the eternal principles of the absolute, a nation's ethical-aesthetic development was linked to an absolute standard of value. In fact, this idea of cultural hierarchy took the place of a belief in biological or racial hierarchy. Cappon, like many of his contemporaries, associated certain character traits with particular nations. The Japanese, for example, combined a European capacity for organization and bravery with a native Oriental cunning and diligence. But beyond this descriptive type of remark about race, he did not attempt to speculate. He did not believe, for instance, that the native tribes of Africa were inherently inferior to whites in either their moral or intellectual capacity: the circumstances of environment and history had simply left them culturally underdeveloped. Similarly, he did not exhibit racial bias against non-Anglo-Saxon immigrants. The problem of the alien was not that he was racially inferior, but simply that he was a cultural stranger unable to appreciate 'the long established traditions of national life.' In his native country he was doubtless a sound and responsible citizen. Though he associated levels of culture with particular peoples, Cappon's view of race was not deterministic. At a precise point in time the culture of a specific group might appear backward when compared to that of another group, but it would not necessarily remain so forever, the inferior product of an inferior race. This conception of the relationship between race and culture was the key to Cappon's theory of history.[24]

'The history of man,' he wrote, 'is a quest for the spiritual infinitude of destiny.' As a nation feared God and attempted to follow the eternal 'law of humanity,' it rose in the scale of civilization. This process of moral progress was best learned through the study of literature, especially the classics. He wrote:

The essential conception of literary education as a whole is that it is the study of man's constant endeavour to keep alive his spiritual life ... no man can have a true understanding of his age and the meaning of its needs and activities, if his literary education is insufficient to enable him to see the present in relation to the whole of which it is a part. The present lives far more of the past than it is conscious of.

History, then, provided certain guidelines for the present. It was essentially a study in idealism, chronicling 'the long history of man's spiritual progress.' Yet Cappon was careful to add that this progress was not without interruption. 'Civilization,' he contended, 'is a middle term between an ideal of progress and the material conditions of nature and man moves with a certain vacillation ... between the two.' If his fallen state led man to occasional periods of regression, his innate idealism inevitably returned him to the path of moral perfection.[25]

Most of Cappon's attitudes towards society, culture, and history were combined in his consideration of one of the most popular topics in the years preceding the Great War: the nature of imperialism. The growth of empires, he held, was among the inevitable 'tendencies of the age,' the 'great phenomenon of our time, just as the evolution of great kingdoms out of feudal duchies and principalities was at the close of the middle-ages.' Beginning in the early nineteenth century, British and French middle-class values began to spread first to most civilized countries and then to underdeveloped colonies. This expansionist impulse was rooted in the 'instinct' of a nation 'to extend its type of civilization, the moral ideals and discipline which it represents over barbarous and rude communities where nothing valuable to humanity is displaced.' It was an attempt 'to put order instead of disorder' and was expressed primarily in cultural terms. The white race had successfully curbed the latent animalism of man, yet retained a large measure of rational freedom. This mixture of the 'moral qualities of moderation, good temper, and a decent respect for justice and humanity ... combined with energy of action' was the secret to Britain's imperial supremacy and the aspect which distinguished it from the barbarous expansion of Napoleonic France or imperial Germany.

The consequence of English rule in culturally underdeveloped areas, among them South Africa and India, was 'a state of law and justice ... on a par with that of the most civilized countries of Europe.' In more developed countries such as Canada, Britain was less a moral tutor than a partner in freedom. To remain outside the Empire was to accept 'the position of a minor state,' while to join with England was to attain to the full freedom of nationhood. Certainly there were pragmatic motives which stressed territorial aggrandizement and economic gain. But Cappon preferred to view the development of a world of balanced empires as a step towards peace and the triumph of the white man's superior culture. His most concise definition of the British Empire seemed to be a summation of his social and cultural philosophy:

The Empire represents an ideal of high importance for the future of civilization, the attempt to assemble in a higher unity than even that of nationality the forces which maintain and advance the white man's ideals of civilization, his sense of justice, his constitutional freedom, his respect for law and order, his humanity. It is an attempt to transcend the evils of nationality ... without impairing the vigour which the national consciousness gives to a people ...To reconcile the principles of Imperial Unity with freedom of national development for all parts capable of using such freedom is the ideal of the British Empire.[26]

By 1930 Cappon's idealistic, Hegelian conception of world history and culture lay shattered in the aftermath of the Great War. He had assumed that imperialism was an inevitable step in the history of man's spiritual progress towards the absolute. With the defeat of Germany he had expected to see the British concept of culture spread its idealism across the globe. Such, however, had not been the result of the war; in fact, as his letters to W.L. Grant illustrated, he knew his particular brand of social idealism had no place in a materialistic, individualistic society. His friend, W.E. McNeill, perceptively remarked that 'he had outlived his generation.' With an air of detached resignation Cappon himself described the intellectual changes of the twentieth century that had left him isolated:

at the turn of the century ... a general change was taking place in the spirit of the age. The current of aesthetic decadentism and brutal naturalism had done little more than ruffle the surface, but the doubt of any absolute truth in our knowledge of the universe, the underlying uncertainty in the mystical tradition of humanity was emerging into a clearer expression of itself. The age had become more questioning, less ready to accept the transcendental answers and solutions, proved inclined to seek what answer could be got in verifiable experiences and realistic values. It was an age for William James and Santayana to speak in rather than for Hegel and Royce, with their philosophy of the absolute.[27]

MAURICE HUTTON
Proceedings and Transactions of the Royal Society of Canada 1940
Photo courtesy Royal Society of Canada

5

MAURICE HUTTON
Classical-Christian Idealist

Maurice Hutton once referred to himself as an ancient Greek born out of his time and place. Had he in fact lived in the classical world, however, he would have found himself as intellectually uncomfortable as he occasionally did in the twentieth century. The Greeks lacked what may have been his most cherished conviction, Christianity, while the modern world was deficient in the intellectual sophistication of the classical period. These two strains in Hutton's thought, Greek philosophy and orthodox Christianity, combined to make of him a Victorian idealist. After 1880 he felt the correspondence between this system of convictions and social reality diminished. A misplaced faith in technological innovation mitigated against the trust in intuition necessary as a foundation for religion, while a false belief that all men were equal ignored the basic distinction between good and bad upon which all morality was based. Liberal rationalism, then, was the force which Hutton felt had made his belief structure an anachronism by 1920. This disintegration was rooted in the extension of scientific empiricism in the late nineteenth century to other phases of knowledge and became overt during the Great War with its emphasis on technological and bureaucratic efficiency. The war, in fact, was a dividing point in Hutton's personal life: though he tenaciously remained a Victorian until his death in 1940, he knew that he and his idealist convictions were out of step with an egalitarian, materialistic age.

I

Maurice Hutton was born at Manchester, England, in 1856. Years after he recalled that he had received 'a start in life no longer in this distracted age generally available: birth, training, and education in an old-fashioned Victorian and God-fearing home.' Indeed, his early years must have been marked by a firm grounding in both religion and literature, for the six Hutton children were 'sworn to temperance, soberness, and chastity,' while he himself 'was a

"walking dictionary"' by the time he was twelve years old. Joseph Henry
Hutton, his father, following the path of both his own father and grandfather,
was a Unitarian minister, though he later became a rector in the Church of
England. Maurice Hutton's uncle, Richard Holt Hutton, was editor of the
Spectator and 'one of the most influential writers on politics, theology, and
literature in the nineteenth century.' His essays, which the young Maurice
must have read, were largely concerned with literary criticism and the controversy between science and religion. It was his uncle's belief, substantiated by
his shift to the Anglican Church, that traditional religious precepts could be
reconciled with, rather than displaced by, scientific knowledge. In such a
family atmosphere of piety and culture, then, Hutton formulated his early
convictions. The profound concern for religion remained throughout his life,
one of the distinguishing features of his thought.[1]

The education begun at home was continued at Magdalen College School.
As 'I look back on ... my own school days,' Hutton recalled, 'some of the men
to whom I am most grateful, are not the amiably selfish who never worried
themselves or me, who never excited me or themselves, but the sarcastic nag-
ging slave drivers...' The rigour of this early training at public school contributed to his success at Oxford. In 1877 he took a first in Classical
Moderations at Worcester College and two years later another in Literae
Humaniores. This period he later referred to as 'that happier age.' It was an
exciting era of religious controversy, especially between Newman and his followers in the Oxford Movement, and the Humanist school represented by Benjamin Jowett, Master of Balliol College, and Mark Pattison, Rector of Lincoln
College. Hutton's sympathies were with the latter group who, on the basis of
their classical studies, stood opposed to church domination and demanded the
right of each man to reason his own rule of life. Hutton's affinity for the
originality and sophistication of Greek philosophy, developed during these university years, was the second major characteristic of his thought.[2]

With his education completed, Hutton was elected a Fellow of Merton College in 1879 and accepted a teaching post at Sheffield. By 'a stroke of luck'
he learned through friends of the vacancy in classics at the University of
Toronto. At this time he found Britain's 'congested and over-peopled cities'
and 'the fierce competition' in business quite uncongenial. He preferred to live
in 'a land with a small population and endless acres,' a land of equality and
prosperity 'for all men of good will.' These considerations, together with the
sound academic reputation of University College, led him to accept the Chair
of Classics in 1880. Despite a nativist outcry in Toronto against the appointment of a non-Canadian, Hutton won immediate popularity and remained, for
the next half century, a familiar figure on the Toronto campus.[3]

When he arrived at University College, he introduced an entirely new atmosphere to the department of Greek. His predecessor, John McCaul, emphasized rhetoric and epigraphy in the tradition of his own training at Trinity College, Dublin. Hutton, in contrast, brought 'the spirit of Oxford "Greats",' with its stress on the philosophy and history of ancient Greece. This approach towards classics was reflected in his four volumes of essays, written during his years at Toronto and published between 1927 and 1930. His scholarship was quite different from the scientific, precise research of German or American classicists. Rather, it was impressionistic, often discursive, and always designed to illustrate a moral lesson. His style was parenthetical, urbane, and usually witty, finding expression on topics as diverse as *Alice in Wonderland* and the Platonic conception of poetry. The attitude which underlay this almost casual approach to scholarship was his concept of education: it was a process designed less for the training of the intellect than to cultivate 'character,' a word which to Hutton denoted an amorphous combination of manners and morals. Teaching became, as a result, 'the noblest of all professions.' Though public esteem was not among the professor's rewards, he enjoyed many other compensations: continual contact with the idealism of youth, a lifelong opportunity to indulge the 'bookworm' impulse, and the responsibility of training the nation's leaders. For these reasons Hutton felt that his life had been 'happy, beyond the ordinary human measure happy' and concluded, 'I never remember a time when I should not have been glad and proud and ambitious to teach Greek in a university...'[4]

Reminiscences from his former students suggest that Hutton had good reasons to feel his academic life had been a success. He was seen as 'a Greek born out of due time' whose personal attempt 'to embody the ideals the classics stand for' was a shining example to students. He combined a capacity for incisive criticism with a wide range of knowledge and a philosophical mind. Witty and entertaining as a lecturer, he took a sincere interest in his students long after they left the university. His classes gave 'polish and letters to raw country boys' and 'stimulated many to think out life's problems with Plato and Aristotle as guides.' In fact, wrote R.H. Coats, the Dominion Statistician, 'we found something which served as a foundation for our subsequent intellectual lives.' If this generalization was accurate, Hutton's influence extended far beyond the confines of University College. Among his students were academics such as F.H. Underhill and C.B. Sissons, as well as C.W. Gordon (Ralph Connor), the author and cleric, B.K. Sandwell, the editor of *Saturday Night*, W.M. Martin, premier of Saskatchewan, and J.C. Breckenridge, general superintendent of the National Trust Company. To several generations of University College students, regardless of their subsequent vocations, Hutton remained a figure of reverence.[5]

His career at Toronto, however, included many activities in addition to teaching. Soon after his arrival he took a keen interest in extracurricular functions, acting in several classical drama productions and conducting non-denominational morning services at the college. He was a regular weekend speaker in rural Ontario towns as part of the university's program of popular lectures and, in fact, later published a volume of these discourses. Perhaps of a more immediate significance to the university was his administrative career. In 1901 he became principal of University College, a post he retained until his retirement in 1929, while during 1906 he was acting president of the university, though he refused to continue permanently in that capacity. His first concern remained the teaching of Greek, for his temperament was that of a scholar rather than an administrator.[6]

In both deportment and demeanour Hutton seemed to typify the Oxford classicist. His face wore an expression of slightly amused detachment. His thinning hair and full, though neatly trimmed moustache were silver grey. This, together with the kindly wrinkles at the corners of his eyes and mouth, gave him an almost angelic appearance. Conservative in manner and dress, yet liberal in his toleration for different opinions, he was a 'humorous whimsical' companion. With his wife, the daughter of John McCaul, and his three children, he seemed to lead a happy existence both in Toronto and at his summer home near James Cappon's at Métis Beach. Perhaps referring to his own experience, he wrote that a good marriage was 'a blessing and a discipline in the best lessons of life, in affection, sympathy, patience, and consideration.' Though he had few very intimate acquaintances, he was a regular member of Goldwin Smith's Round Table dinner group, as well as the Browning Society and the Faculty Union, and was generally considered a genial and entertaining conversationalist. Sir Robert Falconer, the president of the University of Toronto, captured his character by describing him as the paradigm of 'the cultivated English gentleman walking in the path of the just.' Accurate though this assessment was, Hutton's own description was still more revealing. 'I am,' he simply stated, 'a Mid-Victorian.'[7]

Though academic honours came his way in later years, like many other intellectuals of his age Hutton felt increasingly isolated from his society and its thought. It was his opinion that the 'two forces which have fashioned me between them are Victorianism and Democracy.' The former term signified for him an idealism based on education, chiefly classical, and Christian faith, while the latter meant government by freely elected but superior members of society. In the eighteen-eighties the world began to move away from such values, with the result that by the nineteen-twenties Hutton found that he shared a profound 'Victorian pessimism with many other Victorians.' Society, he asserted, was in the midst of 'intellectual chaos.' The university had declined in quality as students increased in quantity. Religious faith was considered 'out of date,' while in its place existed only 'the commercial spirit ... wholly dedicated to the present life and indifferent to any other.' In political affairs rule by 'the some-bodies' was replaced by government by often corrupt and usually ignorant 'no-bodies.' The two forces which seemed responsible for these changes, in Hutton's view, were a foolish egalitarianism and the uncontrolled development of science. As early as 1909 he wrote:

It seems to be coming so close, I mean that great scientific tyranny of the coming socialistic scientific state, and sometimes ... I have fallen only towards morning into an uneasy slumber, out of which I am awakened by the rumble of cart wheels beneath my bedroom windows, why then sometimes I awake with a start of terror and I think this hour of scientific terror has really struck...[8]

It was a relief to retreat from this spectre of impending doom to the pleasures of ancient Greece, in Hutton's words, 'the only society where I seem to be at home.' But in his later years he appeared increasingly discontented, feeling that he and his idealism would be remembered only as a portrait, 'a space six feet by four on a common-room wall ... and identified by a few aging Professors and some white-headed graduates, who will recollect that it belonged to one who once taught a dead language in University College.' Though he claimed his pes-simism was impersonal, essentially a lament for a passing age, the note of personal melancholy was unmistakable. In the final essay in his final book occurred a revealing phrase: he expressed regret that 'the old man ... in an age like ours has often outlived himself and outlived romance: and is only conscious of dull days and apathetic end.' Hutton's own end and, perhaps, the end of a certain idealist tradition in Canada, came in 1940.[9]

II

Maurice Hutton's thought was characterized by the same dichotomy between Hellenism and Hebraism which pervaded the thinking of Matthew Arnold: as a scholar he was aware that man had never established any philosophical absolutes, while as a devout Christian he accepted the transcendental truth of religion. The process of reconciling these two apparently contradictory attitudes constituted the core of his philosophy. He began with the premise that there were certain 'insoluble problems of a moral and emotional order.' Man's grasp of them was at best 'fragmentary,' with the result that truth was 'always relative.' This conclu-sion, however, was hardly an adequate basis for life 'because without belief, life becomes a chaos, a welter, a result of chance and accident.' Fortunately, confu-sion was part of a dialectical process for, Hutton wrote, 'the cure for doubt is more doubt ... since doubt ultimately cures itself even in questions which seem insoluble and the solution which is essential for continued living then imposes itself, just because it is so essential.' What he meant by this assertion, reminiscent of Carlyle's thesis in *Sartor Resartus*, was simply that beliefs rested on faith rather than reason. 'Personally,' he wrote, 'I doubt if the intellectual judgments can be trusted in moral and emotional matters: no, nor even in mere questions of fact.' Instead men must employ the 'Pragmatist test of truth,' for whatever beliefs are suited to an individual's needs 'are, broadly, true.'[10]

Despite his faith in the ability of each individual to devise intuitively his own system of ethics, Hutton seemed convinced that all such systems would not only be reasonable but would also affirm certain moral absolutes. The former characteristic he felt could be derived from an acquaintance with Greek philosophy. From the study of ancient Greece came an appreciation for the intellectual qualities inherent in science and art, a feeling for the logic of history, and a respect for individual freedom. Unfortunately, however, this same intellectual rigour, the emphasis on reason rather than intuition, created a moral vacuum at the heart of Greek thought. Individualism carried to its logical conclusion became simply enlightened self-interest, while the stress on intellectualism precluded an appreciation of religious faith. Certainly Plato's writings, in Hutton's view, evidenced a conception of immortality and God. But the soul he considered only as a segment of the spirit of reason, which ignored the idea of individual personality and heaven, while his view of God gave man excessive free will. Only Aristotle among the Greeks had a rudimentary vision of an omnipotent divinity to whose will man must conform. It was not until Roman civilization emerged that true morality entered the world. Conservative, tenacious, and disciplined, the Roman had a prosaic honesty and an innate respect for law and order. What made the difference between the two societies, Greek and Roman, was the latter's contact with the Christian concept of morality. Only if the intellectualism of classical Greece was tempered with ethics could it provide a beneficial training for life. St Paul, Hutton concluded, 'has contributed to our type of civilization more largely than the Greeks.'[11]

Religion, then, was the missing element in classical thought, the source from which the individual derived his knowledge of certain moral absolutes. It was 'a permanent instinct,' within all men, quite unrelated to intellectual capacity. In recognition of this innate tendency, Christianity viewed man as a creature whose frequent sins were partially mitigated by good intentions. Though perfectibility on earth was impossible, it was the church's duty to teach 'the three decisive Christian virtues': 'faith accomplishes more than knowledge; hope more than experience; charity more than caution.' The essential doctrinal tenets in which these lessons were embodied Hutton summarized as belief in 'the existence of God and the goodness of God, the reality of the Day of Judgment, and of some kind of Heaven and Hell.' He conceded, however, that these convictions were 'by no means confined to the best and latest religion, Christianity.' This realization led him, after the fashion of William James, to the position that Christian creeds 'are only true in some mythical sense; that is ... they are the highest truths a man can reach at present, and true to his heart's needs and the needs of his conscience.' Certainly, 'a few select and academic souls like Aristotle' were able to gratify their spiritual needs without reference to religion. But for the majority of humanity, religion was absolutely essential to give both meaning and morality to existence. 'After all,' wrote Hutton, 'is not Nature the enemy ... both human nature, the beastliness and animalism of man, and Physical nature?' Only by accepting this fact, by viewing earthly life as a punishment, the result of Adam's fall, could existence become at once comprehensible and bearable. From such an orthodox Christian perspective life became 'a halfway house to something better, a precursor of a new start.' It was, essentially, a time of moral preparation for future reward.[12]

From both Christian and classical thought Hutton fashioned his basic philosophic convictions. 'These meeting points,' he wrote, 'these junctions, so to speak, of the divergent highroads of Religion and Intelligence, of Christianity and Literature, spirits never identical ... and indeed often vehemently ... opposed to each other – these junctions have always appealed to me...' But, he cautioned, a 'sober man, who wants to see life as a whole must concern himself with each atmosphere and find some means of reconciling ... the two interpretations of life.' This could best be done by recognizing that classical thought dealt with things of the world, while Christianity was a separate phenomenon upon which the process of reason had no bearing. In matters of ethics, he wrote, 'Beware of the realist ... Better listen to ... the idealist who idealizes virtue.' Only through religious faith could man discern 'the ultimate things ... the ultimate distinction of better and worse, of energy and indolence, of capacity and incapacity, of efficiency and inefficiency, of right and wrong.' Once his intuitive convictions were established, and it was Hutton's assumption that all good men would concur on 'the ultimate things,' he could then depend on his reason to direct his will in daily life. It was precisely because the utilitarians, like the ancient Greeks, attempted to found their basic ethical principles on reason, ignoring the fact that such beliefs 'must rest on foundations closer to rock-bottom: more mystical and metaphysical and instinctive ... on religion in fact,' that their system crumbled into self-interest and materialism. Only an idealism anchored on religious faith and translated into rational conduct could provide, Hutton asserted, the philosophical basis for a moral life.[13]

From this synthesis of religion and Greek intellectualism, Hutton arrived at certain conclusions concerning the nature of man and morality which provided the basis for his social thought. Man, a fallen creature, combined in his soul both barbarism and saintliness. Through the self-control implicit in classical studies and the ethical precepts of Christianity, man could temper his exile with aspirations of perfection. Yet he was faced with a continuing struggle against both his own nature and his environment. The 'natural man' was 'a moral democrat acknowledging no hierarchy in his impulses and instincts, no higher and lower, no better or worse...' Nature itself, as the exile to which Adam had been expelled, was equated with 'plague, pestilence, and famine,' the antithesis of religion. It was, in fact, the existential battle against his own weaknesses and his surroundings which gave meaning to man's existence. Human life, wrote Hutton, 'is dignified by its failures and its tragedies ... If human nature had not this capacity for acute suffering and disappointment ... each would be poorer than he is now.'[14]

Nature, however, even in its brutality, was useful to man. Not only did it provide the basis for 'the most essential of all professions,' farming, but on a more metaphysical level it devised a means to separate the best men from the worst. Though he had no respect for the Darwinian view of man as a sophisticated form of animal life, Hutton accepted the idea that existence was a struggle which only the fit survived. The determining factor in an individual's survival was what he labelled 'character,' a concept to which he often referred but seldom attempted to define. It represented the quality of 'will-power rather than intelligence,' a type of 'moral enthusiasm' which classical Greece lacked and Christian nations possessed. It combined, as Plato suggested, 'manliness, self-reliance, and aggressiveness' with 'gentleness, sweet temper and thought.' An individual possessing such an ideal character became what Hutton designated a 'gentleman.' Moderate and conventional, a gentleman scrupulously adhered to 'convention, caste, and breeding,' without concern for intellectual attainment. What gave a particular individual character, Hutton felt, was a complex interaction of heredity and environment. Canadians as a whole, for example, drew on their racial background. From 'British stock' came 'the aggressive spirit, the self-reliance, the enterprise,' while from the French was derived 'more subtle and delicate intelligence.' Equally important for Canadians, the embodiment of the Platonic 'ideal character,' according to Hutton, was a climate which acted 'as a tonic' to obliterate 'all slackness.' To these general racial and environmental determinants of 'character' Hutton added a number of other influences: family life, religion, and education. Indeed, his attempt to define the moral individual led him to the idea of character; this concept, in turn, was at the basis of much of his social thought.[15]

Many of Hutton's philosophical premises concerning religion and the classics were implicit in his conception of history. He had very precise views as to the nature of written history. As in religion, he felt that there was no possibility of discovering absolute truth in history, for 'all so-called facts are strained through the moulds furnished by the special nature of the writer.' This assertion could be questioned only if history dealt with the mundane details of 'accessions, coronations, royal births and marriages.' Its true focus, however, was 'what people in the mass said and thought ... their religion and ideals of life.' For this reason, as his own scholarship suggested, Hutton rejected the scientific 'school of historians who almost seek to turn history into a record similar to the records of the investigations of the naturalists or mathematicians.' Instead, the proper historian was 'almost a poet,' taking into account, like Carlyle and Froude, 'the character of individual men' and 'the influence of moral and religious ideas.' Whatever method a historian adopted, however, he still faced the problem of causation: he had to choose between a belief in 'fate' or 'the perfectibility of human nature' as the moving force in history. Hutton personally rejected the latter explanation on the assumption that 'human nature is the same in all ages,' while perfection comes only in after-life. It was his conviction that 'Fate leads nations in a cycle: evolution is from one end of the cycle to the other, but the wheels soon revolve full circle, and then evolution is over: at least for that time and that nation.' What seemed to determine the rise of a particular people were the virtues of 'habit and fixed thought,' the 'spirit of obedience and something of the spirit of service.' In other words, history was essentially a continuing morality play, affirming certain universal absolutes in unending cycles. As a result, wrote Hutton, 'the future may guide itself by the experience of the past.' In his opinion, the two supreme guideposts were Greek literature and Christian ethics.[16]

III

Hutton's synthesis of Classical and Christian beliefs provided the basis for his conception of society: it rested on the 'very frail foundation' of religion and democracy. Social morality, he felt, was 'not an intrinsic element in human nature' but stood rather, on a cultivated awareness of 'the value of each individual soul in the eyes of God.' It was this practical Christianity which prevented society from exploding 'into sky rockets of agitation' and, indeed, if it were applied more rigorously, 'all our troubles, social troubles, yellow peril, yellow press, labour wards, politics and corruption would melt away.' This religious emphasis on individual worth was the ethical dimension of the second requisite of society, the Greek belief in democracy. All men, Hutton asserted, were born equal before God, and remained so before the law. But such equality was 'relative': once equality of opportunity was ensured, the individual with character and talent 'naturally forged ahead to greater rewards than the indolent and inept.' The result of this open system was a society divided into classes according to ability and, ultimately, a world divided into higher and lower cultures on a similar basis. It was a simple reflection of the universal and immutable distinction between good and bad. The supreme social virtue in this conception of society became obedience to one's democratically allotted station in life and to the ethical precepts of Christianity. Hutton concluded:

obedience only means ... that quiet, good-natured, amiable and patient performance of common duties in obedience to authority which enables even this mad world somehow still to go, which prevents a society from being blown up sky-high and hill deep by the passions of jealousy, selfishness and dishonesty which have convulsed previous civilization...[17]

Closely linked to this conception of society was Hutton's political philosophy. Politics was an exercise in regulating society on a moral basis, a defence of what he termed 'the ultimate things.' Only by relying on the three virtues 'faith ... custom and stability' could such an objective be reached. This conviction indicated the general orientation of Hutton's own ideology: for practical purposes, though he admired the high aspirations of liberalism, he sided with conservatism. The former he felt represented 'humanitarianism, philanthropy, cosmopolitanism, a single world state and the like.' In marked contrast, conservatism stood for 'the plain humdrum virtues which the world has not yet been able to forego': 'patriotism ... the manliness of man [and] kindliness for the altars of our fathers.' Such views were often the product of 'unthinking loyalty to the past ... or even mere class and economic interests,' but in his own case they were born 'of profound scepticism and doubt ... which reaches so far that it accepts the established always just because it is established and feels that any change may be for the worse...' His conservatism, in addition, included a profound respect for 'the common man.' He was hard-working, religious, and, if lacking in intellect, possessed of the more important traits of common sense and character. These views gave Hutton's toryism a certain egalitarian tinge. As he wrote himself: 'The aristocrat [is] often in this complex world, the practical philanthropist: the theoretic democrat [is] less intent upon serving common people.'[18]

On the basis of his conservative political beliefs, he found much to criticize in the workings of democracy. Paternalistic government, based on a false conception of equality, had not only destroyed the older ideal of self-help among the poor, but by excessively taxing the richer classes threatened to curb their initiative as well. Leadership in most democracies tended to ignore the accumulated wisdom of history, emphasizing instead 'catchwords-cat-calls-clap-trap' to attract voters. That such tactics appealed to the populace was an indication of the declining intellectual standard of civilization. Worse still, it revealed a lack of political principles, a reflection of the low value placed on ethics in modern democracies. Eventually, as 'the most frothy and superficial of the bellmen of democracy,' Walt Whitman, illustrated, the political democrat became a moral democrat and society regressed to a state of barbarism.[19]

Despite these pessimistic views, as Hutton himself asserted, the idea of democracy had profoundly influenced his intellectual development. From both the study of Athenian politics and the memory of the exciting years of Disraeli's reform bills in England, he had developed certain convictions concerning the true nature of democracy. As political realities moved further from his ideal vision, he became at once more attached to his own theories and more critical of existing conditions. He began with the conviction that democracy was not a levelling process. Rather, by emphasizing rewards in return for effort, it attempted to raise all citizens to the status of a 'gentleman or gentlewoman.' Further, democracy was not an end but 'a means ... towards aristocracy: towards choosing the really best men wherever found: not the richest or the best born necessarily ... but the best in common sense, sound judgment, and honesty of purpose and character.' The assumption behind this definition was that men, though equal before God and the law, were born with 'very unequal talents.' The 'divine light ... of proportionate equality' declared that individuals were rewarded 'in proportion to desserts,' from which it followed that it was 'the right of superior character and superior intelligence to direct and govern.' Intellectuals alone did not seem to Hutton to possess the necessary qualities for leadership. Between 1875 and 1905 Paris, for example, had suffered under their guidance 'a shrinkage in political virtue, a lowering of national pride, a gathering indifference to the national name and fame and heritage.' Eventually the French reverted to 'a much older and simpler and more natural' leadership which honoured the family, Nature, and God. Democracy, in fact, depended on the rule of 'landowners and the middle classes.' They were prudent, possessed a sense of history, understood the limitations of government, and respected the rights of those less fortunate than themselves. In effect, Hutton's view of democracy combined both the classical concept of the ruling class as detached philosopher kings and the practical type of upper middle class democracy which had existed in the England of his boyhood.[20]

In his theory of democracy and his rejection of rule by intellectuals, Hutton raised the question of the academics' role in political society. 'The University Professor,' he wrote, 'is in the world, not of it.' Continually concerned with intellectual but insoluble problems, an academic was often led to cynicism. This frame of mind placed him in opposition to the spirit of his time for he was unable to join in popular enthusiasms. Specifically, academics were hostile to both the ethos of commercialism with its emphasis on personal gain, and to a superficial democracy which counted heads rather than what was in them. Detached from the values of their society, the intellectuals could not fulfil a formal role in government. But this same detachment gave them the objectivity to assume an alternate political function. They could serve as advisers to political leaders, helping them to resist rash public demands. More significantly, in political debates they and their students would 'mediate between the merely popular and democratic on one side and the merely reactionary, and bitter and pessimistic on the other.' In short, as a disinterested but informed observer, 'a Professor's business is to interpret the truth of oracles, though it be ... unpopular and unpropitious, and though it lead nowhere but to lamentation.'[21]

Hutton's political thought led him to a consideration of the nature and goals of education since in his view an educated populace was a prerequisite to democracy. Twentieth-century education had produced, he felt, 'universal unsettlement and unrest' and 'removed landmarks and horizons formerly familiar and conceived to be final.' These consequences stemmed from a faulty view of the purpose of education. 'The object of education in its truest sense,' he stated, 'is character building, not the sharpening of wits; for this reason ... the heart of education is religion.' Consequently, formal 'teaching goes for almost nothing; religion can be caught like an infection but not taught, learned through effort and example, but not learned like grammar and Latin.' It was important, as a result, that the schoolmaster exemplify certain morally acceptable traits. He was 'forced to be a conventionalist and formalist,' teaching traditional values and deportment by his own behaviour. Secondly, 'he has a right to be a slave driver and a tyrant' since 'the vital element in education, other than the spiritual element, is the element of logic and discipline.' The assumption which underlay this entire theory of education was that schooling was a process designed to inculcate traditional social values. 'All causes succeed,' wrote Hutton, 'if they are successfully taught to children; no valuable creed fails if children in large numbers have grown up to believe in it; they never lose childhood creeds...'[22]

Of special significance in Hutton's educational thought was the university: public schools created educated citizens, but it was the function of higher education to produce enlightened leaders. Yet universities existed for the study of 'metaphysics in every sense,' for the consideration of 'insoluable problems,' with the result that students were likely to become at first confused and later, cynical. It was the duty of the university to counter this malaise, 'to idealise life' as was done at University College with its 'spirit of Christianity without secularism.' Unfortunately, new subjects such as psychology and political science were not concerned with the idealism which characterized the traditional study of classics and philosophy. Indeed, many younger academics, in Hutton's view, lacked the broad culture of their predecessors. The result was 'a shrinkage in culture and mental discipline' among students, from which it followed that the nation's political leaders were increasingly dissimilar to the nineteenth-century 'statesmen of the old school of the academic type.' Only by returning to the conviction that the university was, in effect, a church, could higher education again become a source of moral inspiration for society.[23]

Hutton's social, political, and educational ideas had led him to a precise concept of the ideal society. It was organically united by a morality based on Christian ethics and an Athenian-like respect for individual freedom. Leaders, though freely chosen in a democratic fashion, were expected to be the nation's best men in terms of 'character.' Such individuals could be relied upon to follow a policy of wise conservatism, avoiding both reaction and undue reform. To help the general populace understand the wisdom of this type of social and political organization, education was designed to inculcate Christian morality as well as a sense of duty and self-discipline. This stable, hierarchical, and traditional society was in many respects an idealized version of the mid-nineteenth-century England in which Hutton had been educated. It reflected his own pious and academic upbringing, his studious years at Oxford, and the level of English society with which he later became familiar. Indeed, he described himself as a 'continuing Victorian' and on that basis, viewing the intellectual changes of the twentieth century, felt 'there is plenty of room for cynicism and pessimism ... for jeremiads...' Many of his essays were exactly that: jeremiads suggesting 'we turn back again to the thoughts of a better world than this.' At the same time, however, he realized that Victorianism was anachronistic. But if Canadians could not return to the values of the mid-nineteenth century, they could at least remain as close as possible to the source of those values: Great Britain. It was his belief that England still retained the primary virtue of the preceding age: moderation. In domestic politics Britain tempered elevated liberal aspirations with conservative practicality, while in international affairs her policy was based on both a desire for peace and a determination to fight in defence of principle. Beneath this political sagacity lay the racial character of the British people, a blend of instinctive wisdom and resolute honesty. It was on the basis of this respect for England's cultural and racial virtue that Hutton became a convinced imperialist.[24]

Canada, he asserted, reflected the British racial heritage in her national character. He realized that certain authorities argued that 'there is no such thing as a national character.' But with other intellectuals educated in an age unfamiliar with social anthropology, he shared a contrary view:

I speak with hesitation and diffidence because no subject is so manifold, so complex, so difficult to analyse and comprehend as national characteristics and racial idiosyncracies: but after a long life spent in comparing Greeks with Romans, i.e. Frenchmen or Irishmen, with Englishmen, I think what I am saying is broadly true.

On this assumption he asserted that Canada displayed the British traits of 'manliness, self-reliance, [and] agressiveness.' It was in her interest to prevent the dilution of this character by the exclusion of undesirable immigrants, among whom Hutton listed 'unbalanced' southern Europeans, 'Jews, and Hindoos or Negroes or Chinamen.' If Canada preserved her racial heritage, or improved upon it by absorbing the intellectual sophistication of the French, she would fulfil an important role in world affairs. The 'old prejudices and misunderstandings' between Britain and the United States could be 'dissipated by Canada the mediator' in preparation for a grand Anglo-Saxon union. Until that distant day, on the basis of her racial heritage, Canada's immediate future lay within the Empire.[25]

The British Empire, however, rested on a much broader foundation than race: to Hutton and many of his contemporaries it was above all a moral or cultural ideal. False imperialism, he stated, was associated with 'the idea of militarism, jingoism, [or] flag-waving.' In contrast, true imperial sentiment was based on 'community of ideals, community of traditions, community of language, community of race and religion: community, in short, of sentiment and origin, community of spiritual atmosphere.' Such an ideal could not be embodied in commercial or defence alliances: education alone could create the sense of collective harmony necessary to maintain the Empire. Indeed, only by viewing the Empire in this fashion could its idealist goals be attained. It was an instrument of cultural tutelage designed to instruct 'inferior' nations such as India in the value of British political practices and social morality. Among the developed nations of the world, the Empire, like its successor, the League of Nations, helped to maintain peace. Finally, for advanced colonies such as Canada, the Empire offered the opportunity to realize full autonomy by sharing with Britain the direction of imperial affairs. To Hutton, then imperialism stood for the practical implementation of his basic values: Christian ethics and political freedom. For that reason he felt that Canada must continue as an integral unit in the imperial structure.[26]

Despite his idealized view of the Empire and its role as a force for international peace, Hutton evidenced a strong interest in military matters. This concern was rooted in his conception of man: though one could 'regulate and chasten' it, he asserted, the martial spirit was an innate facet of human nature. For that reason he believed that the world was not ready for peace. Further, in time of peace, 'literature no less than politics ... is continually falling into ...

idolatries and insincerities.' Military training, however, turned the average young man, even in peace-time, 'from a hooligan into a self-contained, restrained, self-respecting person, of active habits, of punctuality, of obedience, of silence, of all those virtues in which democracy and unrestrained liberty ... are specially deficient.' War itself brought similar benefits. By demanding that each man adhere without question 'to rules and regulations and red tape' it countered the sense of doubt and purposelessness which characterized modern man. Moreover, war was often fought for high moral purposes – to ensure peace, for example – which made it man's highest calling. If sometimes savage and regrettable, then, war had many redeeming virtues for Hutton.[27]

This vision of battle as a grand and glorious affair, born of years of peace and, for some, substantiated by the British defeat of the Boers, was shaken to the core by the carnage of the Great War. At the beginning of the conflict Hutton had exhorted his former students to enlist with the assurance that they would always recall with pride these 'days of youth and romance ... the heroic days of Canada.' At that time, he recalled, it was thought that 'wars were fought by professional soldiers full of love of fighting, full of joy of adventure, full of a certain honourable spirit and chivalry about the rule of fair fighting, full of a very real and universal feeling of sportsmanship and fairplay.' This pre-1914 vision of glory, however, was laid to rest by technological change, for 'science has counted out all individual heroism...' War was no longer a clash between armies, but a global affair, based on mechanized weaponry which destroyed civilians and soldiers alike. What moral benefits the Great War had seemed to promise were negated, leaving only death and destruction in their place. The conflict had begun with the idealistic 'hope and illusion that a new world was to follow.' But disillusionment replaced early optimism, making the period from 1919 to 1922 'the blackest years of most living men's experience.' Though he was a firm supporter of the League of Nations, it was Hutton's private conviction that even blacker days lay ahead. His vision of the ideal society, of the 'ultimate things' in politics and culture, of the British Empire – his Victorian idealism in short – died in the Great War.[28]

The 1920s have often been characterized by the phrase 'revolt of the intellectuals' and the 'disillusionment of youth.'[29] These expressions do not capture, in the case of Maurice Hutton and many of his older academic associates, the changes which the decade brought. In the first place, the intellectual changes did not begin in the 1920s but were evident long before. Secondly, what made the 'revolt' – and in Canada it may have been, until the 1930s, little more than a tremor – of the young intellectuals such as Frank Underhill, for example, so obvious was that the older intellectuals were, in fact, the disillusioned, so much so that their pre-1914 jeremiads almost disappeared. The older men, in effect, abdicated from Canadian academic publications, leaving an intellectual vacuum which the younger thinkers rapidly filled with their own very different ideas. When the older group of intellectuals wrote at all, their articles tended to be somewhat melancholy reminiscences, sprinkled with moral maxims from the Victorian era and drawing unfavourable comparisons between the 1920s and mid-nineteenth-century society. As such, they were testimony to the gradual withering of one strain in the history of Canadian thought: nineteenth-century idealism.

Though he emphasized the social chaos which followed the war, Hutton was very conscious that its origins lay 'back behind 1914.' In fact, the changes began in the 1880s. In the last placid days of the mid-nineteenth century, he wrote:

We had learned from the Greek philosophers and from the New Testament, to find reason and purpose, and mind and God in the world and then Darwin interposed and brought back chance and luck and accident and the doctrine of casual survival of the lucky: until the world has again become all chaos and confusion...

The Great War simply brought this existing crisis to a dramatic head. For the young the conflict 'adjourned ... the season of empty days, and nothing to do worth doing: it gave them at last and for the duration of the war, a sufficient purpose.' Peace, however, 'brought back the old dilemma in its old and acute form: how to kill time': without a theory of life and death, existence became meaningless. Before the onslaught of scientific rationalism, idealist creeds, including Christianity, had, he felt, almost disappeared.[30]

While he retained his personal faith in classical and Christian teachings, by the 1920s the mild 'muckraking' spirit of Hutton's pre-war prose had disappeared. 'I know,' he wrote, 'that he is not a wise man in general who sets himself against the age and the Zeit Geist, who makes no compromise.' The four volumes of essays which appeared between 1927 and 1930 had been written over the preceding quarter century and combined many moods. But the articles written after the Great War differed in tone from his more numerous pre-war essays. The latter were often a subtle form of social criticism, usually drawing on classical sources. 'Plato's Watchdog' (1909), for example, was a study in Platonic terms of the Canadian character which carried a stern warning against non-Anglo-Saxon immigration. His post-war essays, in contrast, tended to be laments for the passing of those institutions and principles which his earlier articles had defended. For instance, in 'The Changes of Forty Years,' appearing in 1922, he sadly noted the decline of both political leadership and scholarship in the wake of Darwinian thought. This change from the social critic to the reminiscent Victorian, common to Andrew Macphail, Archibald MacMechan, and James Cappon as well, amounted to both an admission of defeat for idealism and an abdication of the leading role in Canadian scholarly life. The new ethos was materialism, Hutton felt, a mixture of greedy individualism and naïve faith in technology, while both religion and traditional scholarship were ignored. Set against this creed he knew his articles would appear strangely out of place. Disillusioned, in a sense intellectually obsolete, Hutton's only refuge was his personal idealism. He wrote:

To face the desperate creed ... that the world is an accident or a "dud": or the slip of a prentice God ... requires, I imagine, more courage than to face, after the old fashioned way, the prospect of the Day of Judgment and of the fires of Hell: neither of which prospects are especially Christian or recent, but come freighted with the instincts and traditions of classical and pre-classical antiquity.[31]

ADAM SHORTT
Proceedings and Transactions of the Royal Society of Canada 1931
Photo courtesy Royal Society of Canada

6

ADAM SHORTT

The Emergence of the
Social Scientist

Adam Shortt received what was, in its time, a not unconventional university education: at Queen's and later in Scotland he combined advanced studies in philosophy with equally esoteric investigations in the physical and natural sciences. Indeed, for one whose interests lay in the vague area between the humanities and the pure sciences, there was, in 1880, as yet no recourse to the social sciences. At British institutions, and to a lesser extent in those of the United States, subjects such as political science or economics appeared occasionally in the curriculum. In the relatively traditional academic atmosphere of Canada, however, Shortt was left to discover these disciplines for himself. His training in metaphysics with its focus on human problems and his extensive education in the empirical methods of science combined and were transformed by wide reading in history into a sound knowledge of political economy. Because his exposure to the subject was not based on formal training, he never developed the absolute faith in empiricism which characterized social scientists whose education had been narrowly specialized. It was not unusual for a metaphysical tone or statement to creep into his writing, in contrast, for example, to the work of his fellow political economist, James Mavor of Toronto. Though he was primarily devoted, as he frequently stated, to an objective consideration of social facts rather than theories, through his philosophical impulse he maintained a latent affinity with idealists such as Andrew Macphail. In effect he was a transitional figure, a prototype liberal empiricist educated in an idealist academic tradition yet a pioneer in the development of the social sciences in Canada.

I

Adam Shortt was born in 1859 at Kilworth, Ontario. The mill which his father operated was destroyed by floods four years later with the result that the family eventually relocated in the town of Walkerton. This move proved of considerable importance for Shortt's later attitude towards education. He was prohibited, because he lived beyond the town limits, from attending the village school. Under the guidance of the Reverand George Bell, afterwards registrar at Queen's University, he studied and read at the local Mechanics' Institute. In later years he attributed his distrust of commonly accepted views and penchant for original research to this unorthodox educational background. At the time, however, it seemed that the experience had brought few benefits for he began high school at the bottom of his class. Nevertheless, in 1879 he won a scholarship to Queen's, an event which marked the beginning of a life-long association with that institution.[1]

His choice of Queen's was the result of an address given by Principal George Grant in Walkerton in 1878. His topic, 'the characteristic devotion to education of the Scottish middle classes,' Shortt recalled, 'appealed to every fibre in the personal and national sympathies of my parents and myself.' Though 'previous financial losses and a prominent bank failure' made it 'not quite certain' whether he would 'be able to enjoy a university course,' it was eventually resolved that he would be sent to Kingston to train for the ministry. At this time the university consisted of one building and 194 students. Having visited the campus of the University of Toronto, Shortt was sadly disillusioned with the relatively primitive appearance of Queen's. 'I reached the conclusion,' he recalled, 'that, to save my face, I would stick it out till Christmas, and then quietly transfer to Toronto, where the real and the ideal seemed to be much more in harmony.' With his exposure, however, to teachers such as George Grant, John Watson, and Nathan Dupuis, his disappointment rapidly disappeared and was replaced by enthusiasm for 'the atmosphere at Queen's so free, self-adjustable, and liberal.' He stood near the top of his classes, took an enthusiastic part in such student activities as debates and the college paper, and came to consider his fellows 'the best principled lot of young men I ever was among.' In the process of adjusting to the new academic environment, he began to drift away from his earlier background. To his family he wrote that in Kingston 'it is chiefly the upper crust with whom I am acquainted,' while since 'leaving Walkerton I have taken quite a dislike to the place and the people in it.' Though he retained personal religious practices, perhaps under the influence of Watson's teaching in philosophy, he abandoned his ambition to enter the church. Instead, his future pointed to an academic career, though in an as yet undetermined field.[2]

With an improved financial situation at home, Shortt was able to afford several years of study abroad after taking his first-class degree in 1883. His teacher and friend, John Watson, considered his graduating essay, 'Recent English Psychology,' the 'most complete critical statement of the Psychology of Mr Herbert Spencer to be anywhere found.' With such recommendations he was readily admitted first to Glasgow and later Edinburgh University where he studied philosophy under Caird, physics under Lord Kelvin, and chemistry and botany as well. In 1885 he received his master's degree from Queen's and applied for positions in chemistry at the Ontario College of Agriculture and, later, philosophy at Dalhousie. Though Watson wrote that Shortt's 'knowledge of the literature of philosophy surpasses that of any student who has attended this university in my time,' he was unable to find an academic post. Lonely and miserable in Walkerton, he wrote to his future wife that he would enter Hamilton Teacher's College in the fall of 1885.[3]

Shortt was saved from the high school teaching which had depressed Archibald MacMechan by the intervention of Watson. He arranged for him to teach philosophy at Queen's during the winter term of 1885 and chemistry and botany during the summer session. He continued in this dual role until 1888 when he was asked to substitute for an ailing and unsatisfactory part-time instructor in political science. The funds were available to appoint Shortt to the new John Leys Lectureship in that subject the following year, the same year in which William Ashley began the political economy department at the University of Toronto, and in 1891 he became the John A. Macdonald Professor of Political Science. Works such as Henry George's *Progress and Poverty* were replaced by the most recent books by Alford Marshall, Francis Walker, and Karl Marx. A group of talented students gathered in his classes and left to build outstanding careers. Among the best known were Senator Andrew Haydon, Sir Edward Peacock, a director of the Bank of England, Duncan McArthur, head of the Department of History at Queen's, and O.D. Skelton, Under-Secretary of State. Born of his training in the empirical methods of science and the metaphysical speculations of philosophy, the teaching of political economy seemed to provide for Shortt the ideal career.[4]

Though teaching was first among his interests, he took part in many other activities associated with Queen's. In 1889 he was appointed librarian, in which role he began to collect rare Canadiana. This undertaking was a reflection of his own changing interests: from moral philosophy he had drifted to political theory, then to political economy and finally to economic history. In 1893 he was instrumental in the founding of the Kingston Historical Society, writing the organization's constitution and acting as secretary-librarian. At its meetings he often presented papers, some of which were later published in the *Canadian Magazine* or as part of his seminal series on Canadian currency between 1896 and 1906 in the *Journal of the Canadian Bankers' Association*. Certain of his articles also appeared in the *Queen's Quarterly* which he had helped to found in 1893. He was associated with the journal in an editorial capacity until 1902 and contributed regular 'Current Events' columns for more than a decade. His interest in journalism, however, was by no means confined to academic publications. Two topics in particular made him a well-known commentator on public affairs. His condemnation of Chamberlain's scheme for preferential trade gave him the reputation of an anti-imperialist, while his ridicule of the popular optimism arising from the north-west economic boom made him request, before addressing western audiences, a 'three hour start out of town.'[5]

Despite the fact that he was rapidly becoming a public figure, his existence in Kingston during the 1890s was relatively calm compared to later years in Ottawa. His social life centred on the university, where he belonged to the Saturday Club, with others such as James Cappon and Alexander Macphail, a professor of engineering and brother of Sir Andrew Macphail. In the quiet of the members' homes informal papers were presented on topics of current interest. Shortt's own home, where he lived with his wife and three children, seemed to him ideal for he wrote that 'it is indeed a haven of rest from all the worries and hardness of the outside world.' In 1886 he had married Elizabeth Smith, one of the first three women graduates in medicine at Queen's. Her career paralleled that of her husband for, after teaching medical jurisprudence and sanitary science from 1887 to 1893, her interest turned to active participation in public affairs, particularly public health, immigration, and female suffrage. Among the many organizations with which she was connected were the National Council of Women, the Victorian Order of Nurses, the Ottawa Welfare Bureau, and the Ontario Government Commission on Mother's Allowances. With two such active parents, Shortt noted in 1908, it was fortunate that his children had 'sufficient of their Scottish ancestry in them to take naturally to the pathways of independence and self-reliance.'[6]

The number of students increased at Queen's during the 1890s, necessitating larger classes. The salaries of full professors actually declined while those at the University of Toronto rose, yet Adam Shortt seemed very attached to life in Kingston. To his former student and closest friend, Andrew Haydon, he wrote: 'there is nothing in life so satisfying and uplifting as the hearty and progressive response to one's efforts in stimulating young minds.' Various attempts were made to lure him away from Queen's, among them the offer of 'a special chair in Canadian government & institutions' at Toronto and the presidency of the newly formed University of Saskatchewan. A more interesting suggestion was made in 1904 by the deputy minister of labour, Mackenzie King. He asked Shortt to come to Ottawa to write a definitive 'Industrial History of Canada.' The latter's reply was an emphatic refusal:

I am very much attached to the work of my class-room and the hours I spend with my students, especially my honours students, are the happiest of my life. Mentally they are a continual stimulus to youth and open mindedness. I have always felt and often said, that if I were wealthy enough to choose with perfect freedom what I should do, I should at least never give up my teaching work.

Yet paradoxically this refusal was also a harbinger of his later public service, for it closed with the suggestion that the government should develop closer contact with the university community.[7]

Shortt's career had, in fact, begun to turn towards the civil service. His studies in political thought seemed to him impractical and theoretical. 'I confess,' he wrote to Andrew Haydon, 'that a study of mankind, intensely interesting as it is, yet is apt to develop a cynical streak in one's nature; they do go at it so blindly and persist in climbing over the barbed wire fences instead of going through the gates.' He was tired of being, as he explained to John Willison, editor of the Toronto *News*, 'merely a voice from the wilderness,' and appeared anxious to apply his knowledge of political economy to practical affairs. His first opportunity to realize this ambition came in 1903 when he was appointed chairman of the Ontario Commission to Investigate Railway Taxation. Of greater significance, however, was his work for the Department of Labour under the newly proclaimed Industrial Disputes Investigation Act. This legislation provided for the appointment of a board of conciliation to investigate labour disagreements in public utilities and mines. The board was composed of one representative of the employer, one for the employees, and a chairman selected by the other two members. In the latter capacity during 1907, Shortt sat on 11 conciliation hearings, reaching total agreement in all cases. Yet this very success raised certain pressing questions. Though O.D. Skelton ably took charge of his classes during the investigations, it became clear to him that he could not combine 'the double role of head of a University department ... and meet ... so many outside demands from the government and the public.' In fact, he wrote, 'Some change I fear must take place before long.'[8]

In 1908 Adam Shortt was 49 years of age and had established a sound academic reputation as a Canadian historian. He was described by *Saturday Night* as 'about six feet in height, well built, with a high rounded forehead, bald-head and earnest face,' while his diary recorded that he wore size 9 shoes and 16½ shirts. Infinitesimal though these latter details were, they illustrated a particularly important facet of his character: a predilection for precise and detailed information. It was this characteristic, perhaps encouraged by his extensive training in science, which led him away from philosophy towards economic history and which contributed also to his success as a labour conciliator. It predisposed him, in effect, towards a practical administrative position rather than a purely academic post. In fact, by June 1903, despite his enthusiasm for teaching, he grew restless and recorded in his diary 'the feeling that the summer is rapidly passing and life with it.'[9]

His interest in public administration and his discontent, although mild, at Queen's, led him to accept the position of civil service commissioner in 1908. A combination of his success as a labour conciliator, his national reputation as a scholar and impartial commentator on public affairs, and a wide range of non-partisan political contacts explained his selection.[10] He did not, however, abandon his interest in either academic affairs or scholarly research. In the year of his appointment he published a biography, *Lord Sydenham*, and six years later, *Canada and Its Provinces*, which he edited in association with Arthur Doughty and to which he contributed numerous chapters on economic history. His contacts with other academics were maintained through his membership in learned societies: in 1911 he became a fellow of the Royal Society of Canada, while the following year he was elected president of the newly constituted Canadian Political Science Association and later vice-president of the American Political Science Association. In recognition of his scholarly and public attainments he was offered the presidency of the University of British Columbia and of Queen's, though neither offer was accepted. He did accept, however, both an LLD from Queen's and a CMG in 1911. His academic reputation, it appeared, was not inhibited by his government post.[11]

As civil service commissioner, Shortt was faced with the monumental task of replacing patronage in the public service with open, well-advertised competitions. His memos to Sir Robert Borden on the topic of reform were studded with phrases indicative of an objective, efficient approach to bureaucracy: 'application of scientific processes,' 'simple co-ordinating body,' and 'security for efficiency' were among his common expressions. He quickly established his authority over his co-commissioner and made attempts to draw the university community into the process of reorganizing the civil service. Yet a decade after his appointment, he was still horrified, despite the good intentions of most members of parliament, at 'the extent to which the country and its service suffers from the patronage evil.' Indeed the task of reform seemed hopeless at times, especially with the primitive facilities and minimal staff allotted to his department. Soon after his move to Ottawa he recorded in his diary that he 'Felt tired, seedy & discouraged with the amount of work the battles to fight and the slight effective support.' Even his academic friends, one of whom openly requested a position for his son, did not seem to understand the new principle of impartial appointment to the public service. He was conscious, too, that he grew older and found he derived his greatest pleasure from reading and writing rather than 'the daily grind.' In 1915 he was attacked in the House of Commons by the Honourable Robert Rogers for alleged misconduct in allocating positions.

According to Shortt, the allegations were 'based upon a growing resentment at my persistent obstruction of the element operating the patronage machine,' but were nullified by his offer to resign if improprieties were documented. Of greater significance for Shortt's discontent with his Ottawa position was the War Measures Act of 1914, which allowed the government to disregard the Civil Service Act. By 1918, he wrote to W.L. Grant, his attempt to pattern the Canadian service on 'the British Model' had been subverted by 'the present trashy American model.' Discouraged and perhaps defeated by circumstances beyond his control, he was only too pleased to return to a study of history.[12]

His opportunity to resume his scholarly interests came in 1918. He mentioned to his friend Robert Borden that he regretted, as civil service commissioner, no longer having time to pursue historical research. At the prime minister's request he submitted a memorandum outlining a proposal for the creation of a Board of Historical Publications. Partially in order to appoint Dr Roche, the minister of the interior, to the Civil Service Commission, within a month of the initial conversation Borden named Shortt to the headship of the new organization. His salary continued at the rank of a deputy minister and he was responsible directly to the president of the Privy Council. In Shortt's view:

one may say that the object aimed at by the Board is to put at the immediate and convenient service of all persons in any way interested in Canadian History, the most essential documents bearing on the development of the vital interest of the Canadian people. [This would] give a new interest in our history to those who at present are practically indifferent ... and make for a more intelligent, practical and wholesome national sentiment, thus guarding against the attempt of rash and ignorant enthusiasts to undermine national standards and a wholesome public sentiment.

In effect, the Board of Historical Publications was to be the source of data from which the Canadian people could build a realistic sense of identity.[13]

Of his private feelings towards the position he wrote: 'To me this is of course much more congenial work than the other as it merges in one my personal interests and official duties.' The board published volumes of documents on early currency and constitutional development and provided a place of research training for younger historians. It permitted Shortt to begin research into Canadian economic history on a scale previously impossible for him. As an economic adviser to the League of Nations, he undertook yearly trips to Europe after 1925. On his way to Geneva, through the financial connections of a former student, Sir Edward Peacock, he gained access to and, ultimately, possession of some 100,000 sheets of the Baring Brothers Papers relating to Canadian economic history in the period 1820 to 1870. This acquisition he regarded as his major achievement for he wrote: 'From the character of these papers I have realized that if I had done nothing else than secure the transfer of them to America, my reputation was established for all time.' Indeed, in this estimation he was correct for, as Harold Innis wrote to him four years before his death in 1931, it was as the founder of Canadian economic history that he was to be remembered.[14]

II

In Adam Shortt's thought there were two distinct strains. The first was idealistic and speculative, early expressed in his desire to enter the ministry and later developed in a different direction through the philosophical teaching of John Watson at Queen's and Edward Caird at Glasgow. It led him to consider on a metaphysical level the character of man, his relationship to society, and the nature of morality. An early handwritten essay entitled 'The Philosophy of Moral Obligation' illustrated this element in his thinking. It advanced the Hegelian thesis that man, in coming to know himself, came to know something of one part of the World Spirit, and thereby discovered the essence of morality. Though this belief reappeared in some of his subsequent writing, the essay contained a harbinger of his later lack of interest in metaphysics, for he wrote, 'We cannot, I think, contemplate our position in the sphere of existence ...'[15] This attitude was the key to the second and dominant strain in his thought. It was practical and empirical, born of his early self-education and his formal training in the physical and natural sciences. This frame of mind pervaded most of his writing, stressing the need for a detailed factual approach to existence and refuting conclusions based on mere intuition or sentiment. It explained, too, the drift in his academic interest from moral philosophy to economic history, from the humanities to the social sciences. Led on by his own empirical research, he left far behind the concern for philosophy which once won the unreserved praise of John Watson. Despite his emphasis on scientific method, however, he never entirely escaped the philosopher's propensity to make general assertions as to the nature of man and the universe. As such, he was a transitional figure, related to the older idealist scholarship of Maurice Hutton and James Cappon by his occasional metaphysical statements, yet usually a precursor of a later generation of pragmatic, realistic social scientists which his University of Toronto counterpart, James Mavor, already represented.

It was Shortt's belief that, unfortunately, 'greater numbers of men ... hold their views by faith and not by knowledge.' There were essentially two implications to this epistemological assertion. First, he believed that 'knowledge' referred to factual reality rather than an idealized conception of what one presumed to exist. Only by accurate reference to objective conditions could beliefs find the secure foundation necessary to deal with the practical aspects of existence. He wrote:

I am not one of those who believe in running a country or a great organization on theory. You have to run it on facts ... I have no faith whatever in a policy built on sentiment.

This conviction led naturally to the second implication of his view of knowledge, specifically, a theory of how one came to possess a comprehension of reality. He was willing to concede that on rare circumstances 'receptive minds' could undergo a transcendental experience 'which is apt to reveal for a moment the present and future in the face of the great historic scroll of time.' Generally, however, intuition could not be relied upon to build true understanding; rather, he stated, only close empirical observation of details could lead to knowledge:

the point of view from which I approach ... subjects is that of the historical development. I personally can never understand what a thing means until I have asked myself and others where it began, how it grew up, why it grew up, and what it means today...

This predilection for gaining comprehension through observing reality was the outstanding aspect of Shortt's character. In his teaching he used 'numerous concrete illustrations' to explain the operation of government. His taste in films was limited to documentaries, while in painting he considered impressionism a denigration of true art. In his scholarship, it was Lord Sydenham, the utilitarian reformer, bureaucrat, and economic expert, whose biography he chose to write. For Shortt, then, knowledge could not be equated with intuitively held beliefs, but rather rested upon facts empirically observed.[16]

From his practical knowledge of the details of human history, Shortt felt he could make certain generalizations as to the nature of mankind. Though his statements revealed a training in philosophy, he believed them to be empirical, excusing their metaphysical tone by the assertion that 'between Ethics and Politics [ie, political science] there is common ground.' It was his belief that 'man is a spiritual being' as a result of his 'brotherhood with nature.' As a part of divine creation man possessed 'sympathy,' 'the artistic quality,' and 'religion.' At the same time he displayed the common human faculties of laziness, short-sightedness, and arrogance. Ideally, as the individual's personality developed through a combination of hereditary traits and the proper environmental circumstances, the crude natural man was moulded into a moral being. To Shortt this condition of morality was defined by the exertion of reason resulting in 'self-control, self-respect, and a strong sense of personal responsibility.' Though individual beliefs would differ, it was his conviction that through the universality of reason certain common standards of morality would emerge.[17]

Upon this view of human nature, Shortt based his concept of society. Quoting Aristotle, he felt that 'organized society ... comes into existence to make life possible and continues and develops in order to make life good.' He rejected Carlyle's organic view of social organization which made of the individual simply a small part in a large whole, yet equally, he rejected the extreme individualism of those, like Benjamin Kidd, who considered society a biological phenomenon governed by the survival of the fittest. Instead, he attempted to find a compromise. Since all men were joined in the kinship of nature and developed from this relationship certain common standards of morality, man was basically a social creature. In fact, as Aristotle had long ago suggested, society existed before the individual: it was the influence of society which forced man to develop morality, a means of peaceful co-existence, and thereby realize his true nature. In any civilization, Shortt wrote:

the individuality of each person must be respected ... But this is not the individuality of isolation and independence. It is just because society requires of the individual to forget himself with the social objects and purposes that it can make so much of him in the end, and give him a new and infinitely richer individuality which is the common product of the whole world.

It was this rational, liberal mean between individual freedom and collective existence which led to social progress.[18]

Shortt's view of human nature and of society was an integral part of his conception of the course of world history. At the base of his thinking was the belief that a study of history would reveal that 'the spirit of progress is slowly working out upon the loom of time.' In the seventeenth and eighteenth centuries man had broken from the constraints of medievalism, abandoned the narrow struggle for survival, and set out with the grand purpose of 'subduing the world.' The result of this liberation in thought was the development of modern urban-industrial society, an inevitable step in social progress. At the same time, however, man had failed to develop a new social morality commensurate with the changes in his material circumstances. By the end of the nineteenth century, 'each man [had] become too absorbed in his own specialized factor ... and too little given to the work of co-ordinating results.' Having left the organic medieval world behind, man reached the opposite extreme of total individualism. If this 'vicious' principle were allowed to continue, 'unparalleled progress' would disintegrate in the chaos of revolution. It was necessary, in Shortt's view, to recognize that man and society were mutually dependent. Without radically altering the existing competitive basis of social organization, but rather, by basing change on the lessons of the past, men could be taught the need for combining individual development with social co-operation. Only in this fashion could progress and, therefore, history, resume its course.[19]

Man's knowledge of history was dependent on the insight of the historian. According to Shortt, 'every age demands the rewriting of history to suit its changing tasks and shifting interests.' In the feudal past a knowledge of kings and battles sufficed the needs of society, but the exigencies of the modern democracy demanded a redefinition of the scope of written history. He wrote:

A study of history in its broadest sense is simply the intelligent appraisement of the development of a people or a nation, not merely in its outward political and international relations, but even more particularly in its social, economic, and intellectual progress.

History, to become relevant for the twentieth century, had to exchange an élitist viewpoint for the popular, and a geopolitical focus for a socio-economic perspective.[20]

Though the style and focus of historical literature changed from one generation to the next, the purpose it served and the truths it revealed remained constant. In the process of unravelling a particular sequence of historical events, the historian inevitably arrived at conscious but impartial moral judgements. From the resulting view of the past, a nation derived 'its standards, its self-respect, its conscience.' In contrast, the 'man who is not interested in what preceded him ... will have no conception of what is of permanent value.' History, in effect, was a source of morality; as such, it was the ultimate guide for all questions of social policy. Shortt wrote:

The only satisfactory appeal ... is the appeal to history. ... a properly conceived presentation of historical facts affords an indispensable basis for the satisfactory answer to any intellectual questions which arise ... it affords the only satisfactory data for testing the relative truth of the rival analyses of industrial and political societies of the present day, and the consequent value of practical economic and political programmes which depend upon the soundness of these analyses.

It was not that history repeated itself, but rather, that it taught certain lessons as to the nature of man and society. Moreover, in the course of studying these lessons from the nation's past, it was not merely policy makers who benefited, for citizens developed a sense of their collective identity:

Good citizenship grows out of a patriotic interest in the institutions of one's country and a sympathy with the people who dwell there. Such interest and sympathy are possible in a large measure only to those who are familiar with their country's past.

The facts of history, by providing first, lessons in morality, secondly, a practical guide in matters of public policy, and thirdly, a sense of nationhood, became a man's most important intellectual exercise.[21]

Adam Shortt's fundamental beliefs placed him firmly in the liberal tradition. His thought admittedly shared certain convictions he found in the works of Edmund Burke. Burke placed little faith in 'abstract' reason, preferring a more 'concrete' reason rooted in everyday reality. It was his belief that the individual realized himself through his membership in society, while society itself advanced slowly under the tutelage of a moral élite. The historical process chronicled this advance and represented the principle of reason at work in the world.[22] These similarities, however, were simply shared opinions rather than ideological agreement. Shortt, though he might revere the English constitution, never displayed a traditionalism which feared change or technological innovation. Further, he did not share Burke's belief in natural law, especially that aspect which emphasized the primacy of duties over rights.[23] Though Shortt approached an organic view of society, his first concern always remained the individual rather than the strength of the collectivity. He was too much the liberal empiricist to embrace fundamentally either philosophical idealism or Burkean conservatism.

The individual who seems to have exerted the most influence on Adam Shortt was John Stuart Mill. Educated to accept the doctrine of utilitarianism, Mill subsequently absorbed certain ideas from the German idealists through a reading of Coleridge and Carlyle. Since he tempered a dominant empiricism with an awareness of idealism, Mill's intellectual background was similar to Shortt's and the two men shared certain important social attitudes. Mill argued that political freedom was necessary to allow the highest development of individual character but, like Shortt, he realized that without society the individual could never realize his full potential. Law he regarded as a delicate instrument designed to promote individual freedom within the context of collective existence. As such, the law transcended the purely negative role assigned to it by the classical utilitarians.[24] This view of order in society reflected Mill's hostility to the idea of class: the nation was one body and the economic interest of each citizen was ideally identical to that of the group. Like Adam Shortt, the only élite which he condoned was an intellectual élite, freely chosen as the most able in society and accepted by the population as cultural and political leaders. Such men, Mill believed, might actually arrive at truth through intuition, a process he considered less an innate faculty than a conscious awareness of inner feelings. Under such guidance society would advance in a moral sense, which was the essence of progress.[25] In this general theory of man, society, and the historical process Adam Shortt concurred.

The most significant affinity between Mill and Shortt was in their view of the nature and methods of political economy. John Watson certainly had little sympathy for the empiricist position; indeed, student tradition held that he closed his lectures with the benediction: 'God bless me and Immanuel Kant; damn Comte, Mill and Spencer.'[26] It is also unlikely that Shortt was exposed to Mill's work in economics while at Glasgow for instruction in political economy was not introduced until 1889. But Shortt also studied at Edinburgh University and, while the evidence is uncertain, it seems likely that he would have been acquainted with Joseph Shield Nicholson, who held the chair in political economy from 1880 to 1925.[27] Certainly, Shortt was very favourably impressed by the Scot's treatment of the fundamentals of economics when the first volume of his *Principles of Political Economy* appeared in 1894. Nicholson believed that his work simply developed the principles established by Mill, especially by adding considerable historical documentation. He was careful to avoid reducing economics 'to a branch of applied mathematics' and equally concerned to avoid 'trenching unduly on the domain of ethics, jurisprudence, or politics.' It was his belief that 'political economy is ... a positive science, the object of which is to unfold principles, to discover uniformities, and to trace causal connexions, and not to lay down precepts, set up ideals or pronounce moral judgments.'[28]

In this view of political economy Adam Shortt enthusiastically concurred, describing Nicholson's treatment of the subject as 'eminently sensible.' The volume revealed a 'large and rational spirit best described as philosophical, and yet ... the speculative element is never allowed to run at large, but is kept well in touch with the practical basis and special limitations of the actual economic life of the people.' Too many modern economists, Shortt asserted, attempt to give 'their study the exactness of the physical sciences,' establishing 'arbitrary classifications and laws whose breaches are more numerous than their observances.' Other writers pass 'judgment on the moral or social quality' of economic wants when, in fact, 'the question is hardly one of being right or wrong, but of being rational or irrational.' In 'a work framed on the liberal lines,' Nicholson followed in Mill's path.[29] It was this balance, mid-way between idealism and positivism, which appealed to Shortt. Caught between two opposing schools of thought he became, like John Stuart Mill, a transitional figure, an empiricist with a latent metaphysical bent.

III

Adam Shortt based his social thought on his liberal view of human nature and the course of history. In economics he considered the 'whole commercial network of the country ... one vast co-operative society' requiring only minimal government intervention to function smoothly. Industrialization, far from being a step towards social disintegration, was both an inevitable and progressive step for man. Shortt labelled himself a liberal in politics and, though at times disillusioned with the vagaries of democracy, considered the British system of representative government the highest political achievement of any race. Like most philosophic liberals he saw reason as man's essential guide, stressing, as a result, the importance of education and the contributions of intellectuals to national life. Finally, in the tradition of Manchester liberalism, he was hostile to imperial centralization in any formal or forceful sense, though he was firmly attached to a cultural conception of the Empire. The unifying principle beneath these views was a mean, based on reason, between freedom, whether of the individual, corporation, or nation, on the one hand, and responsibility to the larger collectivity on the other.[30]

Shortt's conception of economic society was derived from his study of history. 'One of the most important social consequences of our modern economic life,' he wrote, 'is the great and still growing dependence of increasing numbers of the community upon the organization of industry.' In contrast to Andrew Macphail, he asserted, 'I have become thoroughly convinced of these points — that the corporations have come upon us in a normal and natural and inevitable manner, that we can not get rid of the corporations without a virtual destruction of our modern form of society.' Not only had the development of industry displaced the agrarian phase in man's evolution, but it had also rendered obsolete economic 'laws' once considered immutable. By the end of the nineteenth century, it was 'truly impossible to have our modern economical life carried any further ... upon the lines that used to determine it by free competition and the opportunity of any individual to go into any business and any trade he pleased.' The older form of competition between small firms familiar to Adam Smith was replaced by competition between a few large corporations for the most efficient means of production and the most rational technological innovations. It was this transformation, resting on the expertise and insight of the businessman, which both explained and necessitated the emergence of men commonly referred to as 'captains of industry.' It was Shortt's opinion that these individuals, far from being condemned as unscrupulous capitalists, were to be praised for their realistic approach to modern business. It was their farsighted desire to change 'the latent wealth of nature into a form available for the satisfaction of human wants', which made them the trustees of the national economy. Viewing industrialism as inevitable and beneficial, Shortt displayed none of the idealists' physiocratic bias against commerce; as a political economist he was forced to consider the real rather than the ideal society.[31]

Unlike many of his contemporaries, Shortt was reconciled to an age of corporate and labour organization with the result that he never advocated a retreat to an agrarian past. He was willing to concede that in an economically immature nation such as Canada, the farmers are 'the most numerous element in the population and their interests are the most vital to the welfare of the country.' Further, he was well aware of the danger of creating through lack of planning 'slums in some of the finest sections of the country.' Finally, he felt that 'there is not any interest ... so varied, attractive and interesting as ... getting back to nature.' Despite these beliefs, however, he wrote, 'I believe we are not going to get the people back to the country.' Rural depopulation and the accompanying growth of urban areas was simply an inevitable consequence of the industrial revolution. The solution to the rural-urban problem was not to oppose the consequences of the machine or the growth of cities, but rather 'to extend ... scientific method of production ... to country products' and to 'redeem life for the city man' by encouraging contact with nature. In effect, Shortt hoped to strike a balance in both rural and urban areas between industrialism and the natural life. Through his compromise, harmony and efficiency would characterize the nation's economy.[32]

If the economic structure of society had changed markedly over the course of the nineteenth century, the economic role of government had also evolved. Man, according to Shortt, had 'only a limited control' over the fluctuations induced by nature in the economy. For that reason, it was his belief that neither laissez-faire nor extensive state control of the economy could be endorsed as absolute principles: each doctrine was useful only under specific circumstances and in relation to particular facts. The true economic duty of the state he defined in a negative fashion:

To teach people how to help themselves is one of the highest and most legitimate functions of government; while the most demoralizing and illegitimate function of a government is either to step in and do the people's work for them, as in undertaking to market their products for example, or in forcing one portion of the people to contribute to the support of another, where the others are not helpless paupers.

Clearly, Shortt's view of economic society accepted the major assumptions of nineteenth-century British liberalism; unlike Andrew Macphail he never permitted his laissez-faire economics to be transformed by a sense of *noblesse oblige* into a form of Tory radicalism.[33]

The use of industrial bounties or protective tariffs to stimulate production clearly contravened Shortt's conception of economic efficiency and paved the way, he felt, for the corruption of politics by business. The solution to the problems of governmental relations with business was neither clandestine agreement nor state ownership, but rather continuous supervision. In the United States, Shortt believed, 'the commission has proved itself the only possible way of dealing with these great corporations.' He continued:

Nobody can follow these workings unless he be more or less of an expert ... that is, special knowledge ... is required to understand any of the great industries or services of modern times ... We should have in this country a body of experts to pass upon the plans and premises that are brought forward by the corporation ... to see that the public are being told the facts...

Just as business was to be placed under close observation, it was time for the government to deal with trade unionism: this could best be done by the incorporation of the unions on a formal basis. This legislation would proscribe practices such as coercion of membership or violation of contracts by creating a legally responsible body, and, at the same time, confer upon the unions a legal status similar to the corporations from which to bargain. While Shortt, like many liberals, believed that only moral reform and not changes in hours or wages could improve the lot of the working man, the incorporation of unions would at least help to rationalize and make more efficient the relationship between capital and labour. Free competition under government surveillance to guard the public interest was the core of Shortt's economic thought.[34]

The principles which underlay his attitude towards the relationship of the state to economic life also determined the nature of his political beliefs. He was, he asserted, a 'Scotch Liberal,' by which he meant that he held individual freedom to be the basic requisite of political organization. The earliest states based their legitimacy on religion, while classical civilization developed in rudimentary form the idea of rule of law. In the modern world, while retaining this respect for law and authority, it was essential 'to regard governments as the instruments of the people, not the people as instruments of the governments ... simply one set of organs among many others, through which people seek to realize themselves.' An essential aspect of this realization was the freedom of each citizen under the law to attain to a station commensurate with his personal capacity. But this freedom was guaranteed by law, rather than by inalienable human rights, and was utilized with varying degrees of success because all men were not equal. The failure to accept these two qualifications, in fact, explained the weakness of the American political system:

It is quite untrue that all men are created free and equal, that they are endowed with inalienable rights such as life, liberty and the pursuit of happiness, that governments are created to secure and preserve these rights, and that they derive their powers from the consent of the governed ... instead of belonging to man by nature, they are slowly and arduously acquired by him, and to be retained and improved demand constant effort through an indefinite future.

Each nation, rather than governing according to universal political principles, slowly evolved a unique system best suited to the character of its people. The highest and most recent form of political organization, in Shortt's view, was the British form of democracy.[35]

The well-being of the majority of the nation's citizens was the principle which underlay democratic theory. In both Canada and Britain this objective had been satisfactorily achieved by striking 'that balance between unrest and progress and conservatism and stability which is the anomaly of the British people.' In fact, it was Shortt's opinion that the Anglo-Saxon race alone possessed the temperament to operate a democratic system. On this assumption, the principles of political organization became a function of racial and geographic circumstances rather than sacred absolutes. For that reason they were not only susceptible to, but indeed, required, constant examination and criticism. As he wrote to Andrew Haydon, 'It is enough to make one despair of democracy to observe how elementary is the stupidity which the common man exhibits when acting in bulk.' International affairs, for example, were conducted on a partisan basis in a democracy, while voters displayed an inordinate propensity to follow the demogogue rather than the best leader. Further, while democratic governments often launched futile attempts to legislate morality, they themselves, as the American example demonstrated, were easily corrupted. To Shortt, then, democracy was in theory man's highest form of political organization and in practice the form most readily abused.[36]

It was this dualistic attitude towards democracy which explained the sociopolitical role he assigned to the expert or intellectual. Andrew Macphail had considered it the duty of the 'best men' to take an active part in political affairs and act as advisers to political leaders; Shortt, in contrast, felt that the intellectual was advised to remain aloof from practical politics, acting instead as an impartial social critic or an expert in the public service. In many respects this dissimilarity in the function assigned to the superior intellect was a measure of the contrast between the idealist and the empiricist approaches to democracy; the former hoped to raise the level of politics to a higher moral plain while the latter focused on the need for efficiency in administration rather than an improvement in party politics. Shortt believed that inevitably various interest groups, whether businessmen or workers, tended to abuse political power for selfish ends, and that the largest group in society, the middle class, was both disorganized and unprotected. It was essential, therefore, that this group be kept informed on important social questions and that their interest be protected by an impartial, efficient government. This, in Shortt's view, was the function of the intellectual.[37]

The university, he asserted, neither courted 'superficial popularity by pandering to low or short-sighted standards,' nor existed 'as a refuge for cloistered scholars.' Ideally, the academic community should 'assist in raising the spiritual tone of the country, and promoting an enlightened and tolerant spirit.' This sweeping objective could be accomplished through a number of activities. The university equipped students 'for dealing with the larger interests of mankind,' rather than merely training them for a specific vocation. Beyond the immediate concern of education, the professor could provide 'an intelligent criticism of the actual conditions of the country' as a guide to public opinion. It was this conviction which led Shortt to join an unsuccessful attempt to launch a nonpartisan journal in western Canada in 1919. It was also the basis for his view of the Canadian Political Science Association from his office as president in 1912. As scholars, its members were in a position to arrive at detached and impartial conclusions which could then by used for 'the information of the public mind.' This was especially true of the social scientist with the empirical approach he used to 'investigate the way of nature and of man'; it made him an ideal member of government commissions and regulatory bodies. Finally, in addition to the educational, journalistic, and advisory functions, the intellectuals had a less overt role: collectively they could form a significant political pressure group. Shortt's support was solicited for at least two such undertakings. In 1915 he and Professor George M. Wrong of the University of Toronto conferred with Clifford Sifton, hoping to form a Good Government League as well as publish a journal devoted to impartial reviews of public policy. Though the scheme quietly collapsed due to insufficient financial backing and the distracting influence of the war, a similar organization was suggested in 1917. Largely at the instigation of certain members of the Department of Political Economy at the University of Toronto, a National Problems Club was proposed to deal with post-war reconstruction. While this plan also was never consummated, it illustrated the academics' propensity to regard themselves as an important though unobtrusive influence on public policy. In this view Adam Shortt concurred.[38]

For many Canadian intellectuals writing in the quarter-century before the Great War, a topic which revealed their basic social assumptions was the nature of the British Empire. Indeed, Shortt was no exception in this respect. His views had been construed as anti-imperialistic, but this interpretation hardly seems complete.[39] He approached the topic of practical imperial relations from an entirely different set of methodological assumptions than did imperialists such as Andrew Macphail and James Cappon and, as a result, arrived at very different conclusions on specific aspects of the imperial question. But beneath these surface disagreements lay a core of shared convictions which ultimately brought Shortt close to the imperialist position and explained his friendships with men like Lionel Curtis and Lord Milner.

On a number of topics assumed to constitute the intellectual basis for an imperialist stance, Shortt's views differed from those of well-known imperialists.[40] Unlike Maurice Hutton he did not consider war a glorious affair. He found no pride in the military aspect of imperial expansion and, instead, soundly condemned the naïveté of those who considered battle a form of moral regeneration. The extravagant eloquence of certain nationalist orators such as might have appealed to Archibald MacMechan he found a suitable object of ridicule, while in his own writing he destroyed a popular contemporary nationalist myth, the vision of Canada as the prolific granary of the Empire. Though he believed, like Andrew Macphail, that each race exhibited distinct characteristics and that the particular genius of the Anglo-Saxon people was a capacity for democracy, he did not use these convictions to support his imperialism. Other races might differ from the English, but this did not mean that they were necessarily inferior. Further, because the British system of government was a function of racial capacity, it could never be exported to non-white colonies. Finally, Shortt's view of the United States differed from that of imperialists such as James Cappon. Both men rejected commercial union, considered the American constitution to be based on false principles, and attributed the degeneration of Canadian politics in part to American influences. Yet it was Shortt's belief that Canadians were essentially an American rather than a British people: the dominant group in Canada's past was the Loyalist strain which, he asserted, was thoroughly American in its political and social orientation. Shortt's assumptions, then, concerning the nature of war, Canadian nationalism, racial character, and the United States differed sharply from those of certain of his imperialist contemporaries; as a result, his views on specific aspects of imperial policy differed as well.[41]

He realized that there were two distinct types of imperialism: expansion into underdeveloped non-Anglo-Saxon territories and control of white colonies of settlement. When the former type necessitated the use of force, he felt, its value was immediately compromised. The Spanish-American War he considered misguided carnage which, like the 'reckless bout of Kiplingism' that explained the Boer War, brought neither peace to the native peoples nor prosperity to the conquering powers. Yet he was willing to admit that imperial control of less developed areas, if peacefully acquired, could bring certain benefits. British rule, based on discipline and order, ultimately proved more humane government for native populations than a national political freedom which was susceptible to abuse. In other words, British or American despotism with a respect for law and human life was superior to an indigenous despotism. It was an exercise in policing a disorderly society, but it was not to be considered a form of tutelage. Shortt firmly believed that a nation's system of government or economic organization – its culture, in effect – could not be exported to another country.[42]

Of more relevance to Canada was the second type of imperialism: control of colonies of Anglo-Saxon settlement. The 'motley collection of visionary schemes for consolidating the Empire' advanced by Canadian and British imperialists Shortt found unappealing. The imperial conference was useful for discussions but any formal alliance was incompatible with the principle of responsible government. An imperial navy he considered reasonable from an economic viewpoint provided the colonies shared in its control. Trade, especially the assumption that Canada could supply food for the Empire, offered no firm basis for imperial consolidation. In this view, Shortt was endorsed by both the imperialist, W.L. Grant, and John Carlton, the liberal continentalist. From a study of history it seemed obvious to him that Canada had become almost independent and would doubtless continue in that direction. This, however, was not the true threat to the traditional connection between Canada and Britain: rather, it was the interference in Canadian affairs promised by the 'New Imperialism' of Joseph Chamberlain which endangered the historic relationship.[43]

These views seemed to consign Shortt to the anti-imperialist side of the debate on Empire: indeed, this was, he wrote, the estimation made of him by the Toronto Empire Club. Yet he joined the British Empire Club himself in 1924 and for the preceding two decades had maintained friendships with a number of important imperialists. He was connected with the Round Table Group in England, through his former student Sir Edward Peacock, and in Toronto, through his friends Arthur Glazebrook, Sir John Willison, and W.L. Grant. These associates acquainted him with Lord Milner, Lionel Curtis, and Philip Kerr. His aid was solicited by Kerr for the founding of the *Round Table Quarterly* in 1910 and five years later he received a rare advance copy of Curtis' controversial book *The Problem of the Commonwealth*. This he obtained from the Toronto historian and ardent Round Tabler, Edward Kylie, who doubtless knew that Curtis had discussed imperial affairs extensively with Shortt in 1911. It seems, then, whatever his views on the folly of preferential trade, that Shortt was not considered an enemy by leading figures in the imperial movement.[44]

The affinity which existed between Shortt and men like Willison and Grant on the imperial question is explained by two facts: first, Shortt believed in a cultural conception of the Empire, and, secondly, the imperialism of most of his colleagues, regardless of their diverse practical schemes for imperial unification, rested on a broadly similar basis. Consequently, his basic imperial views were in harmony with those of men such as Sir Andrew Macphail. It was his opinion that the British Empire 'defies all purely rational analysis and definition.' It was the ill-defined product of the same 'inherent qualities of race' which had created the flexible, informal, English constitution. The guiding principle of the system was the 'free and independent development of the parts, accompanied by constant intercourse and mutual exchange of ideas.' This assumption meant, in effect, that 'the essential unity of the Empire is spiritual' and, therefore, defied expression in mundane schemes of preferential trade. The imperial link, wrote Shortt, 'is based upon the unity of race, language, institutions and traditions and ... expresses itself in the world at large as a type of civilization.' In these assertions he expressed a viewpoint similar to James Cappon's cultural definition of the Empire and Andrew Macphail's spiritual reverence for imperial unity. Though he did not share certain assumptions on which their views were based, and though the process by which he arrived at his conclusions was more pragmatic, his underlying attitude differed little from that of well-known imperialists.[45]

Shortt's social thought was characterized by the same duality which marked his basic philosophy. The first strain was born of the idealistic impulse in his character and philosophic training, expressing itself in the liberal assumption of innate human worth and the ultimate progress of world history. The second tendency, a product of his investigations in physical and social sciences, emphasized reason, expertise, and empirical observation as the basis for all decisions affecting man and society. His conception of economics combined a liberal faith in *laissez-faire* with the rationalist view that maximum efficiency and stability could be facilitated through constant government surveillance. Similarly, in politics he accepted democracy as the system best calculated to permit the individual to realize his potential, yet he also stressed the necessity of expertise in the public service to ensure the effectiveness of democratically derived policies. These assumptions he transferred to his view of international affairs, insisting on the freedom of each nation to develop its own political destiny, but also recognizing that the superior order of British administration was sometimes of benefit to an underdeveloped nation. In effect, Shortt combined liberal social beliefs with a rigorous faith in empiricism.

Unlike certain of his fellow academics, Adam Shortt did not drift into a state of disillusioned reverie during the 1920s. He was, of course, conscious of certain changes in his personal life. His health declined as did the volume of his social engagements and he seemed to lose contact with many old friends. Increasingly, he preferred to work alone in his study, dismissing most forms of external entertainment as superficial. Indeed, when he observed the growth of a city such as London with its 'packed mass of humanity,' he felt a strong attraction to a semi-rural environment. These changes, however, were more a function of age than of intellectual disillusionment and, in fact, did not extend to any of his deeper interests. He pursued his historical research with single-minded enthusiasm, yet found time to teach classes for the Workers' Educational Association and was elected to the presidency of the revived Canadian Political Science Association in 1929. Retaining his post with the Board of Historical Publications, he took annual trips to Europe after 1925, dividing his time between League of Nations activities in Geneva and extensive research in London. When he died at the age of seventy-two, Shortt was plagued with neither disenchantment nor inertia: for him the 1920s brought no sense of obsolescence or defeat.[46]

The difference between Shortt's reaction to society after the Great War and that of, for instance, Archibald MacMechan, was explained by the way in which he approached life: his constant guide was an empirical examination of reality. Though a metaphysical impulse ran through much of his writing, it was not sufficiently prominent to make of him an idealist. He dealt with social questions on an *ad hoc* basis from a empiricist viewpoint bringing few philosophical preconceptions as to the proper ordering of the universe. Consequently, he stood in sharp contrast to the surviving remnant of Victorian idealists who were disappointed to find their world view challenged or ignored in the 1920s. He did, of course, share certain convictions with these men, among which were a mild distrust of democracy, a respect for the cultural aspect of imperialism and a belief that the academic expert could fulfil an important political function. Yet these very similarities also reflected the difference between Shortt and the idealists. For example, his conception of political reform stressed a more efficient bureaucracy rather than, as suggested by Andrew Macphail, a moral elevation of political parties. On the basis of a rational consideration of the facts, he concluded that that hope, regardless of its emotional appeal, simply could not succeed. In effect, then, Shortt was a transitional figure. His metaphysical training gave him a certain affinity with idealists like James Cappon, while his dominant empiricism led him towards a materialist philosophy. It was this frame of mind, securely anchored to reality, which allowed him in later life to confront the problems of social change with objective equanimity. Such placidity, in turn, was a measurement of the contrast between the romantic temperament and that of the social scientist.

JAMES MAVOR
Proceedings and Transactions of the Royal Society of Canada 1926
Photo courtesy Royal Society of Canada

7

JAMES MAVOR

The Empirical Ideal

Towards the end of the nineteenth century the optimism generated by industrial and technological development was clouded by a growing body of social criticism. Conservative racials such as Carlyle and Ruskin were joined by popular commentators, among them Henry George and Edward Bellamy, and later, such socialist critics as Sidney Webb and Bernard Shaw. The combined force of these social thinkers was to draw attention to the worst effects of industrialization. Yet few of them presented detailed, pragmatic plans for social change: they were idealists of various hue and the technical aspects of reform were obscured for them by a pronounced ethical commitment to social amelioration. Into this welter of confusion and criticism stepped a relatively new creature, the social scientist. With emphasis on the empirical study of social problems as the basis for social policy, his thought tended to focus on methodology rather than moral principle. He became, in effect, a spokesman for modern empiricist faith in technology and bureaucracy as the key to social progress. In Canada, one of the first social scientists to express this point of view was the political economist, James Mavor.

I

Mavor was born at Stranraer, Scotland, in 1854, the eldest in a family of nine children. His father, a minister, arrived in the village in 1850 and, after securing the position as master of the free school, married Mary Bride, the daughter of a Dundee sea captain. It was from his mother's vivid accounts of her childhood sojourns in Russia that Mavor developed his subsequent fascination with Asian affairs. These early years he recalled as 'a quiet, agreeable life' in 'a friendly mature and cultivated society.' Indeed, it appears that many of his later economic ideas may have originated from his experiences in Stranraer. Stability and self-sufficiency were the chief characteristics of the area. 'The village,' he wrote, 'was highly self-contained ... Carpenter, smith, saddler, weaver, and shoemaker supplied everything that was necessary.' The surrounding countryside supported a prosperous dairy industry, with no urban industries in the vicinity to attract a landless working class. Though class contours were marked, there were neither indigents nor criminals to disturb the social harmony. Largely Tory in politics, the region was, Mavor concluded, 'homogeneous and contented.'[1]

In 1862 Mavor's family moved to Glasgow where his father had received a teaching post at Free St Matthew's Church, an institution 'of extreme orthodoxy in doctrine, and in its practice of ritual ... of extreme conservatism.' He found that the 'change from the semi-rural and compact society of a country town to a city crowded with an industrial population highly diversified and very individualistic was at first rather depressing.' He considered the two environments quite distinct:

In the country everybody knew everybody else. Everyone had a recognized place in the community. In the town no one knew or cared to know his next door neighbour. In the country there was little ostentatious display of wealth ... definite obligations attached to its possession ... In the town the vulgar display abounds; there is much wealth and poverty. Sense of obligation on the ground of social position has little force, commercial keenness is looked upon with approval; and while there is abundance of caustic wit, there is, in general, slender humour.[2]

Though he became attuned to urban life and later took an active part in schemes of social amelioration, the emotional attachment to the simplicity of a non-industrial environment was an important strain in his subsequent economic thought.

Mavor entered school in 1859 at Stranraer. The subjects he encountered, especially Latin, were both unpleasant and difficult, he found, for they were based on memory rather than comprehension. But his intellectual curiosity had been awakened and he privately read widely in history and geography. Washington Irving, Thackeray, and the *Saturday Review* were among works he later recalled. In Glasgow he entered high school, undertaking formal studies in classics, mathematics, and English grammar. Once again, however, his chief interest lay beyond the classroom, especially at the shop of an optician and instrument maker, patronized by Sir William Thomson (later Lord Kelvin), who allowed him to help with his pioneering experiments in electricity and physics. Regular schooling came to an early end when, as the eldest child, Mavor was sent to work with a Glasgow dry-salter. His education continued, however, for at work he learned of chemistry and foreign trade, while at nights he attended Anderson College, studying physics, chemistry, physiology, and anatomy.[3]

Increasingly his reading turned away from the sciences towards philosophy, especially works by Hegel and Kant. He resumed formal studies at Glasgow University in 1874, taking courses in logic, moral philosophy, and English literature, and meeting Edward Caird, who helped him arrange the various philosophies he had already encountered. He considered Caird 'a man of very fine genius,' while the philosopher said of Mavor 'that his was one of the keenest minds he had ever met.' Not only did this training in philosophy help him arrive at an evaluation of himself and his role in society, but it also acted as a replacement for his earlier religion, which he had come to consider narrow and dogmatic. Though illness prevented him from taking his degree at Glasgow, Mavor had by the late 1870s a sound grounding in both humanities and sciences.[4]

The duality of his education was evident in the variety of his activities after leaving the university. He was editor of the short-lived *Scottish Art Review*, the organ of a group of young Glasgow artists, and at the same time was the assistant editor of an engineering journal, *Industries*. Both interested in social questions and familiar with the empirical methods of science, Mavor drifted naturally towards studies in political economy. As part of his editorial duties he investigated trade unionism, the co-operative movement, and the role of women in the labour force, arriving at the conclusion that the working man bore an insufferable burden. In the 1880s, he recalled, new economic conditions associated with urban-industrial growth and the enfranchisement of the working class led many to demand government intervention to remove old, artificial inequalities. This drift towards socialism was noticeable, 'especially in the minds of members of the universities ... who felt material progress was indeed vain if it did not involve an obvious elevation of life all round.' It was Mavor's own conviction in 1884 that 'There must be a constant effort to correct the prevailing tendency of things.' He joined the Social Democratic Federation and later became a leader of the Glasgow branch of the Socialist League founded by his friend William Morris. His association with such groups not only brought him into contact with social theorists, among them the Russian exile, Prince Kropotkin, and General Booth, the founder of the Salvation Army, but also led him into several campaigns for social reform. He stood unsuccessfully as a Labour candidate and, through his investigations of urban slums, took an active role in the formation of the Glasgow Working Men's Dwellings Company. But even as his contact with the realities of poverty and inequality increased, his sympathy with socialism and, indeed, any reform doctrines rooted in idealism rather than empirical investigation, diminished.[5]

The later 1880s, in fact, seemed to be a period of doubt and change for Mavor. He left journalism for various minor lecturing posts, culminating in his appointment in 1889 as Professor of Political Economy and Statistics at St

Mungo's College, Glasgow. He had few students, however, and found his ideas often unpopular with other members of the faculty. His views on social questions began to shift away from those of his fellows in the Socialist League, which he left in 1886, and emphasized the need for objective and empirical social research without reference to preconceived panaceas. This interest was given practical expression in the type of research in which he engaged, notably his investigations at the request of the British government of the German labour colonies for the indigent. When he entered the Scottish Liberal Club in 1890, he had arrived at the conclusion that only moral reform of the individual could change the condition of society. Even in this realm of moral and spiritual values he seemed confused, questioning the efficacy of prayer and the existence of God. Alienated from his comrades in the reform movement, unhappy in his academic situation, and troubled by inner doubts, Mavor was only too ready to accept a new post in a new environment.[6]

In 1892 William J. Ashley resigned the Chair of Political Economy at the University of Toronto and recommended Mavor, whom he considered 'among the top ten or twelve most distinguished English economists,' as his successor. When he accepted the appointment, Mavor was almost forty years of age. While not a tall man, he was striking in appearance. His hair was grey and, though receding on his high forehead, unusually long. It flowed naturally into his unruly beard and, when combined with his penetrating gaze, accurately reflected the somewhat eccentric character within. He was variously described as a 'kindly genius,' Toronto's 'most picturesque academic personality,' and 'an academic Admirable Crichton.' In the home on University Crescent, where he lived with his wife and three children, 'at any time towards midnight' one could find a collection of 'oddities or celebrities,' wrote his colleague Pelham Edgar, with Mavor 'the centre of geniality and wit.' His friends, Maurice Hutton recalled, were often persons 'without rank or influence or wealth ... to whom he had been drawn by their unconventiality.' Indeed, among his many acquaintances and correspondents were Lord Bryce, Leo Tolstoi, Oscar Wilde, Vilhjalmur Stefansson, and Aubrey Beardsley. His personal enthusiasms indicated a similar eclecticism. He undertook numerous investigatory reports for the Canadian and British governments. He joined several important academic groups, notably the editorial board of the *University Magazine* and the executive of the newly formed Canadian Political Science Association in 1912. Various aspects of Toronto social life also attracted his interest. As a charter member — indeed, according to his own version, a co-founder — of the Round Table literary club, he often met with Goldwin Smith, Edmund Walker, Canon Cody, and others. When the spectacular Victorian era Ball was held in Toronto to celebrate the Diamond Jubilee of 1897, Mavor was chosen to edit the ensuing book of illustrated costumes. From art to economics, from the very poor to the very wealthy, his interests and acquaintances had few limitations.[7]

The range of Maver's interests was reflected in his scholarly publications. His numerous articles could be found in British, Canadian, and American periodicals covering topics from his friendships with men like Sir William Van Horne or Leo Tolstoi to the intricacies of English railway finance. He was best known, how-ever, for his books, among which were *Applied Economics* (1914), *The Russian Revolution* (1928), and *An Economic History of Russia* (1914). The latter work, in two volumes, was a detailed account of Russian economic growth from pre-history to the Bolshevik Revolution. It won extremely favourable reviews in the Anglo-American press and many individuals, including Lord Bryce and Alfred Marshall, sent notes of praise to the author. Similar laudatory reviews and letters greeted the appearance of his autobiography, *My Windows on the Street of the World*, in 1923. Though it lacked comment on Mavor's Canadian career and was, throughout, remarkably impersonal, the book contained accounts of his early years in Scotland and provided a chronology of his later career.[8] In addition to his autobiographical and scholarly works, he published two other books of inter-est: *Government Telephones: The Experience of Manitoba, Canada* (1916), and *Niagara in Politics: A Critical Account of the Ontario Hydro-Electric Commis-sion* (1925). Both studies were intensely hostile to public ownership, asserting that such schemes were less economical and more susceptible to political corrup-tion than privately owned utilities. These sentiments were a measure of how far behind Mavor had left his youthful socialist sympathies and were, perhaps, re-flected in the business friends he cultivated in Toronto: Sir Edmund Walker, Zebulon Lash, and Sir William Mackenzie. His business contacts, in fact, extended well beyond Toronto. The study of government telephones was covertly edited and published by American Telephone and Telegraph Company while his book on hydro, it was later charged, was financed by an American utilities lobby, the National Electric Light Association.[9] From a young reformer of Fabian sympathies in 1885, Mavor became by 1915 an orthodox classical economist dedicated to preserving the capitalistic status quo.

As his reform interest diminished he turned to statistical and geographic studies of economic issues largely unrelated to social reform. Increasingly, he became an ad hoc civil servant undertaking on behalf of federal and provincial governments various studies which called for economic expertise. In 1899, for example, he prepared a study of potential European immigration at the request of Clifford Sifton, the minister of the interior, and also carried out a survey for the Ontario government of British and continental schemes of employers' liability and workmen's compensation. In that same year, through his friend Kropotkin, he learned of the Doukhobor sect's desire to leave Russia. He personally persuaded Sifton to arrange for the settlement of the group with the guarantee of exemption from military service in western Canada. During later outbreaks of 'religious mania' he staunchly defended the Doukhobors as self-reliant and pious, attributing the disturbances to 'propaganda' by 'persons of importance.' In the later 1890s Sifton conferred with Mavor on several topics, but this consultation seems to have ended with the latter's publication of a study undertaken for the British Board of Trade in 1903. It was a survey of potential wheat production in the Canadian north-west. His conclusions not only ran counter to the popular optimism generated by the western 'boom,' but also questioned both the immigration aspect of the Liberal party's 'neo-National Policy,' and the imperialist's concept of Canada as 'the granary of the Empire.' It was his assertion that with large yearly fluctuations in rainfall, differential soil fertility, and a scattered, sparse population, it was unwise to rely on the Canadian north west as a source of wheat. His conclusions provoked considerable press comment in Canada and annoyed Sir Wilfrid Laurier. Perhaps coincidentally, after 1903, the focus of his activities shifted from government investigations to his own research.[10]

In addition to his writing and reports for public bodies, Mavor had extensive duties as professor of political economy at Toronto. During his thirty-year career at the university his attitude towards the post never seemed to advance beyond toleration to enthusiasm. When he arrived in 1892 he seemed to approve of the university but Toronto, and indeed, Ontario, he found parochial and dull. His family remained in Britain where he joined them in the summers until 1896, perhaps indicating that he viewed the Toronto post as a stepping-stone to a higher position. He did apply for several other jobs, among them a commerce professorship at the University of Birmingham and later, the position of deputy master of the Canadian branch of the Royal Mint. Perhaps because these applications were never accepted Mavor was forced to reconcile himself to life in Toronto. By 1919 he felt there was in Canada 'a certain vigorous life ... even in amount of refinement, in spite of the prevalent crudeness inseparable from an immature society.' On his salary of $4000 he felt he was able to live a frugal but acceptable existence in a community which 'differs little from Manchester.'[11]

If Mavor's attitude towards Toronto and the university was sometimes ambivalent, the opinion held of him by his students was equally inconclusive. One student recalled that 'his lectures were 60 minute tours of the world.' On the other hand, another observed that 'his delivery & general style of lecturing is atrocious ... the poorest to which I have ever listened ... he may be an able man, but he can not teach...' Mavor's lack of popularity was confirmed in the student strike of 1895. He attempted to discipline certain students for adding to the Political Science Club's list of speakers a socialist and a trade unionist after he had approved the original draft. In the ensuing protest his lectures were cheerfully boycotted and Mavor developed a dislike for several students, among whom was William Lyon Mackenzie King. It appeared, as was noted at the time of his death, that 'he was more at ease in his study or club than at the lecture desk.'[12]

Even in the club, however, Mavor was not always a genial and generous companion. Though he had a number of close academic friends, notably Pelham Edgar and Andrew Macphail, his relationships with other scholars often became strained and bitter. He quarrelled with Adam Shortt when the latter suggested certain revisions in his contribution to *Canada and Its Provinces*. A similar dispute concerning minute changes in an article submitted to the *University Magazine* led to his resignation from the editorial board and a marked antagonism between himself and Sir William Peterson, then acting editor of the journal. George Wrong he disliked because he felt the latter's attempt to make constitutional history a part of the history department was a direct challenge to the competence of his own department. Even the genial Stephen Leacock, friend of both Edgar and Macphail, fell prey to Mavor's venom. Mavor ranked him at the bottom of a list of five candidates for appointment to McGill in 1901, and at a subsequent meeting of the Royal Society of Canada launched such a devastating commentary on his presentation that Leacock shortly resigned from the Society. It would appear that Mavor's relations with his colleagues were as ambiguous and erratic as with his students.[13]

Mavor died in 1925 at Glasgow. His life was a series of shifting convictions and occupations, likes and dislikes, all marked by the same vehemence and energy. Until approximately 1890 there were two distinct strains to his thinking. The first was scientific, associated with Lord Kelvin and his physics, the drysalter and his chemistry, or Anderson College and its technical subjects. The second was idealist, developed from his reading of Kant and Hegel, broadened by his studies at Glasgow, and fostered by his friendship with Edward Caird. These two strains flowed together to produce an interest in political economy; as a discipline it combined the empirical methods of science with a focus, like philosophy, on man and his problems. Initially, while the idealist element in his political and economic thought predominated, he took part in various campaigns for social reform. But gradually, as he explored a wider range of social problems from an empirical viewpoint, he seemed to lose faith in the reform cause. By 1900 his economic thought was classical liberalism, the antithesis of his earlier Fabian views. Indeed, at the time of his death in 1925, he was aptly described as a 'Scotsman in the direct line of Adam Smith.'[14]

II

In contrast to men like Maurice Hutton or James Cappon, James Mavor subscribed to no elaborate system of personal metaphysics. Exposed to an extraordinary variety of intellectual influences throughout his life, he showed little lasting affinity for idealism and surpassed Mill in subscribing to a rigorous empiricism. His early association with Lord Kelvin contributed little in the way of social thought,[15] but doubtless initiated him into an empirical approach to 'the universe and the laws which regulate it.'[16] Edward Caird turned the young Mavor's mind from purely scientific investigations and made him aware of the emerging school of idealism. After he left the University of Glasgow his closest associates seem to have been socialists of various hue. Together with William Morris and other members of the Socialist League, Mavor signed a manifesto in 1884 'advocating the principles of Revolutionary International Socialism.'[17] But Morris's complete rejection of industrialism, his flirtation with Marxism, and his focus on the aesthetic decadence of nineteenth-century capitalism were convictions that Mavor did not share. The only significant similarity between the two men seems to have been a common disillusionment by 1890 with the socialist organizations in Britain and their revolutionary rhetoric.[18]

Two Russian social theorists may have exerted some influence on Mavor. Peter Kropotkin, 'the anarchist Prince,' first met Mavor while speaking on socialism in Edinburgh. Even in his most radical phase, however, it is doubtful that Mavor was impressed with the Russian's anarchistic theories. In fact, he may actually have been influential in persuading Kropotkin to abandon certain of his extreme ideas. When the latter delivered a scientific paper to the British Association's annual meeting of 1897 in Toronto, he was Mavor's guest. It was after this visit that Kropotkin first expressed hope for regional parliaments in Russia organized on a federal basis as in Canada.[19] Count Leo Tolstoi was the second Russian thinker with whom Mavor was acquainted. The two men shared a pronounced hostility to socialism, but their differences far outweighed their similarities. Tolstoi vigorously opposed industrialism, hated the extension of government bureaucracy, and based much of his thought on a primitive, mystical Christianity.[20] None of these strains of belief is evident in Mavor's thought. In fact, how well he knew Tolstoi is open to question. The only reference the Russian made in his diaries to their relationship suggests that it was rather superficial. He wrote: 'I was about to start work when Mavor, a professor came. He is very lively, but a professor and a supporter of the government and irreligious, the classic type of good scholar.'[21]

His early teachers, his socialist comrades, and his Russian acquaintances seem to have made little impact on Mavor's thought. But his approval of one British social theorist, Charles Booth, provides a clue to the most important influences on his mode of thinking. Though he doubtless considered Booth's religious views extraneous to his social analysis, Mavor agreed that the dynamic of social reform rested on moral regeneration. This conclusion had two important corollaries:

first, it emphasized individual responsibility rather than state aid to individuals; and secondly, it held that the impetus for social reform could come only from the middle class. Not only did Mavor agree with this fundamental aspect of Booth's thought, but he also, like Booth, moved from at least limited socialism in the 1880s to determined economic liberalism by 1910. The most important affinity between the two men, however, was one of method. Booth was among the first men in England to undertake detailed sociological studies based on positivist assumptions. In his investigations of poverty in London he demanded a rigid empiricism, stressing 'scientific facts' and excluding as far as possible subjective judgements. In this approach to sociological enquiry, Booth was a follower of the mid-nineteenth-century French sociologist, Frederic Le Play.[22] This orientation, in turn, explains Mavor's approval of his work and points to what may have been the most important influence on Mavor's own thought.

It would appear that Mavor became acquainted with the Frenchman's thought through an intermediary, his Glasgow friend, Patrick Geddes. Born in Aberdeenshire in 1854, Geddes received his education in biology under Thomas Huxley. He read Carlyle and Ruskin with enthusiasm and used many of the latter's ideas in his subsequent career as a pioneer urban planner. While studying with Huxley he began to attend regular lectures on positivism given by Dr Richard Congreve in London. Already impressed with the views of Comte and Spencer, he travelled to Paris in 1878 and there encountered Edmond Demolins, who introduced him to the sociology of Le Play. The French scholar's approach to society in terms of three factors, place, work, and folk, struck him as analogous to biology's fundamental triad, environment, function, and organism.[23] He quickly absorbed most of Le Play's ideas and 'brought news of the Le Play school to Scotland.' At the Edinburgh Summer School, disciples of the French sociologist were invited to lecture and the concepts were further propagated by Geddes's Sociological Society begun in 1903 and Le Play House founded in 1919.[24] Together with Victor Branford, one of his former students, Geddes became 'the most persistent sympathizer with Positivist sociology' in Britain.[25] It was in this capacity that he doubtless introduced his close friend James Mavor to the methods of Frederic Le Play.

If Mavor knew the details of Le Play's career he must have been impressed by the similarities it displayed with his own life. The Frenchman's early education was scientific, dealing with chemistry and geology at the Ecole des Mines in Paris. He travelled widely in both Russia and Germany, observing social habits and economic organization. During the turbulence of 1848 he sided with the socialists, though in later years this tendency disappeared. His views were solicited by various governments on economic and technological matters, while in academic circles his influence was evident by 1856 when he founded La

Société internationale des Etudes pratiques d'Economie Sociale. The society changed its name in 1886 and by 1892 published two social science journals. Le Play considered the National Association for the Social Sciences in Britain a 'daughter society,' while the Royal Statistical Society and individuals such as Alfred Marshall and Charles Booth acknowledged their debt to his methodology.[26]

Mavor shared a number of Le Play's social views. Both men were convinced that reform ultimately rested on moral regeneration alone. This view was rooted in a vague distrust of human nature and a belief that only an educated élite could guide social progress without a cataclysmic disruption of cultural tradition. Both men were acutely aware of the need to balance freedom with security and order. A stable society was based on private property and initiative, while socialism simply encouraged the weaker members of society in a degenerate life style. Though both thinkers held an affection for the mid-nineteenth-century village economy, they were aware that technological and industrial development was the distinguishing feature of modern society. The most significant similarity between Mavor and Le Play was their view of the methods and application of social science. Both men premised their studies on the conviction that investigations of society, as Le Play stated, 'must be based, not on *a priori* conceptions, but on the methodical observation of facts and on the induction of a rigorous logic.'[27]

Mavor would have fully agreed with Le Play's early declaration: 'I felt that the method of observation applied in the domain of social science had set me on ground as solid in that science as that which I had occupied in the domain of minerology.' The 'test of practical experience' in relation to 'a living organism,' rather than history or literature, Mavor considered the key to all knowledge. Such knowledge was derived through the study of 'facts' from 'a point of view as impartial as possible.' In this process of analysis the 'emotional bias' was negated by 'empirical methods' such that the 'same order of skill with which beasts, birds, fishes, and insects have been classified and arranged is at last being brought to bear on mankind.' For this reason, both men firmly believed that 'Government must become applied social science' through the use of experts to evaluate policy decisions.[28] While their careers and social attitudes showed certain similarities, it was in the empirical approach to social science and the faith in expertise that Mavor and Le Play revealed their greatest affinity.

Though Le Play based his work on the consideration of individual family budgets while Mavor studied the historical development of national economic institutions, both men were convinced that economics was the most fruitful area of investigation in the social sciences. While Mavor considered the discipline justified simply as a disinterested pursuit of knowledge, he believed that the true value of political economy was the light it threw on 'practical problems.' The discipline had developed slowly over the nineteenth century, he recalled, gradually producing an orthodox set of beliefs:

By the seventies, practical and political questions such as free trade, the position of trade unions and the like, as well as theoretical questions in which the non-professional public took some interest, were seen by it as *settled.* The controversies upon them had lasted about seventy years, and there seemed to be no more to be said that was new. For the instruction of youth in accepted doctrines there was available the excellent work of John Stuart Mill, and beyond or behind its conclusions it was deemed necessary to go.

By 1890, under the influence of such critics as Henry George or the 'gas and water socialists,' it became apparent that classical economic laws were not absolute but true only under given historical circumstances. Nevertheless, political economy, because it rested on an 'orderly sequence of ideas,' remained for Mavor a legitimate science. As such, it dealt not with 'what ought to be,' but with reality 'as it actually exists.'[29]

Given the nature of his discipline, the economist had a very important social function. The problems of political economy – government ownership, for example – were essentially 'technical' problems rather than political, dealing with the feasible rather than the ideal. Only the trained economist possessed the expertise to devise public policy on such abstruse matters as currency regulation or the extension of governmental powers. It was incorrect to suggest

that "modern political economists" as a class denounce wise attempts to direct social forces in an upward rather than in a downward direction. What they do, and what it is their function to do, is to point out where a scheme, by too exclusive regard of one element and neglect of others is foredoomed to failure.

It was, in fact, precisely the detached, non-ideological position of the economist, born of his rigorous empiricism, that made him indispensable to the modern industrial economy.[30]

On these assumptions concerning the nature of social science, Mavor based his actions and ideas. In marked contrast to idealists such as Hutton or Macphail, he made few general statements on human nature, the importance of religion, the role of 'character' in politics, or the existence of natural laws. Instead, he issued specific judgements on specific problems often based on his own empirical studies. As his interest increased in such investigation, whether undertaken privately or at the request of a public authority, the idealism which had partially inspired his early commitment to social reform diminished. 'Mature life,' he once wrote, 'is a series of compromises...'[31] Had his former comrades in the Socialist League known of his connections with AT & T or the National Electric Light Association, they might have been shocked at the extent of his own personal compromise.

III

Mavor's social thought, because he subscribed to no metaphysical theories but preferred to base his views on what he considered demonstrable fact, was not only limited to topics related specifically to political economy but was also buried beneath a welter of technical information. Nevertheless, from his numerous articles and books a relatively clear view of man and society did emerge. The concept upon which most of his ideas centred was the nature of political and economic change and the attendant problems of adjusting society to that historical development. He seldom considered the ethical or aesthetic implications of change, in contrast to idealists like James Cappon, choosing instead to regard the problem as essentially an exercise in readjusting the mechanics of society to function in a rational and efficient manner.

This view of social change was rooted in his conception of the major historical developments in western civilization since the medieval period. 'The characteristic social phenomenon of Europe during the past two centuries,' he wrote, 'has been the disintegration of village communities and composite families" This transition was associated with urban industrial development and became particularly overt, according to Mavor, in the period between 1877 and 1890. It was then that the workers and their middle class allies fully realized the weaknesses of industrialism: overpopulation, slum conditions, fluctuating unemployment, and a widening hiatus between rich and poor. Despite this new awareness, however, the basic and inevitable characteristic of modern civilization could not be circumvented: 'In gaining political, in some measure intellectual, social, and industrial liberty, we have lost at once medieval constraint and the medieval guarantee of subsistence.' No utopian schemes of social reform could restore this disintegrating sense of order: ultimately, the loss could only be compensated for through the application of economic expertise to the problems of production and distribution. The result would be a highly rationalized and efficient society which combined not only modern freedom but also a large degree of medieval stability and security. Where Andrew Macphail's search for order led him backward to an agrarian past, Mavor's led forward to an automated and technological future.[32]

Based on this view of the historical development of western Europe, Mavor came to the conclusion that industrialism was 'probably inevitable.' In fact, with the increased individual freedom and impartial rule of law which accompanied it, the 'factory system ... is probably an improvement upon the system which it largely supercedes.' The 'standard of comfort of the mass of the people of the western races has risen during the past fifty years,' he wrote of the period from 1870 to 1920, largely due to technology's ability to increase production. If each individual personally demonstrated a concern for the interest of the group as a whole, he felt, the present system would be ideal. Consequently, it was wrong to generate public hostility to business as had been done by certain irresponsible American reformers. The trust, in fact, was 'an inevitable development of the joint-stock company' while 'the notion' that the state could impede their growth 'is at least doubtful.' To suggest state collectivism as an alternative to big business was simply to transfer control of the companies to national bureaucracies with no guarantee of more equitable or efficient management. In fact, any form of overt state interference with business was a misguided conception of progress: it destroyed the incentive for efficiency, paved the way for political corruption, brought artificial criteria to bear on price levels, and severely restricted competition. The only factor required to make the economic system function in an efficient and rational manner was public and private expertise. Businessmen could hire highly educated individuals divorced from any selfish class interest to set policies for their operations which would be both economical and highly ethical. At the same time, government could supervise the operation of these corporations by commissions using 'impartial inspection under ... intelligent laws.' Such expertise would help the modern industrial state thread a line between misguided socialism and 'the extreme of laissez-faire': it would produce a rational capitalism.[33]

Mavor's view of political organization was a corollary of his economic thought. It stressed the same two concepts of balance between freedom and control and of the necessity for expertise in setting policy. Choosing nineteenth-century Britain as his model, he asserted that an individual's political views were a function of his class position. The views of his class, in turn, were 'determined by tradition touched with selfishness.' The middle class, for example, favoured 'the maintenance of the existing social order ... on the grounds of political and material advantage,' while younger working men, for the same reasons, drifted towards socialism. Politics was not based on a difference in principles, then, but rather on simple economic interests. For this reason Mavor was extremely sceptical of any increase in governmental powers, and devised his definitions of political terms so as to express this scepticism. The 'state' he defined as 'the total of the organs of government' while the 'nation' was 'the total of the inhabitants of the national area.' 'These inhabitants,' he continued, 'constitute the public and the preservation and security of their collective and individual property constitutes the reason for the Government of the state as well as the function of that Government.' Unfortunately, in central Europe during the second half of the nineteenth century this crucial distinction between citizens and state had diminished as governmental powers increased. The result was 'complete subordination of the individual to the state,' and 'enormous industrial and financial power in the hands of governing groups.' Because political groups tended to reflect their class interests, the 'interests of the public are lost sight of in the pursuit of the assumed interests of the state.' The antidote to this deterioration of political organization was to curb the extension of governmental functions, and to replace certain political offices with highly trained, impartial experts. As in his economic thought, Mavor's guiding principles were individual freedom and the necessity for a highly skilled bureaucracy.[34]

The model for political and economic organization which Mavor's thought suggested was an ideal; he recognized that under any system certain inequalities were bound to arise. There had always existed a certain level of poverty which society had supported by alms and charity. But with the coming of the industrial revolution their numbers increased. The factory system, unlike the medieval village community, could not find places for the aged or infirm: these people were left to descend to the lowest level of the social scale. It was Mavor's belief that this initial pauperism was then transferred to subsequent generations as much by heredity as by the influence of the environment. The result was a permanent class of economically depressed persons whose labour productivity was vastly below 'the average level of efficiency' and who had no personal initiative to improve their condition. What made this class a social problem was less their suffering than, first, their latent revolutionary potential and secondly, their potentially degenerating effect on the rest of society.[35]

Various schemes were advanced to rectify the position of the poor, but none seemed as misguided to Mavor in his later years as socialism. The Fabians he considered egocentric, if well-intentioned, while Marxists he dismissed as 'the most bigoted' of 'all groups of men in modern times.' The problem with the socialist position was that it wrongly assumed that the workers' interest could be equated with the general interest. This assumption overlooked the fact that all men were not equal: certain individuals possessed greater talents than others and therefore deserved greater rewards. It further ignored the realities of human nature by presuming that all reasonable men would become ardent socialists if acquainted with its doctrines and that human nature was ultimately capable of temporal perfection. Neither supposition, Mavor asserted, was valid for 'Economic socialism is no barrier against moral individualism.' Indeed, a 'dictatorial person who adopts Socialist instead of individualist opinions remains a dictatorial person.' Socialism failed, then, because it was too theoretical, basing its doctrines on a false view of man rather than addressing itself to the practical problems of financial management and bureaucratic expertise. As a result of these obvious fallacies, he wrote, in western Europe socialist doctrines were never accepted 'with ardour by first-rate minds'; such men, presumably including himself, based their social thought instead on liberalism. That their choice of ideologies was superior to collectivism, he concluded, was amply vindicated by the 'awful warning and example' of the Russian Revolution.[36]

It was Mavor's belief that under an ideal system neither public nor private schemes of poor relief would be required. If each man was aware of his own economic interest and had the political freedom to realize that advantage without endangering society as a whole, the existing economic structure would be ideal. Indeed, the vast majority of British workingmen approached this ideal type of economic citizen. Yet a certain 'submerged tenth' had no real sense of responsibility or initiative; as such they were 'really children and require to be dealt with, if at all, as children.' In previous generations the motive for such concern with the poor had been to increase their productivity, but increasingly certain elements felt 'unalloyed compassion' and many experienced a 'fear of social revolution.' The key to changing the poverty-stricken lay not in altering their environment, as Darwinian biological theory suggested, but rather, elevating their character or 'mental horizon.' This called for a paternalistic discipline, carefully controlled so as to inculcate acceptable values without destroying individual initiative. Such diverse schemes as the eight-hour day, workmen's compensation, or labour arbitration and conciliation obviously did not strike at the core of the problem.[37]

What did, according to Mavor, offer an instructive approach to poverty was the integrated program of the Salvation Army. It was based on the evidence of empirical studies and demonstrated an awareness of 'the unity of life,' a realization that the gratification of material needs had to be accompanied by an adjustment of mental attitudes through education. There was, of course, the danger that reformers would merely attempt to impose middle class morality on the poor, without realizing that the lower levels of society had their own standards suited to their particular social and economic needs. Regardless of this threat, however, the middle class alone had the social conscience required to launch an effective, integrated scheme of reform. For instance, the settlement houses developed by Jane Addams gave by example guidance in practical existence for those incapable of dealing effectively with daily life. On a larger scale, the German system of labour colonies offered 'both work and a healthy mode of existence to those who break down under the strain of independent labour, whether they are unfit or unfortunate.' To Mavor, then, dealing with poverty was a pragmatic response to the exigencies of social change, an effort to ensure the stability of the existing competitive economic system. The moral question 'whether any obligation rests upon society' he considered 'really irrelevant to the issue.' The essence of the 'social question' was simple collective self-preservation:

if for the mass of the people, or if for a large proportion of this mass, spontane- ous regulation does not go on at a faster rate than non-regulative and destructive action, it is clear that society, by voluntary or compulsory action, or by both, apart altogether from any obligation, must interfere to save itself.[38]

Mavor's political and economic ideas explained his general conception of social change and history. 'The oscillation of a pendulum,' he wrote, 'probably affords a more accurate figure of the general movement of mankind than move- ment either invariably upwards or downwards.' Through technological change man had moved forward away from feudalism until the end of the nineteenth century. It then became evident that urban industrialism had brought its own social problems which, if left unattended, led to revolution and the regression of society. None of the various utopian schemes of reform could be relied upon to counter the backward swing of the pendulum: only if man turned to history as his rational guide in economic and political matters could society resume its upward course. The political economist became, in effect, a master mechanic tinkering with the machinery of society only to the degree required to maintain maximum stability and efficiency. Armed with an empirical knowledge of economic history, his vision unclouded by idealistic metaphysics, the social scientist guided society to an orderly and rationalized technological future.[39]

Unlike many of his academic contemporaries, James Mavor did not experience a growing sense of intellectual isolation and disillusionment in the 1920s. He had never written of battle as a glorious affair and consequently did not find his preconceptions destroyed by the carnage of the Great War. Nor had he ever lauded the virtues of the British Empire only to witness it crumble in the geopolitical reorganization after 1919. The literary decadence of the 1890s had not appeared to him a harbinger of degeneration in aesthetics and ethics; indeed, he appeared pleased to have known men like Oscar Wilde, Max Beerbohm, and Aubrey Beardsley. Finally, a return to the agrarian way of life he considered an impossible alternative to modern industrial society and, therefore, felt no con- cern at the growth of technology during the war. In fact, it was his opinion that the Great War had changed little in western social development. With the proper realignment in economic policy designed to counter the growth of governmental power during the war years, political life could be returned to its 'normal' course. Indeed, his support was solicited by businessmen who held similar views, among whom were Edmund Walker and Zebulon Lash, for the Canadian National Reconstruction Groups. What explained Mavor's pragmatic response to the post-war years, compared to the melancholy of Archibald MacMechan or James Cappon, was the fact that he had been since 1890, not only attuned to, but also a factor in the growth of the liberal empiricist faith in technology. Through the empirical studies of social science, he believed, man could locate a rational basis for social policy. With careful administration by experts, this policy could be translated into action designed to guarantee maximization of economic production and political stability. Reconciled to the *Zeitgeist*, Mavor and his empiricism were equipped to survive in a world which ignored or derided the Victorian idealist and his metaphysics.[40]

8

Conclusion:
Conviction in an Age
of Transition

In the quarter century preceding the Great War Canadian intellectuals confronted what they termed a 'Social Crisis.' In common with many of their articulate contemporaries, they believed that accelerated social change had swept aside familiar institutions yet left nothing in their place.[1] Part of this disquiet was rooted in a pastoralism which characterized nineteenth-century Canadian thinking:[2] as social reality departed from an essentially agrarian way of life, traditional values were challenged or abandoned. This was particularly true of individual responsibility, a virtue dear to many Victorians and quite unfamiliar, they regretted, to a new and morally deficient generation.[3] Older Canadians had formulated their ideas on such topics under the guidance of Sir Walter Scott, Robert Louis Stevenson, or Thomas Carlyle.[4] Equally important in the process of attitude formation was the austere and demanding schooling, usually stressing the classics, which many Victorians recalled with more gratitude than affection. Buttressing most of their values was a profound commitment to Christian ethics and, usually, dogma, the product of vigorous family piety in early life.[5] But as these values were corroded by 'a wanton carelessness of spiritual health' and their society physically transformed, many Victorians were driven to animated protest.[6] The urban blight with its 'inferior' immigrants and dreadful sweatshops were frequently seen as a harbinger of American decadence, as were political corruption and the ethos of 'commercialism.'[7] Many Canadians sought an antidote in the venerable British tradition, a mystical blend of Anglo-Saxon superiority and ancient political wisdom.[8] For many, this cultural imperialism became one facet in a general spirit of reform. Such reformation was premised on the leadership of an ethical or intellectual élite and stressed not material change but moral regeneration.[9] In this respect, the intellectuals and their contemporaries shared a similarity of outlook with the American urban progressives[10] and the French-Canadian intellectuals of La Ligue Nationaliste.[11] As well, there were parallels and personal ties with the British followers of Joseph Chamberlain, who frequently combined an interest in empire with an awareness of urgent social problems.[12] Together these various movements represented a turn-of-the-century attempt to retain order in 'the last days ... of an authoritarian world.'[13] To this extent, the Canadian intellectuals were but a small component in a larger upheaval in the English-speaking world.

Underlying this atmosphere of social chaos was an even more profound sense of disintegrating conviction. Until the intellectual quandary was resolved, no solutions could be found to any mere material difficulties. With more than a touch of bitterness, Stephen Leacock readily accepted Arnold Haultain's earlier assertion that the root of the dilemma was epistemological. He wrote:

Our modern scholarship ... has set itself to be so ultra-rational, so hyper-skeptical, that now it knows nothing at all. All the old certainty has vanished. The good old solid dogmatic dead-sureness that buckled itself in the oak and brass of its own stupidity is clean gone ... Everything is henceforth to be a development, an evolution; morals and ethics are turned from fixed facts to shifting standards that change from age to age like the fashion of our clothes; art and literature are only a product, not good or bad, but a part of its age and environment. We have long since discovered that we cannot know anything. Our studies consist only in the long-drawn proof of the futility for the search after knowledge by exposing the errors of the past.[14]

In attempting to expand the limits of truth, the nineteenth century had, paradoxically, destroyed what little certainty it once possessed.

Adrift without a philosophical anchor, Canadian intellectuals were confronted by the legacy of the 'Victorian compromise.' The nineteenth century was an awkward transitional period; it lacked the framework of rationalism associated with the preceding age but was unwilling to accept the relativism which would later characterize the twentieth century. In effect, individuals were obliged to formulate convictions yet were well aware that much of their thought had no secure foundation in widely accepted beliefs. This duality of faith and scepticism explains why older Canadian intellectuals of the period could experience profound personal anxiety and at the same time endorse widely divergent systems of thought with almost evangelical fervour. Andrew Macphail, for example, founded his philosophy on the concept of order inherent in nature while Maurice Hutton, Archibald MacMechan, and James Cappon, less independent thinkers, borrowed their fundamental convictions from the idealism of Plato, Carlyle, and Arnold. John Stuart Mill's empiricism, tempered with metaphysical fragments, provided the basis for Adam Shortt's thought, in contrast to

James Mavor, who adopted the unalloyed empiricism of continental and British positivism. Each individual, then, according to his temper and training proclaimed his own system of conviction as a counter to the chaos of an age of transition.

Despite the diversity of belief evident in the Canadian intellectual community, it is clear that two primary orientations underlay the thought of the period. The first tendency was a variety of idealism which, though often eclectic and amorphous, was readily associated with intuition, romanticism, metaphysics, and Christianity. The second mode of thought, empiricism, was also frequently vague in expression but had obvious connections with positivism, materialism, cultural relativism, and the social sciences. These two sets of intellectual assumptions were marshalled by different men to answer the fundamental question of the Victorian period: what constituted truth and how did man acquire such knowledge.[15] Both systems of thought drew heavily on nineteenth-century epistemology and, in that sense, one was no less traditional than the other. But one system was better equipped for survival in twentieth-century society; to that extent, empiricism must be judged the more modern of the two belief systems. Such success, however, reveals little of the philosophical implications of empiricism nor does it explain those aspects of idealism which account for its demise. Without indulging in the 'doctrinal pedigree hunting' labelled 'one of the silliest manifestations of the colonial mind,'[16] it is essential for an understanding of Victorian Canada to trace the derivation of these two antithetical approaches to thought.

The idealism which pervaded the thinking of men such as Archibald MacMechan had its origin in the academic philosophy current in Britain after 1870. This metaphysical position, in turn, was rooted in an epistemological controversy arising from the middle years of the preceding century. In considering the question of how man came to discern truth, David Hume had arrived, by 1750, at the pessimistic conclusion that reason could determine neither the existence of God nor the purpose of human life. The romantic movement in literature arose in part as an alternative to such scepticism, but academic philosophers refused to accept these emotional intuitive ideas and turned instead to two other theories of knowledge.[17] The first, the common sense school, derived from the work of Thomas Reid and was later developed by Sir William Hamilton. Rejecting Hume's epistemology these men asserted that man lived in a world external to his mind and in no way dependent on this reason for its existence. He came to know the reality of the external world by what Reid termed 'the principles of common sense,' that is, from objective conclusions drawn from ordinary senses. These views, however, enjoyed less academic popularity than a second alternative to scepticism: the empiricism of individuals such as John Stuart Mill.[18] The latter was a direct philosophical descendant of the classical empiricists, basing his thought on their view of the human mind. Man was born with no innate ideas; rather, primary sensory perceptions gained by experience were associated to form more complex ideas. Verification of any such concept depended on experiment and observation while an idea which remained untested was at best an hypothesis. The evidence of orderly design in the universe, for example, might imply the existence of a creative intelligence, but it certainly did not establish the presence of an immanent God.[19] Mill's empiricism, like Hamilton's 'common sense,' placed metaphysics beyond the scope of reasoned knowledge.

The epistemological questions raised by Hume's scepticism were, in effect, avoided rather than answered by the empiricists. Indeed, certain early nineteenth-century English thinkers, notably Thomas Carlyle and Samuel Taylor Coleridge, remained unsatisfied with this British solution and turned instead to the idealism emerging in Germany. It was Immanuel Kant who provided the most convincing alternative to Hume. By synthesizing the empiricists' postulate that experience provides the matter of knowledge with the view of continental rationalism that the form of knowledge is derived from the structure of the mind, Kant established that the basis of scientific thought, reason, is identical to that of metaphysical inquiry. This crucial line of thinking was carried to its conclusion by George Frederic Hegel. If all objects of man's knowledge are products of mind, but not necessarily man's mind, they are the product of an intelligence other than that of a finite individual. This Absolute Mind can be equated with the spirit of reason, making what is real appear rational and permitting man to know all things through the affinity of his own reason with the Absolute.[20] The effort of the German idealists gave metaphysics a basis in reason and allowed it to become, by the mid-nineteenth century, a respectable area of philosophical enquiry. Indeed, a number of early British academic philosophers – James Ferrier at St Andrews, John Crote at Cambridge, James Stirling at Edinburgh – used the German ideas to attack the empiricist position. But idealism found its real home at Oxford during the 1870s. Benjamin Jowett was at Balliol College, as were T.H. Green and A.C. Bradley, while F.H. Bradley was at Merton and Bernard Bosanquet at University College. Though this brand of philosophy declined in the 1890s[21] as a new generation of philosophers – G.E. Moore, Bertrand Russell, Ludwig Wittgenstein – rejected the Hegelian attempt to construct a world view and ignored metaphysics in preference to logic and linguistic analysis,[22] one important individual remained at Oxford to carry on the idealist tradition. In 1893, after twenty-seven years as Professor of Moral Philosophy at Glasgow, Edward Caird returned to the major source of his acquaintance with idealism, Balliol College.

Caird became interested in German idealism through reading Carlyle while a student at Glasgow. Later, studying at Oxford, he became a friend of T.H. Green and came to view the German movement as a part of the larger idealism originating with Plato and developed in Christian theology.[23] It was his belief that Kant had destroyed the subject-object duality of empiricism by proving instead that the mind and the thing were actually a part of one experience. Hegel, in turn, gave a label to this experience by establishing that it was reason which formed the connection between man and the external world. Building on these concepts Caird wrote that 'Idealism must prove the most rigorous Realism.' Since 'moral truth is contained in the first experience of a self-conscious being,' he felt it was the task of the poet and philosopher to awaken man to these precepts. Society he conceived of in organic terms, believing that individual freedom and duty to the collectivity were reconciled in the necessity of coming to know and act in accord with the eternal spirit of reason.[24] Opposed to both empiricism and the 'subjective idealism' of romanticism, Caird was 'the apostle of a new philosophical idealism.'[25] His ideas, as John Watson suggested, were an attempt to 'preserve the essence of religion' by giving it 'a more rational form.' Furthermore, where empiricism demanded knowledge based on objective data and therefore tended to fragment and limit what was regarded as true, Caird's thought led to an organic system of belief equipped to explain the relationship of man to the Absolute.[26] For these reasons his philosophy was particularly appealing to individuals caught in an age of intellectual ferment.

Caird's influence pervaded Canadian academic philosophy. At the University of Toronto, George Paxton Young instructed Archibald MacMechan in the postulates of idealism, while James Cappon at Queen's had been a close friend of Caird at Glasgow. John Clark Murray, Professor of Moral and Mental Philosophy at McGill after 1872 originally subscribed to certain of Sir William Hamilton's ideas but later adopted an eclectic idealism based on Kant and the works of Spinoza and Aristotle. At that time philosophy was compulsory for students at McGill and the young Andrew Macphail was doubtless exposed to Murray's teaching.[27] While Maurice Hutton had no direct contact with Caird, he studied at Oxford during the heyday of Jowett, Green, and the Bradleys and certainly absorbed the Platonic idealism then current. Four of the individuals considered in this study, then, through direct or indirect contact with Edward Caird's thought, reflected the basic precepts of his idealism. In many respects, as one scholar has suggested, 'Philosophically, Central Canada was a colony of Scotland.'[28]

Because he had studied philosophy under both John Watson and Edward Caird, it was natural that Adam Shortt should also absorb certain ideas associated with the idealist school. He considered man 'a spiritual being' who was linked to the Absolute through his reason and a 'brotherhood with nature.' Men were essentially social creatures whose collective moral progress was the basis of the historical process. But Shortt's training in the natural sciences under Lord Kelvin and others may have turned the focus of his thought from metaphysics to empiricism. In the writing of John Stuart Mill, an individual familiar with German idealism as well as British empiricism, Shortt found ideas which were compatible with the duality of his own intellectual background. Both men conceived of political freedom as a prerequisite to the development of the individual, but were equally convinced that without society the individual could never develop his full character. A free society, though classless, ideally was directed by an intellectual élite, whose reasoned guidance would transform a nation's history into a chronicle of progress. The most significant similarity between Mill and Shortt was their view of political economy as a discipline which rested on empirical method rather than idealist visions. It dealt with pure facts, often derived from hsitorical examples, and did not concern itself with theoretical postulates or ironclad laws.[29] Neither an idealist nor a dogmatic positivist, Shortt was, like Mill, a transitional intellectual figure: a social scientist with a vague metaphysical strain.

James Mavor, unlike Adam Shortt, did not temper his empiricism with idealism. He never referred to a 'universal Will' in his writing as did Andrew Macphail, nor did he emphasize the validity of man's intuitive perception of Divine law as did Archibald MacMechan. It was not that he was unacquainted with such concepts for, as his old friend Patrick Geddes wrote to him, 'You know both points of view – the utilitarian and the idealist.'[30] Indeed, his studies at Glasgow and his friendship with Edward Caird combined to give him usually excellent exposure to idealist thought. But Mavor dismissed the idealists and their middle-class allies in various reform movements as ill informed. 'In general,' he wrote, 'their purely classical education predisposed them to look at the problems they encountered in a non-scientific manner and thus they also incurred the reproach of dilettantism.' Carlyle, for example, though he caught the imagination of youth, had little practical impact on social policy because his criticisms were linked to a metaphysical hero worship. Whatever importance 'idealism like that of Rodin, Morris, Ruskin and Tolstoi' possessed lay in its ability to stimulate discussion of social questions and to consider them apart from any particular economic creed such as 'conventional Socialist propaganda.' For his personal system of belief Mavor turned to positivism, especially the work of Frederic Le Play, whom he considered 'a perfect mine of sociological information,' and Charles Booth, for whose 'laborious inductive methods' he had considerable respect.[31]

Mavor was hardly a disciple of Le Play, but it is obvious that under the influence of the latter's methodology he joined the ranks of late nineteenth-century positivism. This system of thought represented 'a certain philosophical attitude concerning human knowledge,' 'a collection of rules and evaluative criteria' to distinguish that which is true knowledge. Building on the early empiricist tradition of Bacon, Locke, and Hume, Auguste Comte coined the term positivism in his attempt to classify and study all aspects of human social behaviour. Ultimately sociology would emerge as man's highest intellectual achievement, the basis of both a 'religion of humanity' and all rational legal systems. Various thinkers seized on Comte's attempt to rid social science of its metaphysical tones by emphasizing empirical method. Herbert Spencer, for example, though he rejected the utopianism of Comte along with conventional religion, borrowed a number of positivist assumptions. In particular, he based his theory on the belief that all changes in the universe could be reduced to the same mechanical operations, a form of neutral evolution to which the subjective labels 'good' and 'bad' did not apply. A variety of other British Victorian thinkers – John Stuart Mill, Frederick Harrison, Harriet Martineau, Beatrice Webb – read and approved of certain aspects of positivism.[32] By the turn of the century, it was the established credo of most social scientists,[33] emphasizing empirical method and stripped of the utopian, system-building idiosyncrasies of Comte and Spencer. While certain branches of social science would drastically change with the introduction of the concept of irrational man by Freud and others after the Great War,[34] the positivism of men like Charles Booth would also continue well into the middle of the twentieth century.[35] James Mavor was a representative of this modern strain of positivism.

The late nineteenth-century Canadian academic community was clearly characterized by two antithetical modes of thought: idealism and empiricism. This division, in fact, represented the fundamental duality of the Victorian world view, a duality which separated Herbert Spencer's evolutionary positivism from Matthew Arnold's plea for a less materialistic culture. The idealists were willing to accept on faith certain universal principles from which they reasoned their conscious attitudes towards existence. Andrew Macphail, for example, stated with conviction his 'credo,' his 'philosophy of life,' and upon these largely intuitive assumptions constructed a social theory which reconciled a particular view of God and man to the society around him. In marked contrast, the empiricists, by rejecting the validity of intuitive postulates, rejected the very foundations necessary for the creation of a metaphysical system. James Mavor, for instance, seldom made explicit his personal view of human nature and never incorporated it into a comprehensive philosophy; he preferred, instead, to emphasize the method by which he approached a specific and limited problem. When this type of thought was borrowed from the natural sciences and applied to human affairs, the empiricists entered a domain previously ruled by the metaphysicians. Through this trespass the social sciences were born and, though the twentieth century would see a radical shift in the conception of the human mind to account for the subconscious, empirical method remained the basis for all such studies. Method, in effect, replaced principle as the significant aspect of the social scientists' approach to existence, leaving a metaphysical vacuum at the core of their thought.

The idealists were well aware of the relativistic threat imposed by empiricism and, to that extent, were considerably more percipient than the early social scientists. Admittedly, the empiricists deserved credit on two grounds. First, the empirical approach was often well equipped to devise technical solutions to immediate social problems. Secondly, and more significantly, the empirical method cut through Victorian pretense to make explicit what the nineteenth century feared to admit: the very narrow limits of man's established knowledge. But these accomplishments were more than balanced by the deficiencies inherent in a rigid empiricism. Where the idealists appeared dogmatic, the empiricists were directionless, applying their methodology in an *ad hoc* fashion. The result was a narrowness of focus and a refusal to confront the underlying issues which gave rise to specific problems. Moreover, by stressing reality as it was rather than as it might be, the empiricists were trapped in an inertia which precluded ever guiding society towards an ideal goal. The empiricists' investigations tended, as well, to fragment knowledge by compartmentalizing the various aspects of social existence. This fragmentation, in turn, created discrete disciplines which purported to deal with human affairs in a scientific fashion yet considered man in mono-dimensional terms. Most serious of all, empiricism was blind to the implications of its own solitary principle. Though arguing that principles constituted a bias, empiricism itself was premised on an ideal conception of the human mind. Man, it assumed, could not only discern aspects of truth through an inherent power of inductive reason, but could also apply this knowledge to society by the legislative process. Refusing to accord respectability to the idealists' assumptions and cloaking their own in the rhetoric of objectivity, the empiricists were little better than intellectual hypocrites. Committed to methodology, empiricism flaunted its lack of preconceptions; this deficiency, in turn, opened the door for the relativism characteristic of much modern scholarship and social policy.

A synthesis of the empiricists' efficient knowledge with the idealists' commitment to principle, however desirable, was quite impossible, for by 1900 idealism was a dying system of belief. In part this was a reflection of the emergence of an urban industrial society which placed a premium on planning and cost benefit analysis rather than metaphysical declarations. Important also were changes in religion and literature, for Victorian idealism had found allies in writers such as Arnold and Tennyson, who could not be replaced altogether by Shaw or Eliot. Of more fundamental significance was the death of idealism in British academic circles. Cut off from its acknowledged roots, Canadian idealism found no alternative buttress, for in the United States academic idealism died with Josiah Royce and on the continent it was superceded by existentialism and later, phenomenology. As well, discoveries in physiology and psychology cast doubt on the idealists' conception of the human mind while the developing disciplines of anthropology introduced a cultural relativism quite at odds with the absolutism of the idealists' great systems. The final sign of impending defeat was the ease with which the empiricists posed debates in their own terms. This was the striking irony, for example, of the idealist defence of the classics. Their position was lost when they attempted to prove that a knowledge of Greek equipped a young man for the world of business as well, if not better, than a command of mathematics.[36] By stressing relevance and practicality as the points at issue, the empiricists were easy victors. By 1914, then, it was obvious that the idealist approach to thought and reality had all but succumbed to the empiricist attack.

The debate between the idealist and empiricist positions was carried beyond the academic circle to a wider audience through articles and addresses on topics such as imperialism, urban development, or political corruption. Though the philosophical orientation of the author was often implicit, his approach to the topic discussed seldom left any doubt as to basic assumptions. In considering the Empire, for example, Andrew Macphail's idealism led him to view imperialism as an emotion akin to religion, while Adam Shortt's empiricism forced him to debunk preferential trade schemes which contravened his view of economic practicality.[37] Discussions of specific topics were less important in the long run to Victorian intellectuals than was the opportunity to express their fundamental convictions. It was for this reason that they conceived of the academic as a moral tutor rather than an instructor in a specific subject. It explains, further, why the intellectuals were willing to alienate themselves from practical politics and, for the most part, confine themselves to academic journals rather than the public hustings. In effect, whether idealist or empiricist, they considered intellectual orientation inseparable from political or cultural debate. Education, for instance, became not simply a means of ensuring a well-informed populace, but was itself an expression of primary social and philosophical values. This same argument could be applied to discussions of imperialism, political reform, free trade — indeed, to virtually any of the topics considered by these nineteenth-century intellectuals. In their view it was essential that Canadian society formulate a set of correct assumptions on which to base a response to the dislocation of an age of transition.

With this sense of urgency behind them, the academics were willing to abandon their scholarly interests and concern themselves with explaining social issues to their contemporaries. To a certain extent they achieved this end. In the two decades prior to the Great War, their ideas were disseminated in a variety of ways to a diverse audience. On a popular level their views were published in periodicals such as the *Canadian Magazine,* they spoke before clubs in many centres across Canada, and newspapers carried reports of their more controversial statements. This was particularly true of Adam Shortt, whose views were cited by Oliver Asselin, the *Grain Growers' Guide,* and the *Dominion Grange,*[38] and of Andrew Macphail, who also found a receptive audience among western farmers, and especially in the eccentric visionary, E.A. Partridge.[39] On a more academic level the intellectuals edited and published in both the *Queen's Quarterly* and the *University Magazine.* While their circulations were small, these two journals monopolized the field of Canadian academic publication from 1890 to 1920. In the case of the latter periodical, its subscribers ranged from Governor-General Grey to W.C. Good, the farm radical, and subscriptions were sent to readers in both the United States and Great Britain. Books also were an important method of conveying ideas. Andrew Macphail's work, for example, prompted controversial reviews in English and American periodicals, while Maurice Hutton's collections of essays were often revised versions of lectures presented to rural Ontario audiences. As teachers, according to the testimony of former students, the academics were frequently remembered for their outspoken opinions. Frank Underhill, for example, writing in 1946, recalled his 'thrill of appreciation' at Hutton's remarks on the dullness of Canadian politics delivered thirty years earlier.[40] It is evident, too, that certain academics offered advice to political figures such as Sifton, Laurier, and Borden. Shortt and Mavor, indeed, acted in official capacities to devise policies on the civil service and immigration respectively. Politicians, students, fellow academics, and a wider popular audience were all exposed in some degree to the ideas of the six intellectuals.

The Great War, however, brought with it a change in both the volume and focus of the intellectuals' writing. Andrew Macphail, for example, forsook the editorship of the *University Magazine* for overseas service while his friend MacMechan, eager for vicarious participation, turned his energies to a chronicle of the Halifax explosion. This wartime shift of interest created a hiatus with the social criticism of the pre-war years from which the writing of the academics never recovered. But while the war may have destroyed the continuity of publication, a more important explanation for the change in emphasis was to be found in the men themselves. By 1920 most of them had reached their early sixties and found the topics they had debated in their heyday – imperial unity, female suffrage, university training for the working man – were no longer considered relevant. Indeed, the Victorian authorities such as Caird, Mill, or Bagehot with whom they buttressed their assertions were disparaged by Freud, Keynes, and other iconoclastic twentieth-century intellectuals. In a sense, too, the fundamental battle of the period had been decided: the idealists were defeated and the empiricists, secure as victors, slipped into relative complacency. Ironically for the late Victorian empiricists, however, their status was threatened by modernity as well. In the 1920s it was increasingly difficult to stumble into a career in disciplines such as political economy without lengthy and specialized training.[41] For both idealists and empiricists, then, the 1920s brought profound changes.

Though there were personal differences in the response of the intellectuals to the post-war era, these were outweighed by marked similarities. James Mavor was spared a sense of growing isolation by his death in 1925 but Adam Shortt, living another half dozen years, retreated to archival research and published almost nothing in this period. Archibald MacMechan's social commentary, never prolific, ended abruptly in 1920 with his views on Canada as a vassal state. The works he published in the following thirteen years were collections of maritime adventures often written in an earlier and, doubtless, more congenial time. Andrew Macphail continued his prolific volume of publication well into the 1930s but the old crusading style had been left, with much else, in the soggy fields of France. Increasingly, before his death at 74 in 1938, his interest turned from contemporary affairs to critical biography. Though he published his excellent study of Bliss Carman in 1930, James Cappon wrote his last 'Current Events' column for the *Queen's Quarterly* in 1919, the same year the *University Magazine* came to an end. Indeed, when he died in 1939 at the age of 85, Cappon had published virtually nothing over the preceding two decades. Finally, Maurice Hutton produced several volumes of essays in the twenties but most of the material had been written and frequently published in the pre-war period. Born at the end of the Crimean War and alive to witness the beginning of the Second World War, it was not unnatural that Hutton should find himself composing tributes to departed colleagues and occasionally given to melancholy reminiscences. In a period of intellectual transition these Victorians had made explicit their fundamental convictions to help fellow Canadians grope towards a more tranquil future. In the post-war years changing criteria of relevance saw their causes ignored and, on occasion, derided.[42]

By remaining true to their convictions, the older intellectuals found themselves incompatible with a changing Canadian academic environment. The *Canadian Forum*'s desire to appear 'progressive' and its attack on the 'Maple-leaf' school of writers were attitudes which must have perplexed Andrew Macphail. Similarly, the facile attempt by the *Canadian Mercury* in 1928 to dismiss the Victorian period in Canada as one of 'no real social criticism and no real quest for human values' must, had he read it, have caused Maurice Hutton considerable dismay.[43] By 1930 the *Queen's Quarterly* and the new *University of Toronto Quarterly* shared few of the attitudes of earlier academic publications. Even those areas upon which most intellectuals had agreed were neglected or disputed. History was no longer universally looked upon as the model for human behaviour but, from the depth of the Depression, could be dismissed as gigantic folly. The slowly evolving British constitutional tradition, in particular, was stripped of its mystique and in the debate on dominion-provincial relations, exposed in all its rigid inadequacies.[44] Indeed, young and pragmatic economists seldom expressed the moral hesitation which had marked earlier considerations of positive government.[45] Perhaps most significant of all, the new inhabitants of academic Canada showed singularly little appreciation for the intellectual turbulence of the pre-war years. As early as 1919 one writer asserted that it had been 'a period of stability' while two decades later another myopically observed that it was a placid age 'responsive to our aims and efforts.'[46] Perhaps the only belief which linked the new spirit to that of the earlier academics was the firm conviction that the intellectual existed primarily to advise and criticize the society around him.[47] But such agreement was of little comfort to the older intellectuals who, finding the new views at best puzzling and more often abhorrent, were unlikely to consider them proper advice for a society in crisis. By a cruel irony, what had begun as an alienation by choice gradually became an alienation enforced by circumstance. It was isolation from which they would be rescued by history alone.

Notes

CHAPTER ONE   INTRODUCTION: 'A SEARCH FOR AN IDEAL'

1 Arnold Haultain, 'A Search for an Ideal,' *Canadian Magazine* XXII 5 (1904)
  427-8
2 Arnold Haultain, *A Selection from Goldwin Smith's Correspondence* (New York
  1913) xix-xx
3 Walter Houghton, *The Victorian Frame of Mind* (New Haven 1957) xv, 1, 11-21;
  Jerome H. Buckley, *The Victorian Temper* (Cambridge, Mass. 1951) 1-13
4 See J.A.V. Chapple, *Documentary and Imaginative Literature, 1880-1920*
  (London 1970); Raymond Chapman, *The Victorian Debate: English Literature
  and Society, 1832-1901* (London 1968); J.A. Lester, *Journey through Despair,
  1880-1914: Transformation in British Literary Culture* (Princeton 1968);
  H. Stuart Hughes, *Consciousness and Society: The Reorientation of European
  Social Thought, 1890-1930* (New York 1961)
5 Samuel Hynes, *The Edwardian Turn of Mind* (Princeton 1968)
6 Goldwin Smith, *Reminiscences* (New York 1910) 329-32, 412-13
7 Henry F. May, *The End of American Innocence: A Study of the First Years of
  Our Time, 1912-1917* (New York 1959) x, 10-30, 168-9
8 Morton White, *Social Thought in America: The Revolt against Formalism*
  (Boston 1957) 6-12. Note also R.J. Wilson, *In Quest of Community, Social Philosophy in the United States, 1860-1920* (New York 1968)
9 Frederic C. Jaher, *Doubters and Dissenters: Cataclysmic Thought in America,
  1885-1918* (New York 1964) 9, 18
10 Ramsay Cook, 'Stephen Leacock and the Age of Plutocracy, 1903-1921,' in
   John S. Moir, ed., *Character and Circumstance* (Toronto 1970) 167
11 H.B. Neatby, 'Politics: The Opiate of the 1930's,' *Canadian Forum* L 591
   (1970) 18

12 R.J.D. Page, 'Canada and the Imperial Idea in the Boer War Years,' *JCS* V 1 (1970) 41. See also Michiel Horn, 'Visionaries of the 1930's: The League for Social Reconstruction,' in Stephen Clarkson, ed., *Visions 2020* (Edmonton 1970) 263; F.W. Watt, 'Critic or Entertainer: Stephen Leacock and the Growth of Materialism,' *Canadian Literature* 5 (1960) 36; F.H. Underhill, *In Search of Canadian Liberalism* (Toronto 1961) 5, 18.

13 Munro Beattie, 'Archibald Lampman,' in Claude T. Bissell, ed., *Our Living Tradition,* First Series (Toronto 1957) 72; Claude T. Bissell, 'Literary Taste in Central Canada during the Late Nineteenth Century,' *CHR* XXXI (1950) 244

14 Carl Berger, *The Sense of Power: Studies in the Ideas of Canadian Imperialism, 1867-1914* (Toronto 1970) 177; Alan Bowker, introduction, *The Social Criticism of Stephen Leacock: The Unsolved Riddle of Social Justice and Other Essays* (Toronto 1973)

15 W.S. Wallace, *A History of the University of Toronto, 1827-1927* (Toronto 1927) 143, 106, 185; Wilhelmina Gordon, *Daniel M. Gordon, His Life* (Toronto 1941) 218, 189; D.D. Calvin, *Queen's University at Kingston, 1841-1941* (Kingston 1941) 111; Cyrus Macmillan, *McGill and Its Story, 1821-1921* (Toronto 1921) 253, 262, 263

16 Queen's University Archives, Daniel M. Gordon Papers, E.D. McClaren to Gordon, 4 April 1906

17 Gordon, *Daniel M. Gordon* 233

18 University of Toronto Archives, James Mavor Papers, Robert Falconer to Mavor, 11 July 1921

19 Gordon Papers, memorandum entitled, 'Comparative Salaries, Toronto and Queen's, 1890-1910'; M.C. Urquhart and K.A.H. Buckley, eds, *Historical Statistics of Canada* (Toronto 1965) 99, 111, 292

20 Wallace, *A History of the University of Toronto* 20; Gordon Papers, Gordon to Chancellor Nathaniel Burwash, 11 Mar. 1908; Sir William Peterson Papers, Peterson to Maurice Hutton, 25 Jan. 1906

21 Stephen Leacock, 'The Apology of a Professor,' *UM* IX 2 (1910) 176, 178. A similar view was expressed much earlier by Archibald Lampman in 'At the Mermaid Inn' in the Toronto *Globe,* 2 Apr. 1892.

22 Berger, *The Sense of Power* 72-3; Carroll Quigley, 'The Round Table Groups in Canada, 1908-38.' *CHR* XLIII 3 (1962) 205, 218; Michiel Horn, 'The League for Social Reconstruction, 1932-36,' *JCS* VII 4 (1972) 4

23 Malcolm Ross, 'Goldwin Smith,' in Bissell, *Our Living Tradition;* Sandwell's comment quoted in Northrop Frye, Conclusion, in Carl F. Klinck, ed., *Literary History of Canada* (Toronto 1965) 839; European, British, and American intellectuals were equally alienated in this period. See Hughes, *Consciousness and Society* 51; Hynes, *The Edwardian Frame of Mind* 51; George Watson,

The English Ideology: Studies in the Language of Victorian Politics (London 1973) 245, 258; Christopher Lasch, *The New Radicalism in America, 1889-1963: The Intellectual as a Social Type* (New York 1965) xii, xv.

24 Andrew Macphail, 'The Navy and Politics,' *UM* XII 1 (1913) 17

25 Sir Robert Falconer, 'From College to University,' *UTQ* V 1 (1935) 2

26 Sir Robert Falconer, 'Glimpses of the University at Work from 1907 until the World War,' *UTQ* XI 2 (1942) 396, 398

27 N.F. Dupuis, 'The Conservative and the Liberal in Education,' *QQ* IX 2 (1901) 122. For an estimation of Dupuis by a traditionalist see James Cappon, 'In Memorium,' *QQ* XXV 2 (1917) 132. See Laurence R. Veysey's account of this conflict in the United States in *The Emergence of the American University* (Chicago and London 1965) especially 38-40, 59, and 193.

28 Milton Rokeach, *Beliefs, Attitudes and Values: A Theory of Organization and Change* (San Francisco 1969) chapter 1, offers suggestive comments on the concept of 'conviction.'

29 T.A. Goudge, for example, in 'A Century of Philosophy in English-Speaking Canada' (*Dalhousie Review* XLVII [1967-8]) refuses to accord the idealist philosophers serious consideration, instead dismissing their work as 'Rhetorical phrases, purple passages, and edifying "uplife" ... ' (538). In this connection see Carl L. Becker, *The Heavenly City of the Eighteenth-Century Philosophers* (New Haven 1932) chapter 1.

30 John Higham, 'Intellectual History and Its Neighbours,' *Journal of the History of Ideas* XV 3 (1954). In writing this type of history, single references to specific sources do not always suffice. Facing this problem in 1939 with the publication of his *New England Mind*, Perry Miller, the first American scholar to refer to his work as 'intellectual history,' chose to deposit separate volumes of references in the Harvard library. The present study adopts the device of cumulative notes on the assumption that only by viewing a number of sources taken together is a particular idea clearly documented.

31 It should be obvious that this study is not an exercise in collective biography. See Lawrence Stone, 'Prosopography,' in Felix Gilbert and Stephen Graubard, eds, *Historical Studies Today* (New York 1972).

32 Arnold Haultain, *Of Walks and Walking Tours: An Attempt to Find a Philosophy and a Creed* (London 1914) 40

CHAPTER TWO   ANDREW MACPHAIL: THE IDEAL IN NATURE

1 Alice Chandler, *A Dream of Order: The Medieval Ideal in Nineteenth-century English Literature* (Lincoln 1970) 196; Herbert L. Sussman, *Victorians and*

the Machine: The Literary Response to Technology (Cambridge, Mass. 1968) 77, 82; Leo Marx, *The Machine in the Garden: Technology and the Pastoral Ideal in America* (New York 1964) 216

2 Information on Macphail's early life comes from his autobiographical work, *The Master's Wife* (Montreal 1939). See also his articles 'The Old School House,' *Saturday Night* LIII 9 (1938) and 'Prince Edward Island,' *Proceedings of the Canadian Club of Toronto, 1911-12* IX (Toronto 1912). In the Sir Andrew Macphail Papers, held privately in Montreal by Macphail's daughter, Mrs Dorothy Lindsay, see William Macphail to Macphail, 2 Nov. 1904, and a typed manuscript, 'The Man and the Machine.'

3 Andrew Macphail, 'The Old College,' *Saturday Night* LII 28 (1938) 1-2; *The Master's Wife* 178

4 On Macphail's early teaching see *The Master's Wife* 181-3, and in the Macphail Papers, Macphail to the Hon. Thomas McNutt, nd [1935?], Macphail to William Macphail, 11 Sept. 1882, and William Macphail to Macphail, 1 Feb. 1883. For his latter attitude to medicine see his articles: 'An Address on the Sources of Modern Medicine,' *Canadian Medical Association Journal* XXVIII 3 (1933); 'The Healing of a Wound,' *ibid.* XXX 6 (1934); 'American Methods in Medical Education,' *British Medical Journal* 3 Sept. 1927; 'The Attainment of Consideration,' *ibid.* 15 Nov. 1902.

5 Macphail, *The Master's Wife* 184-6. On Macphail's early journalism see Macphail Papers, scrapbook of Montreal *Gazette* articles, and editor of the Chicago *Times* to Macphail, 16 Sept. 1890.

6 On early financial details see *The Master's Wife* 188 and Macphail Papers, William Macphail to Macphail, 31 Oct. 1889.

7 J.A. Stevenson, 'Sir Andrew Macphail,' *Canadian Defence Quarterly* XVI 2 (1939) 210. See also Pelham Edgar, 'Sir Andrew Macphail, 1864-1938,' *PTRSC,* Series III, XXXIII (1939) 148.

8 See note 7 and the following: Pelham Edgar, 'Sir Andrew Macphail,' *QQ* LIV 1 (1947); Archibald MacMechan, 'Andrew Macphail,' in *Late Harvest* (Toronto 1934); Stephen Leacock, 'Andrew Macphail,' *QQ* XLV 4 (1938); 'H.E.M.' on Macphail in the *Canadian Medical Association Journal* XXXIV 5 (1939); Andrew Macphail, 'John McCrae: An Essay in Character,' in John McCrae, *In Flanders Fields and Other Poems* (Toronto 1920); E.A. Collard, 'Voices from the Past,' *McGill News* LIII 5 (Nov. 1972). The final reference suggests that Macphail's lectures were considered rather dull by students.

9 The alumnae publications were *The University of Toronto Review* and *The Queen's Review*. On Macphail as founder of the *University Magazine* see Edgar, 'Sir Andrew Macphail' 148.

10 James Mavor Papers, Macphail to Pelham Edgar, 14 Nov. 1910. In 1909 the University of Toronto contributed only $750 despite the journal's financial difficulties. University of Toronto Archives, Sir Robert Falconer Papers, Falconer to Macphail, 22 Feb. 1909

11 The prominence of McGill men has been noted by F.H. Underhill, *The Image of Confederation* (Toronto 1964) 42. Among them were Stephen Leacock, John McNaughton, William Peterson, and F.P. Walton; also Montreal lawyers F.W. Chipman and Archibald McGoun.

12 Macphail Papers, Andrew Macphail, 'Business and Politics,' typed manuscript, nd, 3

13 Andrew Macphail, 'The Navy and Politics' 17

14 Andrew Macphail, 'Certain Varieties of the Apples of Sodom,' *UM* X 1 (1919) 46

15 University of Toronto Archives, George M. Wrong Papers, Macphail to Wrong, 8 Jan. 1913

16 Macphail wrote to Sir Wilfrid Laurier: 'For I think it is the true theory of politics that each man who has a thing to say should say it freely and as well as he can as an assistance to a statesman in shaping his career.' PAC, Sir Wilfrid Laurier Papers, Macphail to Laurier, 6 Oct. 1909. He advised Laurier on the naval question and Sir Robert Borden on the Maine-New Brunswick border. PAC, Sir Robert Borden Papers, Macphail to Borden, 7 July 1918.

17 Andrew Macphail, 'John McCrae: An Essay in Character' 52

18 Macphail wrote to Sir William Peterson that 'the safe rule of editing' was that 'it is easier not to publish a thing than to undo any harm which may arise from publishing it.' Peterson had to warn Macphail against allowing the journal to appear too one-sided and to distinguish his own views from the journal's. McGill University Archives, Sir William Peterson Papers, Macphail to Peterson, 27 Nov. 1908, and Peterson (and F.P. Walton) to Macphail, 1 Dec. 1911

19 Leacock, 'Andrew Macphail,' 450; also Edgar, 'Sir Andrew Macphail, 1864-1938,' 148

20 See, for example: 'A Westerner,' 'Imperialism, Nationalism, or a Third Alternative,' *UM* IX 3 (1910); Andrew Macphail, 'A Voice from the East,' *UM* IX 4 (1910); William Peterson, 'True Imperialism,' *UM* IX 4 (1910).

21 Obituary for Sir Andrew Macphail, *Saturday Night* LIII 48 (1938) 1

22 See, for example, the first sentence of his essay on Sir Henry Wilson in *Three Persons* (London 1929) 3: 'The Irish have always had a sure instinct in murder.'

23 Leacock, 'Andrew Macphail' 448; Lorne Pierce, introduction to Macphail's 'Sir Gilbert Parker: An Appraisal,' *PTRSC*, Series III, XXXIII (1939) 123; Dalhousie University Archives, Archibald MacMechan Papers, MacMechan to Macphail, 27 Sept. 1914

24 Andrew Macphail, 'The Peace and Its Consequences,' *UM* XIX 2 (1920) 120-1; circulation figures are from Macphail Papers, Macphail to Mavor, 13 Sept. 1913; MacMechan Papers, Macphail to MacMechan, 12 Jan. 1912; Mavor Papers, Macphail to Mavor, 2 Nov. 1919

25 Revenue figures are from Falconer Papers, Macphail to Falconer, 6 May 1919 and Falconer to Macphail, 6 May 1919; Macphail Papers, Macphail to Mavor, 17 Sept. 1913; Mavor Papers, Macphail to Mavor, June 1913; Peterson Papers, Peterson to Maurice Hutton, 12 Mar. 1909; Peterson to Macphail, 28 Feb. 1918; Peterson to MacMechan, 8 Nov. 1918. The publisher named was George Morang.

26 For example, Peterson and Mavor had a major quarrel over a minor revision made by Peterson in an article submitted by Mavor. Peterson Papers, Peterson to Mavor, 11 Feb., 21 Feb., and 5 Apr. 1916

27 Macphail's bitterness towards the University of Toronto is found in a letter in the Mavor Papers, Macphail to Mavor, 3 Oct. 1920. The increased cost are explained in the Falconer Papers, Macphail to Falconer, 6 May 1919.

28 MacMechan Papers, Macphail to MacMechan, 8 Jan. 1920

29 MacMechan Papers, Macphail to MacMechan, 4 Oct. 1919

30 Mavor Papers, Macphail to Mavor, 3 Oct. 1920; Peterson Papers, Peterson to Macphail, 29 Apr. 1918 and Peterson to MacMechan, 8 Nov. 1918

31 MacMechan Papers, Macphail to MacMechan, 27 Mar. 1927

32 Pelham Edgar, 'Andrew Macphail, 1864-1938' 149

33 Mavor Papers, Macphail to Mavor, 9 Feb. 1914; Public Archives of Canada, Grey of Howick Papers, Grey to Sir A. Bigge, 7 Apr. 1909

34 Peterson Papers, Macphail to Peterson, 9 Dec. 1913; Macphail Papers, Lord Grey to Macphail, 7 Apr. 1909.

35 Partridge quoted Macphail extensively in his *War on Poverty* (Winnipeg 1926) 84, 89, 96, 114. The *Grain Grower's Guide* for 21 Feb. 1912 approved of Macphail's criticisms of Canadian politics in an article in *Saturday Night.* John Strachey was a close associate of Macphail, acting as an informal literary agent and often publishing articles by Macphail in *The Spectator.* See Macphail Papers, Strachey to Macphail, 27 Nov. 1908.

36 Andrew Macphail, 'Canadian Writers and American Politics,' *UM* IX 1 (1910); Macphail Papers, Grace Richie-England, President Montreal Local Council of Women to Macphail, 20 Mar. 1914 (the offensive article appeared in the *UM* XIII 1 [1914]); MacMechan Papers, Macphail to MacMechan, 13 Feb. 1909

37 The examples chosen are but a few of many reviews of the *University Magazine* found in the Macphail Papers. The Charlottetown *Guardian,* 22 Dec. 1908, Toronto *Globe,* 17 Dec. 1908, and Montreal *Herald,* 18 Dec. 1908, all reviewed Macphail's 'Why the Conservatives Failed' (VII 4 [1908]). The London *Spectator* reviewed his 'Patience of England' (*UM* VI 3 [1907]) on 2 Nov. 1907. The Boston

Herald gave an unfavourable review to his 'Canadian Writers and American Politics' on 10 Feb. 1910.

38 MacMechan Papers, Macphail to MacMechan, 15 Dec. 1913

39 One of his most controversial books was the *Official History of the Canadian Forces in the Great War, 1914-19, the Medical Services* (Ottawa 1925), in which he was critical of both Sir Sam Hughes and the surgeon-general, Dr Herbert Bruce. See the Montreal *Gazette,* 16 & 17 July 1925, for an example of the controversy. Of greater public notice was his *Three Persons,* described by the London *Mercury* as 'the most devastating review published in the last hundred years' (reported in the Montreal *Gazette,* 16 Apr. 1929). Both reviews are in the Macphail Papers.

40 An obituary in the Montreal *Daily Star,* 24 Sept. 1938, contains a summary of this type of information. See also the obituary in the *Canadian Medical Association Journal* XXXIX 5 (1938), by C.F. Martin. It contains the account of an attempt on Macphail's life by a mentally deranged assassin in 1921.

41 MacMechan Papers, Macphail to MacMechan, 4 Apr. 1926 and 26 Nov. 1917; Andrew Macphail, 'The Immigrant,' *UM* XIX 2 (1919)

42 PAC, Sir Arthur Currie Papers, Alexander Macphail to Currie, 27 May 1920, containing a copy of a letter from Andrew Macphail to Alexander, 24 May 1920; MacMechan Papers, Macphail to MacMechan, 23 Jan. 1923; Andrew Macphail, 'John McCrae: An Essay in Character' 86; 'Women in Democracy,' *UM* XIX 1 (1920); Macphail Papers, Macphail to Lord Beaverbrook, 23 Oct. 1930; Andrew Macphail, 'Art in Democracy,' *Dalhousie Review* IV 2 (1924)

43 Stephen Leacock, though an affectionate friend of Macphail, thought his agrarian bias was a 'whimsical make-believe' and didn't seem to appreciate the philosophical unity of Macphail's thinking. He wrote: 'What Andrew really thought of life in general I didn't know, and never knew, and I doubt if he did.' See Leacock, 'Andrew Macphail' 451 and 446. (Cf. Carl Berger, *The Sense of Power* 46.) Pelham Edgar, who apparently had access to some of Macphail's papers when writing, shows a more sophisticated appreciation of Macphail's philosophy in his 'Sir Andrew Macphail' 21.

44 Andrew Macphail, 'A History of the Idea of Evolution,' *DR* V 1 (1925-6); 'John Wesley' in *Essays in Puritanism* (Boston 1905) 337-8; 'The Attainment of the Idea of Evolution' 26. Evolution is described as creation by Macphail in 'Women in Democracy.'

45 Macphail, 'A History of the Idea of Evolution' 30, 29, 30-2

46 Andrew Macphail, 'The Fallacy in Theology,' in *Essays in Fallacy* (New York & London 1910) 195-8; 'The American Woman,' in *ibid.* 17; 'Jonathan Edwards,' in *Essays in Puritanism* 20; *The Bible in Scotland* (London 1931) 70. This attempt to separate reason and emotion in the religion-evolution controversy

was hardly unique. See Bert Loewenberg, 'The Controversy over Evolution in New England, 1859-73,' *New England Quarterly* VIII 2 (1935).

47 For the parallels with the emotional and ethical aspects of Puritanism see J.F. Maclear, ' "The Heart of New England Rent": The Mystical Element in Early Puritan History,' *Mississippi Valley Historical Review* XLII 4 (1956). That Macphail was well acquainted with Puritanism is evident from his romantic novel *The Vine of Sibmah* (London 1906), set in Cromwellian England and his volume of essays on New England, *Essays in Puritanism*. Occasionally the language of covenant theology slips into Macphail's writing, for example, in reference to the imperial connection in 'The Dominion and the Spirit,' *UM* VII 1 (1908).

48 Macphail, 'The Fallacy in Theology' 215; 'Women in Democracy' 12; 'Unto the Church,' *UM* XII 2 (1913); 'A History of the Idea of Evolution' 26

49 See Walter Houghton, *The Victorian Frame of Mind* 36-8, 144-54, Richard Hofstadter, *Social Darwinism in American Thought* (Boston 1967) 24-30, and Paul Boller, *American Thought in Transition: The Impact of Evolutionary Naturalism, 1865-1900* (Chicago 1969) 22-46.

50 Andrew Macphail, 'Evolution and Life,' *Annals of Medical History,* New Series I 5 (1929); 'I Believe, This is My Credo, My Philosophy of Life,' Montreal *Herald,* 10 Dec. 1934

51 Macphail, 'Jonathan Edwards' 29; 'Women in Democracy' 9; 'The Immigrant' 136; 'The Burden of the Stuarts,' *Quarterly Review* CCLIV 504 (1930) 218

52 Macphail, 'The Dominion and the Spirit' 22; 'Certain Varieties of the Apples of Sodom' 30; 'Walt Whitman' in *Essays in Puritanism* 279; 'Women in Democracy' 5

53 Macphail, 'Unto the Church' 364; 'John Wesley' 337; 'Jonathan Edwards' 20; 'The Fallacy in Theology' 348, 226, 225

54 Macphail, *The Master's Wife* 45, 46; 'The Attainment of Consideration' 1614; 'Business and Politics' 4

55 Macphail, 'The Immigrant' 136; 'Women in Democracy' 3-4; 'The Patience of England' 384-5; 'Loyalty to What,' *UM* VI 2 (1907); 'The Dominion and the Spirit' 20; 'Women in Democracy' 4; 'Jonathan Edwards' 29

56 Andrew Macphail, 'Sir Henry Wilson,' in *Three Persons* 73; 'On Certain Aspects of Feminism' 88; 'Prince Edward Island' 50-1

57 Macphail, 'Prince Edward Island' 49-51; 'The Conservative,' *UM* XVIII 4 (1919) 424; 'The Fallacy of Education,' in *Essays in Fallacy* 116, 155; 'History of the Idea of Evolution' 27; 'On Certain Aspects of Feminism' 88

58 Macphail, 'The Fallacy in Education' 182, 105, 109, 103, 141, 185; 'The Hand or the Book,' *DR* VI 2 (1926-7)

59 Macphail, 'The Fallacy in Education' 120, 117, 122, 121, 109, 110, 116, 187

60 Macphail, 'The Dominion and the Spirit' 11, 23; *Three Persons* 73; 'Conservative-Liberal-Socialist,' *UTQ* III 3 (1933-4) 278, 279; 'John Wesley' 288; 'The Immigrant' 162
61 Macphail, 'The Fallacy in Education' 141; 'Protection and Politics,' *UM* VII 2 (1908) 250; 'John McCrae: An Essay in Character' 918; 'Patriotism and Politics,' *UM* XIII 1 (1914) 3; 'Unto the Church' 356-7; 'Women in Democracy' 8
62 Macphail, 'The Fallacy in Education' 185; 'The Dominion and the Spirit' 16-17
63 Macphail, *The Master's Wife* 114. Macphail's knowledge of Scottish theology is evident from *The Bible in Scotland*. His parallels with Edward Caird are evident by comparing his concepts of religion and the natural order to those described by Caird's former student, James Cappon, in 'Edward Caird: A Reminiscence,' *QQ* XVI 3 (1909), and 'A School of Idealism: Meditatio Laici' in *Philosophical Essays Presented to John Watson* (Kingston 1922).
64 Macphail, 'John Winthrop,' in *Essays in Puritanism* 149, 71-2; 'The Fallacy in Theology' 348, 220; 'Unto the Church' 360, 356; 'The New Theology' *UM* IX 4 (1910) 690, 687, 695; 'The Psychology of Canada,' in *Essays in Politics* (London 1909) 193
65 Macphail, *The Bible in Scotland* 19, 123, 50; 'Unto the Church' 361, 364; 'The Fallacy in Theology' 225, 324; 'John Wesley' 337, 338. See also Mavor Papers, Macphail to Mavor, 23 Jan. 1925, where he predicts a revival.
66 Macphail, 'Women in Democracy' 14; 'Greek Medicine,' *QQ* XLIII 1 (1936), 25; 'Conservative-Liberal-Socialist' 284; 'The Dominion and the Spirit' 22; 'Theory and Practice,' *UM* XII 2 (1913) 381; 'Certain Varieties of the Apples of Sodom' 30; 'John Winthrop' 146; 'The Psychology of the Suffragette,' in *Essays in Fallacy* 86
67 Macphail, 'Loyalty – To What?' 148; 'Women in Democracy' 2; 'New Lamps for Old,' *UM* VIII 1 (1909) 29; 'Consequences and Penalties,' *UM* XIII 2 (1914) 170.
68 Andrew Macphail, 'Family and Society,' *Quarterly Review* CCLXVIII 532 (1937); *The Master's Wife* 189, 96, 90, 141, 186; 'The Immigrant' 153-4; 'The Tariff Commission,' *UM* XI 1 (1912) 32; 'Women in Democracy' 10; 'The Dominion and the Spirit' 23
69 Macphail, *The Master's Wife* 23, 148, 112, 114. It would appear that Macphail's wife, the former Georgina Burland of Montreal, fit his conception of an ideal woman. Macphail's sister described her in these terms: 'I find she has the same good old fashioned principles and beliefs that I have...' Macphail Papers, Margaret Macphail to Macphail, 7 Aug. 1896
70 Andrew Macphail, 'The American Woman,' in *Essays in Fallacy* 17, 49, 16; 'The Psychology of the Suffragette' 79-81; 'Women in Democracy' 5; 'On certain Aspects of Feminism' 84, 90; *The Master's Wife* 106

71 Macphail, 'Prince Edward Island' 52; 'On Certain Aspects of Feminism' 84, 81, 78; 'The American Woman' 10, 11; 'The Psychology of the Suffragett' 85

73 Macphail Papers. Andrew Macphail, 'The Whole Duty of the Canadian Man,' typed manuscript (1908) 4; 'Family and Society' 216; 'The American Woman' 11

73 This tradition in the United States is examined in Morton & Lucia White, *The Intellectual versus the City, from Thomas Jefferson to Frank Lloyd Wright* (Cambridge, Mass. 1962) and in England in Alice Chandler, *The Dream of Order: The Medieval Ideal in Nineteenth-Century English Literature.*

74 Louis Hémon, *Maria Chapdelaine, a Romance of French Canada,* trans. by Sir Andrew Macphail (Montreal, Toronto, London, & New York 1921); MacMechan Papers, Macphail to MacMechan, 8 Jan. 1921

75 Mavor Papers, Macphail to Mavor, 10 Feb. 1914; Macphail, 'The Peace and Its Consequences' 21-2; 'Theory and Practice' 382; 'Conservative-Liberal-Socialist' 285, 283, 281; 'The Women of Moscow,' *Saturday Night* L 43 (1935). On the 'Red Tory' in England see J.H. Buckle, *The Victorian Temper: A Study in Literary Culture* 18 and in Canada see Gad Horowitz, *Canadian Labour in Politics* (Toronto 1968) chapter 1.

76 Macphail, 'The Immigrant' 149-51, 157; 'The Cost of Living,' *UM* XI 4 (1912) 541; *The Master's Wife* 18; 'The Dominion and the Spirit' 12; 'The Patience of England' 285; 'Why the Conservatives Failed,' *UM* VII 4 (1908) 533; 'Family and Society' 216; 'The Fallacy in Education' 187; 'The Conservative' 421; 'Women in Democracy' 8.

77 Macphail, 'The Cost of Living' 536; 'Family and Society' 218; 'The Psychology of Canada' 239; 'The Dominion and the Spirit' 10, 14, 23; 'Loyalty – To What?' 150-1; 'The Immigrant' 91; 'The Cost of Living' 537; 'Conservative-Liberal-Socialist' 281. As a cure for the depression, Macphail urged imitation of the French-Canadian 'back to the land' movement. Montreal *Star,* 14 Dec. 1934. John Ruskin, whom Macphail often echoed, had urged similar schemes in Britain half a century earlier. See Chandler, *A Dream of Order* 207.

78 Macphail, 'The Dominion and the Spirit' 14. Many of Britain's idealists joined Arnold and Macphail in expressing hostility to the city. See Houghton, *The Victorian Mind* 79.

79 Macphail, 'The Immigrant' 157, 155, 137, 142, 149; 'The Cost of Living' 536, 541; 'The Tariff Commission' 26; 'On Certain Aspects of Feminism' 23; 'The Dominion and the Provinces,' *UM* XII 4 (1913) 554

80 Macphail, *The Master's Wife* 169; Toronto *Daily Mail and Empire,* 25 Feb. 1932; Stevenson, 'Sir Andrew Macphail' 210; Macphail, *The Bible in Scotland* 118; 'Art in Democracy' 180

81 Macphail, 'The Machine and the Man' 6. 'The Dominion and the Spirit' 12; 'Prince Edward Island' 55; 'The Immigrant' 155; 'The Hand or the Book' 220; 'The Cost of Living' 531-2, 540, 539; 'The American Woman' 11

82 Macphail, 'Prince Edward Island' 55; 'Patriotism and Politics,' *UM* XIII 1 (1914) 5, 10; 'The Conservative' 421; 'The Dominion and the Spirit' 12; 'Protection and Politics,' *UM* VII 2 (1908) 252; MacMechan Papers, Macphail to MacMechan, 24 Apr. 1914; 'Consequences and Penalties' 172. The intellectual hostility shown by Macphail to businessmen was, in part, a reflection of his own unfortunate experiences in the business world. In addition to the problems created for the *University Magazine* by the alleged duplicity of George Morang (see above, note 25), Macphail was associated with Archibald MacMechan, Stephen Leacock, and a few other Canadian writers in a firm called Publishers' Press. Its function was to match the authors' manuscripts with interested publishers. It appears to have operated on its initial capital until the manager, Epstein, having collected a large salary, declared the group insolvent and its backers liable for the debts incurred while operative. See MacMechan Papers, Macphail to MacMechan, 17 Jan. 1912 and MacMechan to Macphail, 29 Nov. 1911. MacMechan seems to have lost $1000 in the venture.

83 Macphail, 'Women in Democracy' 5, 7, 8; 'Canadian Writers and American Politics' 6; 'Art in Democracy' 172; 'The Tariff Commission' 26; 'Why the Conservatives Failed' 543; 'Why the Liberals Failed,' *UM* X 4 (1911) 579; 'Unto the Church' 356-8; 'On Certain Aspects of Feminism' 83, 79-30

84 Macphail, 'New Lamps for Old' 29; 'Protection and Politics' 250; 'Certain Varieties of the Apples of Sodom' 33; 'Women in Democracy' 2; 'Consequences and Penalties' 172; 'Patriotism and Politics' 3; 'Theory and Practice' 395, 381; 'Why the Conservatives Failed' 530, 529; 'The Navy and Politics' 3, 21, 22; Wrong Papers, Macphail to Wrong, 8 Jan. 1913; 'The Conservative' 419, 422; 'Conservative-Liberal-Socialist' 263. Macphail's own political activity was largely confined to journalism and offering advice to political leaders (see above, note 16). Only once did he take a hand in 'practical politics' — campaigning successfully for a brother's election in a PEI constituency in 1911. MacMechan Papers, Macphail to MacMechan, 20 and 25 Nov. 1911

85 Macphail, 'Women in Democracy' 6; 'Conservative-Liberal-Socialist' 264; 'The Dominion and the Spirit' 20, 19, 15; 'New Lamps for Old' 20, 21; 'Theory and Practice' 381-2, 86; 'Art in Democracy' 176; 'Patriotism and Politics' 3. For Carlyle, see Crane Brinton, *English Political Thought in the Nineteenth Century* (New York 1962) 172, and Basil Wiley, *Nineteenth Century Studies, Coleridge to Matthew Arnold,* (London 1949) 130

86 Macphail, 'A Voice from the East' 520; 'Loyalty — To What?' 142, 151, 150; 'Why the Liberals Failed' 580; 'The Navy and Politics' 19; 'The Dominion and

the Spirit' 21, 19; 'The Psychology of Canada' 194, 208-9, 207, 244; 'The Patience of England' 282; 'Why the Conservatives Failed' 539; 'What Canada Can Do,' *UM* VI 4 (1907) 405; 'The Whole Duty of the Canadian Man' 13; 'The Freedom of England' *Quarterly Review* CCLV 505 (1930) 2-3; 'The Hill of Error,' *UM* XII 4 (1913) 537

87 Macphail, 'The Dominion and the Spirit' 15; 'The Psychology of Canada' 236-7, 224, 231; 'Canadian Writers and American Politics' 7, 11, 12; 'Patriotism and Politics' 2-3; 'New Lamps for Old' 21, 29; 'John Winthrop' 123-4; 'Certain Varieties of the Apples of Sodom' 44; 'The Patience of England' 290; 'The Cleansing of the Slate,' *UM* X 2 (1911) 183-4; 'Consequences and Penalties' 168

88 Macphail, 'The Machine and the Man' 4

89 Macphail, 'Consequences and Penalties' 167; 'John Wesley' 278, 280; *The Bible in Scotland* 119; 'Conservative-Liberal-Socialist' 284; 'Sir Gilbert Parker: An Appraisal' 124; 'History of the Idea of Evolution' 30; 'John Winthrop' 73-9; 'The Reading of History,' *JCMA* XXIX 6 (1933) 671; *The Medical Services,* 8; 'Art In Democracy' 173; 'The Cost of Living' 542; 'The Fallacy in Education' 171; 'The Immigrant' 161

90 Wrong Papers, Macphail to Wrong, 8 Jan. 1913; Charlottetown *Guardian,* 18 June 1910; Toronto *Daily Mail and Empire,* 5 Dec. 1934; Currie Papers, Alexander Macphail to Currie, 27 May 1920 containing a copy of a letter from Andrew Macphail to Alexander, 24 May 1920; Macphail, *Medical Services* 8. See Stow Persons, 'The Cyclical Theory of History in Eighteenth Century America,' *American Quarterly* VI (Summer 1954).

CHAPTER THREE   ARCHIBALD MAC MECHAN: ROMANTIC IDEALIST

1 This description of MacMechan is based in part on three articles: G.G. Sedgewick, 'A.M.,' *DR* XIII 4 (1933), C.L. Bennet, 'Dr Archibald MacMechan,' *The Alumni News, Dalhousie University* XIX 3 (1962) and Wilhelmina Gordon, 'Archibald MacMechan,' *QQ* 40 (1933). See also Halifax *Herald,* 8 Aug. 1933.

2 Sir Robert Borden Papers, MacMechan to Borden, 29 Oct. 1926; Archibald MacMechan Papers, Private Journal, 23 Jan. 1893 to 22 Dec. 1895, 23 Oct. 1894 (hereafter cited as Journal I); 'The Late Rev. John MacMechan,' *The Presbyterian* (January 1903); D.C. Harvey, 'Archibald McKellar MacMechan,' *PTRSC,* Series III, XXVIII (1934) 8; Archibald MacMechan, 'Picton Boys Sixty Years Ago,' Picton *Gazette,* 28 Dec. 1930

3 Archibald MacMechan, 'Afoot in Ultima Thule,' *DR* III 1 (1923) 97; 'The Malvern Festival of 1932,' *DR* XIII 2 (1933) 207; 'Book and Beaver,' Montreal *Standard,* 26 May 1906 (hereafter cited as 'B & B'); 'The Dean's Window,'

Montreal *Standard,* 4 Apr. 1908 (hereafter cited as 'TDW'); 'B & B,'
23 Mar. 1907

4 Thomas Carlyle, *On Heroes, Hero-Worship, and the Heroic in History,* edited
by Archibald MacMechan (Boston 1901) dedication; MacMechan Papers,
Journal I, 28 June 1893; Private Journal, 14 Sept. 1917 to 1 Apr. 1920, 21 June
1919 (hereafter cited as Journal III); Private Journal, 21 Oct. 1921 to 6 May
1923, 14 May 1922 (hereafter cited as Journal V)

5 MacMechan Papers, Mrs Jean Willets (MacMechan's daughter), 'A Portrait in
Prose,' typed manuscript, nd, 1-2; Archibald MacMechan, 'Virgil,' in *The Life
of a Little College, and Other Papers* (Boston & New York 1914) 277-9; 'The
Ghost of a Garden,' in *The Porter of Bagdad and Other Fantasies* (Toronto
1891) 67-8

6 MacMechan Papers, MacMechan to Jessie McNab, 17 Jan. 1885; Archibald
MacMechan, 'This is Our Master,' in *The Life of a Little College* 151; 'The Porter of Bagdad,' in *The Porter of Bagdad and Other Stories*

7 MacMechan Papers, MacMechan to Jessie McNab, spring 1884; 16 Nov. 1884;
1 Nov. 1885; 27 Feb. 1885; Journal I, 1 Jan. 1894; MacMechan to McNab,
12 Apr. 1888; 26 June 1888; 27 May 1888; 21 Feb. 1888; 6 Jan. 1888; 24 May
1889; 13 July 1889

8 Archibald MacMechan 'The Day in Dolcefar,' in *The Book of Ultima Thule*
(Toronto 1927) 133; MacMechan Papers, Journal I, 23 June 1893; MacMechan
to Jessie McNab, July 1890; 1 Jan. 1893; 19 Nov. 1894; MacMechan to Edith
MacMechan, dated 1907

9 MacMechan Papers, Journal I, 28 June 1893; Journal III, 25 Dec. 1919; 17 Mar.
1920; Private Journal, 17 June 1916 to 13 Sept. 1917, 8 Aug. 1917, 25 Oct.
1916 (hereafter cited as Journal II); Private Journal, 14 Oct. 1929 to 28 Nov. 1930,
20 Nov. 1929 (hereafter cited as Journal IX); Private Journal, Oct. 1925 to 15 Nov.
1928, 25 Dec. 1926, (hereafter cited as Journal VII). Delusions of povery seemed
common among academics of this period. MacMechan's salary was $2000 in
1889, $3500 in 1920, and $3800 in 1930. To this was added income from various
writing and lecturing activities which amounted in 1926, for example, to $1860.
This information is found in the MacMechan Papers, MacMechan to Jessie
McNab, 24 May 1889; Private Journal, 2 Apr. 1920 to 30 Sept. 1920, 23 Aug.
1920 (hereafter cited as Journal IV); Journal IX, 24 June 1930; Journal VII,
1 Dec. 1926.

10 MacMechan Papers, Archibald MacMechan, 'Address on Receiving LLD from
Dalhousie,' typed manuscript, 16 May 1933, 1-2; Archibald MacMechan,
'The Life of a Little College,' in *Life of a Little College* 13, 25, 27; MacMechan
Papers, MacMechan to Jessie McNab, 13 July 1889; Journal I, Feb. 1894;
24 Apr. 1894; Journal II, 6 Oct. 1916; Willets, 'A Portrait in Prose' 3; Sedgewich,

'A.M.' 453; Gordon, 'Archibald MacMechan,' 635-8; Bennet, 'Dr Archibald MacMechan' 5; MacMechan Papers, MacMechan to Jessie McNab, 12 Apr. 1888; Private Journal, 1 Oct. 1928 to 13 Oct. 1929, 24 Feb. 1929 (hereafter cited as Journal VIII).

11 MacMechan Papers, Journal I, 19 Feb. 1895; W.D. Wallace to MacMechan, 25 Aug. 1922; Journal VII, 6 Aug. 1927; quoted in Thomas Raddall's introduction to a collection of MacMechan's stories, *Tales of the Sea* (Toronto 1947) xiv. See bibliography for a list of MacMechan's books.

12 MacMechan Papers, Elizabeth Shortt to MacMechan, 14 Dec. 19??; James Mavor to MacMechan, 24 Oct. 1923; Journal V, 30 Aug. 1922; D.C. Harvey, 'Archibald McKellar MacMechan' 8; Archibald MacMechan, 'Virgil' 283

13 MacMechan Papers, Journal I, 28 Oct. 1894; MacMechan scrapbooks, particularly C, E, and F; Harvey, 'Archibald McKellar MacMechan' 8

14 Sedgewich, 'A.M.' 455; Archibald MacMechan, 'The Reviewer,' Halifax *Herald*, 8 Oct. 1892; MacMechan Papers, Journal IV, 17 Mar. 1920; Archibald MacMechan, 'My Townsmen of the Olden Times,' in *The Book of Ultima Thule* 83; Queen's University Archives, Lorne Pierce Papers, MacMechan to Lorne Pierce, 29 Jan. 1929, PAC, Sir John S. Willison Papers, MacMechan to Willison, 8 Feb. 1920

15 Archibald MacMechan, 'The Reviewer,' Halifax *Herald,* 8 Oct. 1892; George M. Wrong Papers, MacMechan to Wrong, 1 Oct. 1914; MacMechan Papers, Journal III, 2 Nov. 1917; 21 May 1919; Journal IV, 20 Apr. 1920; Journal VIII, 6 Jan. 1929; Journal V, 4 May 1923; Journal IX, 23 July 1933

16 Archibald MacMechan, 'This is Our Master' 161, 156, 153, 161-3; 'A Green Ribbon,' in *The Porter of Bagdad* 72; MacMechan Papers, notebook entitled 'Pass Metaphysics, Lecture 1, Oct. 7, 1878'; MacMechan to Jessie McNab, 11 Mar. 1889; John A. Irving, 'The Development of Philosophy in Central Canada from 1850 to 1900,' *CHR* XXXI 3 (1950) 261-4

17 Archibald MacMechan, 'Alfred Tennyson, Artist,' *UM* VII 2 (1908) 74; 'This is Our Master' 151; introduction to Thomas Carlyle, *Sartor Resartus* (Boston 1897) liii, xiv, liv, lxii, lxvii, lxiv-lxviii; introduction to Thomas Carlyle, *On Heroes, Hero-Worship, and the Heroic in History* (Boston 1901) lxxxvi, lxxxv, lxxi-lxxvii. In 1933 MacMechan still revered Carlyle: 'Read more of Carlyle in the night. No one like him.' MacMechan Papers, Journal IX, 27 Apr. 1933

18 Archibald MacMechan, 'TDW,' 9 May 1925; 'TDW,' 23 May 1914; 'TDW,' 9 Nov. 1910. On Chesterton see Christopher Hollis, *G.K. Chesterton* (London 1950) and *The Mind of Chesterton* (London 1970); Gary Wills, *Chesterton: Man and Mask* (New York 1961).

19 Archibald MacMechan, 'Concentration,' in *The Porter of Bagdad* 142; 'Alice in Wonderland,' *UM* VII 3 (1908) 474; 'The Vanity of Travel,' *UM* XI 2 (1912) 294; *Sagas of the Seas* (New York, London, and Toronto 1923) 42; 'Entrevues,'

in *The Porter of Bagdad* 126; 'TDW,' 29 June 1918; 'Storia Di Christo,'
DR II 2 (1922) 292

20 Archibald MacMechan, 'By a Summer Sea,' in *The Book of Ultima Thule* 227-8;
'Old St Paul's,' in *ibid.* 172; MacMechan Papers, MacMechan to Jessie McNab,
18 Mar. 1894; MacMechan, 'TDW,' 19 Mar. 1927; 'Thoreau,' in *The Cambridge
History of American Literature* II (New York 1918) 12

21 MacMechan Papers, Journal III, 3 Dec. 1917; Journal II, 8 Aug. 1917; 'TDW,'
23 July 1910; 'TDW,' 16 May 1914; MacMechan Papers, Journal I, 30 Sept.
1894; Journal VIII, 19 Oct. 1930; MacMechan to Jessie McNab, 6 Jan. 1888;
MacMechan to Andrew Macphail, 19 May 1928

22 Archibald MacMechan, 'Spring in Ultima Thule,' in *The Book of Ultima Thule*
189-90; 'The Ghost of a Garden' 68; *The Winning of Popular Government:
A Chronicle of the Union of 1841* (Toronto 1916) 80; 'TDW,' 16 May 1914,
'TDW,' 14 Mar. 1911; 'TDW,' 9 Nov. 1910; 'TDW,' 29 June 1924, 'TDW,'
18 Dec. 1926; MacMechan Papers, MacMechan to Andrew Macphail, 23 Nov.
1911 and 11 Apr. 1910; Archibald MacMechan, 'Painted Music,' *DR* V 3 (1925)
347-8; 'Canada as a Vassal State,' *CHR* I 4 (1920) 347-52

23 MacMechan, 'Alfred Tennyson, Artist' 71; *Headwaters of Canadian Literature*
(Toronto 1924) 116; 'The Reviewer,' Halifax *Herald,* 17 Dec. 1892; 8 Oct. 1892;
10 Dec. 1892; introduction, *Sartor Resartus* 1; 'Introduction,' *Select Poems of
Alfred Tennyson* (Boston & London 1907) lv. On Ruskin's aesthetics see Herbert
L. Sussman, *The Victorians and the Machine: The Literary Response to Tech-
nology,* chapter 3; Alice Chandler, *A Dream of Order: The Medieval Ideal in
Nineteenth Century English Literature,* chapter 6; and especially Jerome H.
Buckley, *The Victorian Temper: A Study in Literary Culture,* chapter 8.

24 MacMechan, *Headwaters of Canadian Literature* 176, 116, 124; 'Introduction,'
Select Poems of Alfred Tennyson xxi; 'Alfred Tennyson, Artist' 64, 68-9, 54, 75;
'The Reviewer,' Halifax *Herald,* 8 Oct. 1892; 'TDW,' 5 Sept. 1925. MacMechan's
concept of the writer as the leader of society was an echo of the high place
accorded the man of letters by Carlyle in his *On Heroes, Hero-Worship, and the
Heroic in History.* See Walter Houghton, *The Victorian Frame of Mind, 1830-
1870* 153. On Arnold see Vincent Buckley, *Poetry and Morality* (London 1959)
68-75.

25 Archibald MacMechan, 'In Memory of Scott,' *DR* I 2 (1921) 124; *Late Harvest;*
MacMechan Papers, Journal V, 15 Feb. 1923; Journal VII, 22 Sept. 1927; Mac-
Mechan, 'The Vanity of Travel' 291, 'TDW,' 21 Dec. 1907

26 Archibald MacMechan, 'Titania,' in *The Porter of Bagdad* 10; 'The Vanity of
Travel' 294; 'The Dip in the Road,' in *The Porter of Bagdad* 100-1; 'The Coast
of Ultima Thule,' *DR* VI 3 (1926) 280; 'Alice in Wonderland' 16; MacMechan
Papers, Journal I, 19 Feb. 1895; 'TDW,' 9 Nov. 1910

27 MacMechan, 'Afoot in Ultima Thule' 100-1, 97; 'Alfred Tennyson, Artist' 52, 57; MacMechan Papers, Archibald MacMechan, 'Radio Lecture,' 6 Aug. 1924, typed manuscript; 'The All-Mother' in *The Porter of Bagdad* 63; 'By a Summer Sea' 227-8; 'The Dip in the Road' 118-19

28 MacMechan, *Headwaters of Canadian Literature* 15, 16, 41; 'Via London,' in *Sagas of the Sea* 103; Borden Papers, MacMechan to R.L. Borden, 29 Nov. 1928; Archibald MacMechan, *There Go the Ships* (Toronto 1928) 11; Pierce Papers, MacMechan to Lorne Pierce, 29 Jan. 1929; Archibald MacMechan, *Old Province Tales* (Toronto 1924) 186

29 For a good example of the privateer as hero see MacMechan's 'Godfrey of the Rover,' in *Old Province Tales*; for the merchant as hero see 'The Rise of Samuel Cunard,' *DR* IX (1929); for the shipbuilder as hero see 'The Great Ship,' *DR* VIII 2 (1928); for the sailor as hero see 'An Able Seaman,' in *Sagas of the Sea*. The character flaws of evil men are emphasized in 'The Saladin Pirates,' in *Old Province Tales*, while MacMechan's view of the Indian is evident in 'The Payzant Captivity,' in *ibid.*, and of the Greek in 'The "Lennie" Mutiny,' also in *ibid.* For an example of the natural leaders and the disciplined followers see 'The Saga of "Rudder" Churchill,' in *ibid.*, while providential intervention is stressed in 'A Master Mariner,' in *There Go the Ships*.

30 Archibald MacMechan, 'How Prentice Carried His Dispatches,' in *Sagas of the Sea* 25; 'The Discipline of H.M.S. "Atalante",' in *ibid.* 101; 'The Sack of Lunenburg,' in *ibid.* 64; 'An Able Seaman' 147; 'The Coasts of Ultima Thule' 280; 'The Nova Scotia-ness of Nova Scotia,' *CM* XXV 2 (1905) 165; 'Ab Urbe Condita,' *DR* VII 2 (1927) 198

31 Archibald MacMechan, 'The Payzant Captivity' 53; 'The Captain's Boat,' in *Sagas of the Sea* 125; 'The "Lennie" Mutiny' 322, 325, 347; 'The Two Games,' in *The Book of Ultima Thule passim;* 'TDW,' 6 Sept. 1913; 'Canada at War,' *The Nation* CL (Jan. 1916) 10; MacMechan Papers, Archibald MacMechan, 'The Halifax Disaster,' unpublished typed manuscript, chapter 20

CHAPTER FOUR   JAMES CAPPON: THE IDEAL IN CULTURE

1 W.E. McNeill, 'James Cappon, 1854-1939,' *PTRSC*, Series III, XXXIV (1940) 97; H.J. Morgan, *Canadian Men and Women of the Time* (Toronto 1912) 198; James Cappon, 'Current Events,' *QQ* XI 4 (1904) 432 and XII 3 (1905) 316 (reference to the 'Current Events' column in the *Queen's Quarterly* will hereafter be cited as 'CE'); MacMechan Papers, Cappon to MacMechan, 19 Jan. 1915; W.E. McNeill, 'James Cappon,' in R.C. Wallace, *Some Great Men of Queen's* (Toronto 1941) 74; James Cappon, 'A School of Idealism: Meditatio Laici' *passim*

2 Cappon, 'A School of Idealism: Meditatio Laici' 2; McNeill, 'James Cappon, 1854-1939' 97, 98; R. Bruce Taylor, 'Memoirs,' unpublished, typed manuscript in Queen's University Archives 297; James Mavor, *My Windows on the Street of the World* I (London & Toronto, nd [1923]) 213; PAC, George Munro Grant Papers, John Watson to Grant, 17 July 1888; MacMechan Papers, MacMechan to Jessie McNab, 7 Aug. 1888

3 McNeill, 'James Cappon, 1854-1939' 97, 98, and a copy of the Varley portrait facing page 97; McNeill, 'James Cappon' 85-6, 89; James Cappon, *Bliss Carman* (Toronto 1930) 132

4 McNeill, 'James Cappon, 1854-1939' 98; McNeill, 'James Cappon' 88; Lorne Pierce Papers, W.L. Grant to Pierce, 6 Jan. 1929 and Wilhelmina Gordon to Pierce, 18 June 1929; Lorne Pierce, 'The Makers of Queen's, James Cappon, MA, LLD, FRSC,' *Queen's Review* III 6 (1929) 192; Cappon 'Bliss Carman's Beginnings,' *QQ* XXXVI 4 (1929) 645; James Cappon, *What Classical Education Means* (Kingston, nd) 195; 'Democracy and Monarchy in the Modern State,' *QQ* XXIV 1 (1916) 99; PAC, William Lawson Grant Papers, Cappon to Grant, 9 Sept. 1919

5 McNeill, 'James Cappon, 1854-1939' 97; Lorne Pierce Papers, S.W. Dyde to Pierce, 6 June 1929; PAC, Sir Sandford Fleming Papers, Cappon to Fleming, 6 Dec. 1906; James Cappon, 'Some Considerations on Queen's Position,' *QQ* XVII 2 (1909) 154; 'The Situation at Queen's,' *QQ* XVII 3 (1910) 206, 209; Fleming Papers, Cappon to Fleming, 4 Mar. 1909

6 Queen's University Archives, Adam Shortt Papers, Cappon to Shortt, 11 June 1910; Queen's University Archives, Queen's Quarterly Treasurers Account, 1893-1902, containing also 'Secretarial Notes' from 1893 to 1907; McNeill, 'James Cappon' 80; W.L. Grant Papers, Cappon to Grant, 9 Mar. 1907

7 PAC, William Lyon Mackenzie King Papers, Cappon to King, 4 Apr. 1905; Wilhelmina Gordon, *Daniel M. Gordon: His Life* (Toronto 1941) 218, 241; Queen's University, *Report of the Principal, Session 1911-12* 9; Daniel M. Gordon Papers, Cappon to Gordon, 1909; Queen's University, *Report of the Principal, Deans and Treasurer, Session 1915-16* 13; McNeill, 'James Cappon, 1854-1939' 98; 'James Cappon' 76-7; Lorne Pierce Papers, W.L. Grant to Pierce, 6 June 1929; W.L. Grant Papers, Cappon to Grant, 19 Sept. 1919; PAC, Sir John S. Willison Papers, Cappon to Willison, 14 Apr. 1919

8 McNeill, 'James Cappon, 1854-1939' 97, 100; Cappon, 'CE' XXV 1 (1917) 91, 104; Cappon, 'CE' XI 3 (1904) 338; W.L. Grant Papers, Cappon to Grant, 19 Sept. 1919 and 16 Dec. 1927

9 MacMechan Papers, Cappon to MacMechan, 19 Jan. 1915; Cappon, *Bliss Carman* 100, 238, 261, 262; Cappon, 'A School Idealism: Meditatio Laici' 5; Cappon, 'Edward Caird: A Reminiscence' 266, 267. See also John Watson, 'Edward Caird as a Teacher and Thinker,' *QQ* XVI 4 (1909).

10 James Cappon, 'CE' XXIII 3 (1916) 340-1; 'CE' XXIII 2 (1915) 222; 'CE' XXV 1 (1917) 94; 'A School of Idealism: Meditatio Laici' 31, 20; *Bliss Carman* 53; 'Edward Caird: A Reminiscence' 281, 278

11 Cappon, 'CE' X 4 (1903) 501; 'Democracy and Monarchy in the Modern State' 99; 'CE' XXV 1 (1917) 108

12 Cappon, 'CE' XI 3 (1904) 338; 'Bliss Carman's Beginnings' 643; *Britain's Title in South Africa* (London 1901) 331; 'CE' X 3 (1903) 391; 'CE' XI 3 (1904) 336; 'CE' XXV 3 (1918) 362; 'CE' XXVI 3 (1919) 343, 344, 345; 'CE' VII 2 (1899) 158

13 Cappon, 'CE' XXVI 3 (1919) 344-5

14 Cappon, 'Democracy and Monarchy in the Modern State' 78, 83; 'CE' XXVI 3 (1919) 346; 'CE' XXIII 3 (1916) 340-1; 'CE' XVI 3 (1909) 385; 'CE' XXV 1 (1917) 93; *Bliss Carman* 283, 289

15 Cappon, 'CE' I 4 (1894) 330; 'Democracy and Monarchy in the Modern State' 101; *What the Present War Means* (Kingston 1914) 9-10; 'CE' XV 3 (1908) 243-4; 'CE' XI 4 (1904) 434-6; 'CE' X 3 (1903) 385; 'CE' XXV 1 (1917) 121

16 Cappon, 'CE' XIV 4 (1907) 338; 'CE' XXIV 3 (1917) 387; 'Democracy and Monarchy in the Modern State' 99; 'CE' XXV 1 (1917) 108; *Bliss Carman* 195-6; *Roberts and the Influence of His Times* (Toronto 1905) 6-7

17 Cappon, 'CE' X 3 (1903) 390; 'The Great American Democracy' *QQ* XI 3 (1904) 307; 'CE' XII 2 (1905) 319; 'CE' XIX 3 (1912) 291; 'CE' XVI 4 (1909) 386; 'CE' X 3 (1903) 392; 'CE' XIX 3 (1912) 298-300; 'CE' VII 2 (1899) 158; 'CE' XI 1 (1903)

18 Cappon, 'CE' XXVI 3 (1919) 347; 'The Great American Democracy' 310

19 Cappon, 'Democracy and Monarchy in the Modern State' 110-11; *Britain's Title in South Africa* 322-3. On this aspect of Arnold see Basil Wiley, *Nineteenth Century Studies: Coleridge to Matthew Arnold* (London 1949) 257-60.

20 Cappon, 'CE' XI 4 (1904) 431, 432; *What Classical Education Means* 194-5; Queen's University, *Report of the Principal, Session 1915-16* 12; Cappon, *Bliss Carman* 7; 'CE' XIV 3 (1907) 239.

21 James Cappon, 'Literature for the Young: Notes on the High School Reader,' *QQ* I 1 (1893) 31, 29, 26-8; 'Facts and Comments,' *QQ* XIII 2 (1905) 174; *What Classical Education Means* 191-3, 204

22 Cappon, 'Bliss Carman's Beginnings' 645, 639; *Bliss Carman* 142, 3, 143, 294, 332, 192, 8; Lorne Pierce Papers, W.L. Grant to Pierce, 6 June 1929

23 Cappon, 'CE' XXV 1 (1917) 91-2, 108; *Bliss Carman* 52, 294, 97; 'CE' XII 3 (1905) 313-14, 319

24 Cappon, 'CE' XII 2 (1904) 216-17; *Britain's Title in South Africa* 322-3; 'The Great American Democracy' 310

25 Cappon, *Bliss Carman* 21; *Britain's Title in South Africa* 159; 'CE' XXIII 3 (1916) 340; 'CE' XXV 1 (1917) 93; *What Classical Education Means* 195; 'CE' XI 4 (1904) 430; 'CE' XIII 3 (1915) 222-3

26 Cappon, 'CE' X 3 (1903) 386-7; 'CE' XXVI 3 (1919) 340-2; 'CE' VII 2 (1899) 158; *Roberts in Relation to His Time* 74-5; 'CE' XXIII 3 (1916) 339; *Britain's Title in South Africa* 325; 'CE' XXIII 2 (1915) 223-5; 'CE' X 3 (1903) 388, 391; 'Canada's Relation to the Empire,' *QQ* XIX 2 (1911) 98

27 Cappon, 'CE' XXIII 3 (1916) *passim;* see above, note 8, for reference to letters to W.L. Grant; McNeill, 'James Cappon, 1854-1939' 100; Cappon, *Bliss Carman* 239

CHAPTER FIVE
MAURICE HUTTON: CLASSICAL-CHRISTIAN IDEALIST

1 Maurice Hutton, 'A Professor's Valedictory,' in *The Sisters Jest and Earnest* (Toronto nd [1920] 110, 112, 105; Malcolm Wallace, 'Principal Maurice Hutton,' *UTM* XL 7 (1940) supplement, unpaged [2]; A.J. Church, 'Richard Holt Hutton,' in *Memories of Men and Books* (London 1908) 203; Gaylord C. LeRoy, 'Richard Holt Hutton,' *Publications of the Modern Language Association* LVI 3 (1941) 810-13

2 Maurice Hutton, 'On Schoolmasters,' *QQ* XIV 2 (1906) 86-7; R.A. Falconer, 'Maurice Hutton, 1854-1940,' *PTRSC*, Series III, XXXIV (1940) 111; Hutton, 'A Professor's Valedictory' 110; 'Some Oxford Types,' in *Many Minds* (London 1927) 159

3 Falconer, 'Maurice Hutton, 1854-1940' 111; D.R. Keys, 'Principal Maurice Hutton,' *UTM* XXVIII 9 (1928) 415; Maurice Hutton, speech reported in 'Principal Hutton is Guest of Honour,' *UTM* XXVIII 8 (1928) 372, 374; University of Toronto Archives, Letters and Journals of Sir Daniel Wilson, 16 Oct. 188; W.S. Wallace, *A History of the University of Toronto, 1827-1927* (Toronto 1927) 102

4 Falconer, 'Maurice Hutton, 1856-1940' 111, 112; Keys, 'Principal Maurice Hutton' 416; Maurice Hutton, 'Oxford and Toronto Undergraduates,' in *The Sisters Jest and Earnest* 134; 'Address to the Women Graduates of the Normal School, Toronto,' *UTM* IX 3 (1909) 108; 'On Schoolmasters' 89; 'A Professor's Valedictory' 105, 116; 'Speech at the Art Dinner, 1909,' *UTM* IX 6 (1909) 217-18

5 A Group of Classics Graduates, *Honours Classics in the University of Toronto* (Toronto 1929) 56, 57, 62, 37, 58, 69-83

6 Keys, 'Principal Maurice Hutton' 415; Letters and Journals of Sir Daniel Wilson, 14 Apr. 1882; Maurice Hutton, 'Popular Lectures,' in *Many Minds;* Falconer,

'Maurice Hutton, 1856-1940' 113; Sir Robert Falconer Papers, Hutton to
Falconer, 29 July 1917; Maurice Hutton, 'Thought and Action,' in *Many Minds*
259-61. The references to Hutton's non-denominational services is taken from a
letter from F.H. Underhill to the author, 4 July 1971.

7 Falconer, 'Maurice Hutton, 1856-1940' 114; Maurice Hutton, 'The Religious
Interpretation of Life and Its Atmosphere,' in *The Sisters Jest and Earnest* 235;
Mavor Papers, notebook of T.A.T. Haultain concerning the Round Table Literary
Club; C.W. Parker, *Who's Who and Why* (Toronto 1914) 891; Maurice Hutton,
'Alice,' in *The Sisters Jest and Earnest* 57

8 Maurice Hutton, speech, reported in 'The University Dinner to Dr Hutton,'
UTM XXIX 5 (1929) 183; 'The By-Products of Democracy,' in *All the Rivers
Run into the Sea* (London 1928) 157; 'The Changes of Forty Years,' *UTM*
XXII 8 (1922) 344, 345; 'A Professor's Valedictory' 123; 'Reflections of a
Professor of Greek,' Address to the University Women's Club of Ottawa,
4 Nov. 1929 (Ottawa, nd) 3; 'Fifty Years' Retrospect,' in *The Sisters Jest and
Earnest* 140; 'Worldliness and Other-Worldliness,' in *All the Rivers Run into the
Sea* 8; 'On Taking Orders,' *UTM* XXXI 6 (1931) 269; 'Address to the Women
Graduates of the Normal School, Toronto' 114

9 Maurice Hutton, 'The Dream of Greek Letters,' *Canadian Magazine* XVII 1
(1901) 55; 'The Classics,' in *The Sisters Jest and Earnest* 276; 'A Professor's
Valedictory' 123; 'The Religious Interpretation of Life and Its Atmosphere' 198

10 Maurice Hutton, 'Address at the Annual Reception of the Students of the First
Year on October 3, 1905,' *UTM* VI 1 (1905) 2; 'Address to the Incoming Students of the First Year, October 3, 1907,' *UTM* VIII 2 (1907) 75, 76; 'The Folly
of the Wise,' *Proceedings of the Canadian Club, Toronto, 1922-23* (Toronto
1923) 217; 'Language Study – The Classics,' *UTM* XIX (June 1919) 297; 'The
Religious Interpretation of Life and Its Atmosphere' 237; 'The University Dinner
to Dr Hutton' 184. On the Hellenism-Hebraism dichotomy in Arnold's thought
see Kenneth Allott, *Matthew Arnold* (London 1955) 18 and Basil Wiley, *Nineteenth Century Studies, Coleridge to Matthew Arnold* 257-60.

11 Hutton, 'Reflections of A Professor of Greek' 15; 'The Classics' 278-81: 'Hellen-
ism in Character,' *The Greek Point of View* (London 1925) 103-5; 'Virtue is
Knowledge,' in *ibid.* 54, 57; 'Greek Religion,' in *ibid.* 157-8; 'Virtue and Art,'
in *ibid.* 91-2, 101; 'Socrates and Plato as Theists,' in *ibid.* 153; 'The Englishman:
The Frenchman: The Roman: The Greek,' in *Many Minds* 194-5; 'Hellenism,'
UTM II 7 (1902) 188

12 Hutton, 'Worldliness and Other-Worldliness' 40; 'Virtue and Art' 87; 'Address to
the Incoming Students of the First Year, October 3, 1907' 79; 'The Religious
Interpretation of Life and Its Atmosphere' 172, 263; 'The Necessity of Religion,'

in *The Sisters Jest and Earnest* 99, 100; 'Theology in the Doldrums,' in *All the Rivers Run into the Sea* 229, 231

13 Maurice Hutton, speech, reported in 'The University Dinner to Dr Hutton' 183; 'The Religious Interpretation of Life and Its Atmosphere' 219; 'Address to the Incoming Students of the First Year, October 3, 1907' 76; 'Militarism and Anti-Militarism,' *UM* XII 2 (1913) 190; 'The Best Policy,' in *Many Minds* 281-2; 'Virtue is Knowledge' 54-6

14 Maurice Hutton, 'The Philosophy of Political Parties,' in *All the Rivers Run into the Sea* 105; 'Address to the Incoming Students of the First Year, October 3, 1907' 76, 78; 'In Paris,' in *All the Rivers Run into the Sea* 65; 'Theology in the Doldrums' 229, 221

15 Hutton, 'The Philosophy of Political Parties' 117; 'The Wisdom of the Vulgar,' *Proceedings of the Canadian Club, Toronto, 1921-22* (Toronto 1923) 170; 'Address to the Incoming Students of the First Year, October 3, 1907' 72-3; 'Hellenism' 190; 'Plato's Watch Dog' *UM* VII (1908) 521-2; 'On Schoolmasters' 95; 'Virtue is Knowledge' 51; 'The Englishman,' in *All the Rivers Run into the Sea* 85; 'The Canadian National Character,' *Empire Club Speeches, 1903-04* (Toronto 1904) 68-71; 'Oxford and Toronto Undergraduates' 134; 'Address to the Women Graduates of the Normal School, Toronto' 109

16 Maurice Hutton, 'Thucydides and History,' in *Many Minds* 29-31, 57-9, 53; 'The Mind of Herodotus,' in *ibid.* 17; 'Militarism and Anti-Militarism' 196

17 Hutton, 'Worldliness and Other-Worldliness' 9; 'Francis Bacon,' in *Many Minds* 96; 'The Greek City State,' in *The Greek Point of View* 38; 'Address to the Incoming Students of the First Year, October 3, 1907' 79; 'Speech at the Graduating Class Dinner,' *UTM* XI 7 (1910-11) 277; 'A Professor's Valedictory' 114

18 Hutton, 'The Greek City-State' 9, 16; 'Virtue and Art' 82; 'The Philosophy of Political Parties' 104; 'The Philosophy of Our Political Parties,' *UM* VIII 4 (1909) 582-3; 'Thucydides and History' 44; 'The Wisdom of the Vulgar' 168, 170; 'The Religious Interpretation of Life and Its Atmosphere' 179; 'All Men are Either Platonists or Aristotelians,' *UM* VIII 3 (1909) 417

19 Hutton, 'Address to the Women Graduates of the Normal School, Toronto' 113; 'The By-Products of Democracy' 135-6, 144, 125; 'Speech at the Arts Dinners, 1909' 212; 'The Greek City-State' 10-11

20 Hutton, 'The University Dinner to Dr Hutton' 183; 'Address to the Women Graduates of the Normal School, Toronto' 111; 'The By-Products of Democracy' 156, 157, 139, 160; 'Virtue is Knowledge' 58

21 Maurice Hutton, 'Speech at the University College Dinner,' *UTM* XI 3 (1910-11) 69, 70; 'Address to the Annual Reception of the Students of the First Year on

October 3, 1905' 3; 'Address at the Annual Reception of Students of the First Year on October 2, 1906,' *UTM* VII 1 (1906) 3, 5; 'Quality and Equality,' in *Many Minds* 276; 'Speech at the Arts Dinner, 1909' 212-13; 'Theology in the Doldrums' 221

22 Maurice Hutton, 'Signs of the Times,' *Proceedings of the Sixty-Fourth Annual Convention of the Ontario Educational Association* (Toronto 1925) 134; 'The New Minister of Education,' *UTM* XVIII 9 (1918) 340; 'The League of Nations and Its Relation to the Public Schools,' *Proceedings of the Sixty-Fifth Annual Convention of the Ontario Educational Association* (Toronto 1926) 86; 'On Schoolmasters' 85-6; 'Language Study — The Classics' 300; 'National Leagues,' in *All the Rivers Run into the Sea* 278

23 Hutton, 'The Best Policy' 287; 'Address at the Annual Reception of the Students of the First Year on October 2, 1906' 2; 'Address at the Annual Reception of the Students of the First Year on October 3, 1905' 3, 6; 'Address to the Senate of the University of Saskatchewan,' *UTM* VIII 6 (1908) 198, 200; 'The Changes of Forty Years' 345; 'Fifty Years' Retrospect' 140, 142; 'The Retirement of Dr Burwash,' *UTM* XIV 1 (1913); 'Speech at the Arts Dinner, 1909' 213

24 Hutton, 'On Taking Orders' (1931) 270; 'Signs of the Times' 136; 'Address to the Incoming Students of the First Year, October 3, 1907' 76; 'Address to the Women Graduates of the Normal School, Toronto' 115; 'The British and the German Mind,' *UM* XIV 3 (1915) 344; 'The Englishman' 78-80

25 Hutton, 'Hellenism in Character' 105; 'The Englishman' 84; 'Plato's Watchdog' 521, 525, 527; 'In Paris' 66; 'The By-Products of Democracy' 124; 'National Leagues' 254

26 Hutton, 'Thucydides and History' 52; 'The By-Products of Democracy' 151; 'National Leagues' 248, 253, 254; 'Kipling,' in *Many Minds* 124; 'Fifty Years' Retrospect' 155

27 Hutton, 'Militarism and Anti-Militarism' 195; 'Objects of the Canadian Defence League,' in *Addresses Delivered before the Canadian Club of Montreal, Season 1912-13* (Montreal, nd) 119; 'A Text from Pericles,' in *All the Rivers Run into the Sea* 97, 102; 'To the Alumni Leaving for the Front,' *UTM* XV 6 (1915) 270.

28 Hutton, 'The British and the German Mind' 336; 'To the Alumni Leaving for the Front' 271; 'The League of Nations and Its Relation to Public Schools' 84-5, 87; 'Theology in the Doldrums' 225, 227

29 The interpretation of the 1920s as a period of intellectual rebellion and youthful disillusionment began, in America at least, with Frederick Lewis Allen's *Only Yesterday* (New York 1931), and was substantiated by later works such as Lloyd Morris's *Postscript to Yesterday: American Life and Thought, 1896-1946* (New York 1947). Recently, however, this image of the decade has begun to change. Henry May's *The End of American Innocence* (New York 1959)

correctly established that a pronounced change in American intellectual life was evident as early as the turn of the century. Most recently, Roderick Nash's *The Nervous Generation: American Thought, 1917-1930* (Chicago 1970) has suggested that most young Americans in the 1920s were neither in revolt nor particularly disillusioned, but retained most of the values and beliefs of the preceding generation.

30 Hutton, 'The By-Products of Democracy' 132; 'The Changes of Forty Years' 345; 'The Folly of the Wise' 224; 'Reflections of a Professor of Greek' 11-12
31 Hutton, 'A Professor's Valedictory' 105; 'Plato's Watchdog' 527; 'The Changes of Forty Years' 344-5; 'Reflections of a Professor of Greek' 1; 'Dedication to the Memory of Ruth Hutton,' in *The Sisters Jest and Earnest* 11

CHAPTER SIX
ADAM SHORTT: THE EMERGENCE OF THE SOCIAL SCIENTIST

1 Andrew Haydon, ' "The Makers of Queen's", Adam Shortt, CMG, MA, LL D,' *Queen's Review* II 6 (1928) 171; W.A. Mackintosh, 'Adam Shortt,' in R.C. Wallace, *Some Great Men of Queen's* (Toronto 1941) 115; Andrew Haydon, 'Adam Shortt,' *QQ* XXXVIII (Autumn 1931) 609
2 Adam Shortt, 'Random Recollections of Queen's,' Part I, *QQ* XXVII (April 1920) 353, 356-7; Part II, *QQ* XXVIII (October 1920) 133; PAC, George Munro Grant Papers, list entitled 'Thirty-Ninth Session, 1879-1880,' Adam Shortt Papers, Shortt to 'Home,' 13 Oct. 1879; 5 Mar. 1880; 24 Jan. 1880; 16 Apr. 1880; 14 Feb. 1880; 7 Feb. 1880; 19 Mar. 1880; George Bell to Shortt, 30 Aug. 1883; Haydon, ' "The Makers of Queen's"...' 172
3 Haydon, ' "The Makers of Queen's"...' 172; Mackintosh, 'Adam Shortt' 611; Shortt Papers, John Watson, report on the 'Prize Essay,' 23 Apr. 1883; Watson to Shortt, 24 Apr. 1885; A.C. Fraser to Shortt, 12 July 1886; Watson, letter of reference, 15 July 1885; Shortt to Elizabeth Smith ? July and 23 July 1885
4 Shortt Papers, 25 Dec. 1885; Haydon, ' "The Makers of Queen's"...' 173; W.A. Mackintosh, 'Adam Shortt, 1859-1931,' *Canadian Journal of Economics and Political Science* IV 2 (1938); Mackintosh, 'Adam Shortt' 118, 123
5 Mackintosh, 'Adam Shortt, 1859-1931' 167; Queen's University Archives, minute book of the Kingston Historical Society, especially the entry for 24 Nov. 1893; Arthur Lower, 'Adam Shortt, Founder,' *Historic Kingston* 17 (1968); 'Adam Shortt,' obituary, *Journal of the Canadian Bankers' Association* XXXVIII 3 (1930-1) 247; *Queen's Quarterly* treasurer's accounts, 1893-1902 and Secretarial Notes; Shortt Papers, Shortt to Haydon, 7 Jan. 1894; Shortt, 'Canada and Mr Chamberlain,' *CM* XXII 2 (1903); Shortt, 'Some Observations on the Great

North West,' *QQ* II 3 (1895) and III 1 (1895); 'Canada's Industrial and Economic Growth,' *Addresses Delivered before the Canadian Club of Toronto, 1927-28* (Toronto 1928) 68

6 Queen's University Archives, correspondence and minutes of the Saturday Club; Norman Miller, 'The Story of the Saturday Club,' in *Lest We Forget* (Kingston 1969); Shortt Papers, Shortt to Andrew Haydon, 13 Oct. 1902; typed description of Elizabeth Shortt, nd; diary 1907-8, 21 Feb. 1908

7 Daniel M. Gordon Papers, memorandum, Comparative Salaries at Queen's and the University of Toronto, 1890-1900 and memorandum, Registration to 22 Jan. 1907; Shortt Papers, Shortt to Andrew Haydon, 24 Apr. 1903; Shortt to Elizabeth Shortt, 17 Sept. 1908; Shortt to M. Wickett, 11 Mar. 1905; William Lyon Mackenzie King Papers, C.F. Hamilton to Shortt, 14 Dec. 1904; Shortt to Hamilton, 19 Dec. 1904

8 Shortt Papers, Shortt to Andrew Haydon, 31 July 1895; Sir John S. Willison Papers, Shortt to Willison, 25 Apr. 1903; 'Adam Shortt,' obituary, *Journal of the Canadian Bankers' Association* 248; University of Saskatchewan, Adam Shortt Papers (hereafter cited as Shortt Papers [U of S]), 'Canadian Industrial Disputes Act,' typed manuscript nd, 2; Mackintosh, 'Adam Shortt' 124; Shortt Papers, diary 1907-8, 20 Jan. and 28 Mar. 1908

9 'A Queen's Professor in Toronto,' *Queen's University Journal* XXV 11 (13 Apr. 1898); Shortt Papers, cover of diary 1909; diary 1907-8, 20 June 1908; A.R.M. Lower, *My First Seventy-Five Years* (Toronto 1967) 125

10 Shortt Papers, diary 1907-8, 20 Feb. 1908 in which Shortt mentioned his national reputation and Shortt to Elizabeth Shortt, 4 July 1926, in which he mentioned his many Liberal and Conservative contacts

11 K.W. Taylor, 'The Founding of the Canadian Political Science Association,' *Canadian Journal of Economics and Political Science* XXXIII 4 (1967) 583; Shortt Papers, diary 1912, 16 Nov. 1912: Shortt to Elizabeth Shortt, 30 Oct. 1910; Archibald MacMechan Papers, journal 17 June 1916 to 13 Sept. 1917, 27 Sept. 1916

12 Sir Robert L. Borden Papers, Shortt to Borden, Memorandum on Improvements Required in the Dominion Civil Service, nd, R.L. Borden to Elizabeth Shortt, 7 Aug. 1931; Shortt Papers, Shortt to Elizabeth Shortt, 16 Sept. 1908; Shortt to G.A. Warburton, 4 Jan. 1918; diary 1909, 3 Apr. 1909; 31 Mar. 1909; 2 Oct. 1909, diary 1912, 25 Feb. 1912; Sir William Peterson Papers, Peterson to James Cappon, 25 Jan. 1909, Peterson to Shortt, 2 June 1910; William L. Grant Papers, Shortt to Grant, 18 Mar. 1915; Shortt to Grant, 16 Mar. 1923; Haydon, 'Adam Shortt' 619

13 Shortt Papers (U of S), Shortt to Walter Murray, 20 Dec. 1929; Shortt Papers, Shortt to E.R. Peacock, 19 Jan. 1918; Shortt to R.L. Borden, 3 May 1921

14 Shortt Papers, Shortt to David Kinley, 11 Feb. 1918; Shortt Papers (U of S), Shortt to W.B. Munro, 14 Aug. 1930; Shortt to C.H. Cahan, 17 Sept. 1930; Harold Innis to Shortt, 27 Dec. 1927; Lower, *My First Seventy-Five Years* 123, 127

15 Shortt Papers (U of S), Adam Shortt, 'The Philosophy of Moral Obligation,' handwritten manuscript, nd, 3, 7, 24

16 Adam Shortt, 'Current Events' (hereafter cited as 'CE'), *QQ* VI 2 (1898) 160; 'Canada's Industrial and Economic Growth' 67, 74; *Lord Sydenham* (Toronto 1910) 352, 3, 22, 83; 'Taxation of Corporations,' *Addresses Delivered before the Canadian Club of Toronto, 1905-06* (Toronto 1906) 17; Shortt Papers, Shortt to W.J. Dunlop, nd; Shortt to Elizabeth Shortt, 17 Apr. 1926 and 17 June 1928

17 Adam Shortt, 'The Nature and Sphere of Political Science,' *QQ* I 2 (1893) 98; 'CE' IX 2 (1901) 234; Shortt Papers (U of S), 'The Origins of Organized Society or the State,' typed manuscript, nd, 9, 16, 8; 'CE' X 2 (1902) 240; 'Some Aspects of the Social Life of Canada,' *CM* XI 1 (1898) 4; Shortt Papers, 'Personality as a Social Factor,' baccalaurete address, 13 June 1909, Thomas S. Clarkson Memorial School of Technology, reprinted from the *Clarkson Bulletin* VI 3 (1909) no pagination; 'Legislation and Morality,' *QQ* VIII 4 (1901) 354

18 Adam Shortt, 'Municipal Taxation in Relation to Speculative Land Values,' *The Annuals of the American Academy of Political and Social Sciences* LVIII (1915) 1; 'The Origins of Organized Society or the State' 19, 16, 8; 'Social Evolution, According to Mr Kidd,' *QQ* II 4 (1895); 'The Nature and Sphere of Political Science' 98

19 Shortt Papers (U of S), Adam Shortt, 'Some Characteristics of Canadian Economic History,' handwritten manuscript, nd, 2, 3; 'The Social and Economic Significance of the Movement from the Country to the City,' *Addresses Delivered before the Canadian Club of Montreal, Season 1912-13* (Montreal nd) 65-6; 'Personality as a Social Factor'; Shortt Papers, 'What is Socialism?', newspaper clipping of an address, 1887; 'Should We Revise the Constitution of Queen's?,' *QQ* VIII 2 (1900) 112; 'The Origins of Organized Society or the State' 18

20 Adam Shortt, 'The Significance for Canadian History of the Work of the Board of Historical Publications,' *PTRSC*, 3rd Series XIII (1919) 103; *Life of the Settler in Western Canada before the War of 1812,* Bulletin of the Departments of History and Political and Economical Science in Queen's University, Kingston 12 (July 1914) 1

21 Shortt Papers, George Wrong to Shortt, 16 Apr. 1923; Shortt, 'CE,' VI 1 (1898) 84; 'The Educational Value, from a National Point of View of the Canadian Archives,' Dominion Educational Association, *Minutes of Proceedings, 1907*

(Toronto 1908) 79; 'The Significance for Canadian History of the Work of the Board of Historical Publications' 104; introduction, *Canada and Its Provinces* I (Toronto 1913) viii

22 Charles Parkin, *The Moral Basis of Burke's Political Thought* (Cambridge, Eng. 1956) 30-6, 109-18, 126

23 B.T. Wilkins, *The Problems of Burke's Political Philosophy* (Oxford 1967) 248

24 George Sabine, *A History of Political Theory*, 3rd ed. (New York 1961) 706, 709, 712-13

25 J. Hamburger, *Intellectuals in Politics: John Stuart Mill and the Philosophic Radicals* (New Haven & London 1965) 102-3, 98; Frederick Copleston, *History of Philosophy* VIII (London 1966) 52; J.B. Ellery, *John Stuart Mill* (New York 1964) 50

26 Irving, 'The Development of Philosophy in Central Canada from 1850 to 1900' 272

27 James Coutts, *A History of the University of Glasgow* (Glasgow 1909) 459; A. Logan Turner, ed., *History of the University of Edinburgh, 1883-1933* (Edinburgh 1933) 234. Evening classes were given in political economy at Glasgow from the 1830s to about 1860. See David Murray, *Memories of the Old College of Glasgow* (Glasgow 1927) 105-6, 113.

28 Joseph Shield Nicholson, *Principles of Political Economy* I (New York 1894) v-vi, 16

29 Adam Shortt, 'Some New Books in Political Science,' *QQ* I 3 (1894) 228-30. See also his 'The Basis of Economic Value,' *QQ* II 1 (1894).

30 Adam Shortt, 'Co-operation,' *QQ* V 2 (1897) 133; Shortt Papers, diary, 1910, 28 Jan. 1910

31 Adam Shortt, 'The Incorporation of Trade Unions,' *CM* XX 4 (1903) 361; 'Taxation of Corporations' 17-18; 'In Defence of Millionaires,' *CM* XIII 6 (1899) 497, 493, 495-6; 'CE,' IX 3 (1901) 326

32 Adam Shortt, 'CE,' XI 2 (1903) 216; 'Canada's Industrial and Economic Growth' 76-7; 'Social and Economic Significance of the Movement from the Country to the City' 71, 69, 66, 70

33 Adam Shortt, 'CE' XI 3 (1904) 110; XI 2 (1903) 215; 'Recent Phases of Socialism,' *QQ* V 1 (1897) 19-21; 'Some Observations on the Great North-West,' Part II, 22

34 Adam Shortt, 'CE' IX 4 (1901) 326; XI 2 (1903) 216-17; 'Taxation of Corporations' 19, 20; 'The Incorporation of Trade Unions' 361-2; 'CE' X 3 (1903) 399, 398

35 Shortt Papers, diary, 1910, 13 Jan. 1910; Shortt, 'The Origins of Organized Society or the State' 1-3; 'The Nature and Sphere of Political Science' 96; 'In Defence of Millionaires' 494; 'CE' VI 4 (1899) 321-2; 'Phases of Democracy since the War,' *Empire Club Speeches, 1926* (Toronto 1927) 30-2

36 Shortt, 'Nature and Sphere of Political Science' 93; 'Phases of Democracy since the War' 29, 30; Shortt Papers, Shortt to Andrew Haydon, 16 Apr. 1895; Shortt, 'CE,' XII 3 (1905) 323; 'Personality as a Social Factor'; 'Legislation and Morality' 356-7; 'CE' X 4 (1903) 509-10

37 Adam Shortt, 'CE' II 1 (1894) 78. For Macphail's views see above chapter 2.

38 Adam Shortt, 'Principal Grant,' QQ X 1 (1901) 1-2; 'CE' XIII 2 (1905) 188; 'Some Aspects of the Social Life in Canada' 7; 'CE' XIII 1 (1905) 72; Shortt Papers, Shortt to Major D.E.M. Stuart, 4 Mar. 1919; Shortt, 'Aims of the Political Science Association,' Proceedings of the Canadian Political Science Association I (1913) 9, 16; King Papers, Adam Shortt to C.F. Hamilton, 14 Dec. 1904; George M. Wrong Papers, Wrong to Clifford Sifton, 31 May 1915 and Shortt to Wrong, 7 July 1915; PAC, Adam Shortt Papers (hereafter cited as Shortt Papers [PAC]), R.M. MacIver et al. to Shortt, 8 Mar. 1917

39 Shortt is viewed as an anti-imperialist by Carl Berger in his book of readings Imperialism and Nationalism, 1884-1914: A Conflict in Canadian Thought (Toronto 1969) 64-5.

40 Carl Berger in The Sense of Power: Studies in the Ideas of Canadian Imperialism, 1867-1914 suggests that militarism, pride in Canadian nationality, a belief in Anglo-Saxon superiority, and anti-Americanism were essential components in the imperialist belief structure.

41 Adam Shortt, 'CE' VI 2 (1898) 156 and XIII 1 (1905) 75; 'CE' X 4 (1903) 507-8; Imperial Preferential Trade from a Canadian Point of View (Toronto 1904) 57; 'Phases of Democracy since the War' 29, 30, 31; 'CE' I 3 (1894) 250; VI 4 (1899) 321; X 4 (1903) 509; 'Some Aspects of the Social Life in Canada' 3-4

42 Adam Shortt, 'CE' VI 4 (1899) 321, 322; X 1 (1902) 119; VI 2 (1898) 158; 'Phases of Democracy since the War' 29

43 Adam Shortt, 'The Colonial Conference and Its Functions,' QQ XIV 4 (1907) 1, 3-5; 'Some Aspects of the Imperial Problems,' CM XVIII 4 (1902) 328, 329; Shortt Papers, W.L. Grant to Shortt, 5 Feb. 1904 and John Carleton to Shortt, 28 Nov. 1904; Adam Shortt, 'Britain's Treatment of Canada,' Addresses Delivered before the Canadian Club of Toronto, 1913-14 (Toronto 1914) 69; Shortt Papers, Canada and Chamberlainism, pamphlet reprint from the London Daily Chronicle, 1905, published by the Liberal Publication Department (London 1905) 5

44 Shortt Papers, Shortt to E.R. Peacock, 6 Mar. 1926; Secretary of the British Empire Club to Shortt, 29 Oct. 1924; E.R. Peacock to Shortt, 22 Dec. 1908; Philip Kerr to Shortt, 20 Apr. 1910; Edward Kylic to Shortt, 16 June 1915; Lionel Curtis to Shortt, Feb. 1911; Arthur Glazebrook to Shortt, 28 Dec. 1910. For a description of the Round Table Movement and its Canadian membership

see Carroll Quigley, 'The Round Table Groups in Canada, 1908-38,' *CHR* XLIII 3 (1962) and James Eayrs, 'The Round Table Movement in Canada, 1909-1920' *CHR* XXXVIII 3 (1957).

45 Shortt Papers, Adam Shortt, 'The International Position and Prospects of Canada,' pamphlet reprint of an address at the Institute of Politics, Williamstown, Mass. (Summer 1922) 1; 'CE,' *QQ* VI 1 (1898) 81; 'Some Aspects of the Imperial Problem' 331; Sir Sandford Fleming Papers, Shortt to Fleming, 4 Nov. 1905

46 Shortt Papers, Shortt to J.A. Wilbur, 26 July 1924; Shortt to Lorraine Shortt, 18 Sept. 1923; Shortt to A.J. Glazebrook, 21 Nov. 1925; Shortt to Elizabeth Shortt, 16 June and 22 June 1929; Shortt to G.M. Wrong, 20 Sept. 1921; Shortt to W.A. Childs, 24 Mar. 1927; Shortt to W.J. Dunlop, nd; R.H. Coates to Shortt, 25 May 1929; Shortt Papers (U of S), Shortt to Elizabeth Shortt, 19 June 1927; Shortt to W.B. Munro, 14 Aug. 1930

CHAPTER SEVEN   JAMES MAVOR: THE EMPIRICAL IDEAL

1 James Mavor, *My Windows* I, 21, 32, 24-6, 4, 31, 19, 17; Pelham Edgar, 'James Mavor,' *PTRSC,* Series III, XX (1926) 14

2 Mavor, *My Windows* I, 46

3 *Ibid.* 32, 33, 43-9

4 *Ibid.* 57, 58, 73; Maurice Hutton, 'James Mavor,' in *The Sisters Jest and Earnest* 169; James Mavor Papers, 'A Letter of Application and Testimonials by James Mavor to the Principal and Governing Body of University College, Liverpool.' Mavor was given the degree of PH D by the University of Toronto in 1912. Toronto *Daily Star,* 24 Jan. 1912

5 Mavor, *My Windows* I 234-5, 147-9, 176-8, 159-61, 244; II, 31; 'Labour and Politics in England,' *Political Science Quarterly* X 3 (1895) 502-3; Mavor Papers, Robert Brodie to Mavor, 19 Sept. 1914

6 Mavor, 'The Relation of Economic Study to Public and Private Charity,' Inaugural Lecture before the University of Toronto, 6 Feb. 1893, *Annals of the American Academy of Political and Social Science* IV (July 1893) biographic note; Mavor Papers, Patrick Geddes to Mavor, 15 Jan. 18?; Mavor, *My Windows* I, 180, 297-9, 217; 'The New Crusade,' *Universal Review* VIII (Sept.-Dec. 1890); 'Setting the Poor on Work,' *Nineteenth Century* XXXIV, No. CC (Oct. 1893); Mavor Papers, Holmes Ivory to Mavor, 10 Apr. 1890; Mavor Papers, 'Ballade of the Inwardness of Things,' in a notebook marked 'Verses by J.M., 1892'

7 Obituary, Toronto *Daily Star,* 2 Nov. 1925; Andrew Macphail, 'John McCrae: An Essay in Character,' in John McCrae, *In Flanders Fields and Other Poems* 98;

Edgar, 'James Mavor' 13, 14, 15; Hutton, 'James Mavor' 168; Mavor, *My Windows* I, 258; II, 131; Mavor Papers, Andrew Macphail to Pelham Edgar, 14 Nov. 1910; K.W. Taylor, 'The Founding of the Canadian Political Science Association' 583; James Mavor, ed., *Book of the Victorian Era Ball* (Toronto 1898). Mavor's claim that he was a co-founder of the Round Table Club is sharply contradicted by a notebook found in the Mavor Papers kept by T.A. Haultain, the group's secretary. It suggests that Smith chose all the members, ignoring those nominated by an unidentified companion.

8 James Mavor, *Applied Economics* (New York 1914); *The Russian Revolution* (London 1928); *An Economic History of Russia* (New York 1914); 'Van Horne and His Sense of Humour,' *Maclean's Magazine* XXXVI 22 (1923); 'Count Leo Tolstoi, 1899-1910,' *Canadian Forum* I 10 (1921); 'The English Railway Rate Question,' *Quarterly Journal of Economics* VIII 3 and 4 (1894). Reviews of *An Economic History of Russia* appeared in *The Scotsman* 25 May 1914; *The Nation,* 30 Jan. 1915; Boston *Herald,* 8 Aug. 1914. Review of *My Windows* appeared in *Times Literary Supplement,* 18 Oct. 1923; *The Scotsman,* 18 Oct. 1923; the *New Statesman,* 17 Nov. 1923; The Boston *Herald,* 13 Feb. 1924. Pelham Edgar noted the impersonal tone of the autobiography (Mavor Papers, Dorion Hope to Mavor, 20 June 1923), as did Archibald MacMechan ('The Dean's Window,' Montreal *Standard,* 1 Dec. 1923), while Patrick Geddes, an old friend from Glasgow, complained of the lack of Canadian material (Mavor Papers, Geddes to Mavor, 16 Nov. 1923).

9 James Mavor, *Government Telephones* (New York 1916); *Niagara in Politics* (New York 1925). Mavor's business friendships are evident from a variety of letters in his papers, for example, H.H. Macrae to Mavor, 24 Aug. 1918 and Francis Hankin to Mavor, 20 Feb. 1919. The connection between Mavor and AT & T is established by numerous letters between Mavor and S.L. Andrew in 1916 while the connection with the National Electric Light Association was revealed by C. Alfred Maguire, vice-chairman of Ontario Hydro, and reported in the Toronto *Daily Star,* 15 Feb. 1934.

10 Mavor, *My Windows* I 376-7; II 1-6, 23-30, 197-8; Sir Clifford Sifton Papers, Mavor to Sifton, numerous letters in 1898-9 and 22 Oct. 1900, 21 Oct. 1902; Sir Robert Falconer Papers, broadsheet by Mavor entitled 'An Open Letter to Sir Thomas White, Acting Prime Minister of Canada,' dated 1 May 1919, concerning mistreatment of the Doukhobors; Mavor Papers, William R. Lang to Mavor, nd [fall 1903?]. Mavor's 'Agricultural Development in the North-West of Canada, 1905 until 1909,' *Report of the Seventy-Ninth Meeting of the British Association for the Advancement of Science, 1909* (London 1910) was a substantiation of his earlier *Report to the Board of Trade on the North-West of Canada, with Special Reference to Wheat Production for Export,* British Parliamentary papers, Cd. 2628 (London 1905).

11 Mavor Papers, Margaret Ashley to Mavor, 15 Nov. 1892; Mavor, *My Windows* I, 327, 311, 217; Mavor Papers, J.B. Douglas to Mavor, 31 Mar. 1896; J. A. Muirhead to H.H. Mavor, 18 June 1901; Arthur Ponsonby to Mavor, 20 Aug. 1906; Falconer Papers, Mavor to N.A. Smith, 29 June 1919

12 Obituary, Toronto *Daily Star,* 2 Nov. 1925; Adam Shortt Papers, Cecil Lovel to Shortt, 2 Dec. 1894; H.S. Ferns and B. Ostry, *The Age of Mackenzie King: The Rise of the Leader* (London 1955) 19-25; 'Professor James Mavor,' *Journal of the Canadian Bankers' Association* XXXIII 2 (1926) 149

13 Shortt Papers (PAC), Mavor to Shortt, 15 Jan. 1913; Mavor Papers, Mavor to Sir William Peterson, 3 Apr. 1916; Sir William Peterson Papers, Peterson to Mavor, 5 Apr. 1916; Falconer Papers, Falconer to Mavor, 25 June 1910; James Loudon Papers, George Wrong to the vice-chancellor, 5 June 1905; Peterson Papers, Mavor to Peterson, 29 Apr. 1901; Pelham Edgar, *Across My Path* (Toronto 1952) 94

14 'Professor James Mavor,' *Journal of the Canadian Bankers' Association* 148. Cf. comments made by Mavor's daughter in Herbert Whittaker, 'Dora Mavor Moore: Zeal and Achievement Earn Tribute for Toronto Theatre's Great Lady,' Toronto *Globe,* 20 Nov. 1971.

15 J.G. Crowther, *British Scientists of the Nineteenth Century* (London 1935) 202

16 Sir William Thomson and P.G. Tait, *Elements of Natural Philosophy* I (Oxford 1873) ch. 3; Sir William Thomson, *Popular Lectures and Addresses* I (London 1889), especially 'The Six Gateways of Knowledge' (1883)

17 Cited in Philip Henderson, *William Morris: His Life, Work, and Friends* (London 1967) 274. See also J. Bruce Glazier, *William Morris and the Early Days of the Socialist Movement* (London 1921) 15.

18 Philip Henderson, *William Morris* (London 1952) 6, 29; R.P. Arnot, *William Morris* (London 1964) 19; L.W. Eshleman, *A Victorian Rebel: The Life of William Morris* (New York 1940) 314

19 George Woodcock and Ivan Avakumovic, *The Anarchist Prince: A Biographical Study of Peter Kropotkin* (New York 1971) 210, 274; J.N. Hulse, *Revolutionists in London: A Study of Five Unorthodox Socialists* (Oxford 1970) 75

20 Romain Rolland, *Tolstoi,* trans. by Bernard Miall (New York 1972 [1911]) 26; Otta Heller, *Prophets of Dissent* (New York 1918) 192-203

21 Leo Tolstoi, *Last Diaries,* trans. by Lydia Weston-Kesich, ed. by Leon Stillman (New York 1960) 169, entry for 30 Aug. 1910

22 H.W. Pfautz, ed., *Charles Booth* (Chicago 1967) 32, 15, 37, 45; Charles Booth, *Life and Labour of the People in London* XVII (London 1903) 203-4

23 Abbie Ziffren, 'Biography of Patrick Geddes' in Marshall Stalley, ed., *Patrick Geddes: Spokesman for Man and Environment* (New Brunswick, NJ 1972) 5-10.

See also Philip Mairet, *Pioneer of Sociology: The Life and Letters of Patrick Geddes* (London 1957) ch. 3.

24 Dorothy Herbertson, *The Life of Frederic Le Play* (Ledbury, Herefordshire 1950) 115

25 W.M. Simon, *European Positivism in the Nineteenth Century* (Ithaca 1963) 235

26 Herbertson, *The Life of Frederic Le Play* 12-20; M.Z. Brooke, *Le Play: Engineer and Social Scientist* (London 1970) 120, 131, 135

27 Brooke, *Le Play* 100-5; Herbertson, *The Life of Frederic Le Play* 16

28 Herbertson, *The Life of Frederic Le Play* 23, 97; Mavor, *Government Telephones* V, vii; 'The Relation of Economic Study to Public and Private Charity' 40; 'The New Crusade' 525, 538

29 Mavor, 'The Relation of Economic Study to Public and Private Charity' 34-5; *My Windows* I, 171, 173, 183; *Applied Economics* I, 197

30 Mavor, *My Windows* II, 162, 400; 'Labour and Politics in England' 501; 'The New Crusade' 536-7

31 Mavor, *An Economic History of Russia* II, 3

32 Mavor, *My Windows* II 154; 'Labour and Politics in England' 502; *My Windows* I, 152; 'The New Crusade' 530

33 Mavor, 'The Relation of Economic Study to Public and Private Charity' 50; *Applied Economics* 534, 341, 265, 201, 350-1, 358; 'Recent Financial Movements in the United States,' *Economic Journal* XIV (June 1904) 177; *Government Telephones* 7, 164, 4, 2; 'The Intelligentsia and Revolution,' *UM* XII 2 (1913) 311-12

34 Mavor, 'Labour and Politics in England' 492, 497, 491; *Niagara in Politics* 4; *Government Telephones* 1, 2; *Applied Economics* 413

35 Mavor, 'The Relation of Economic Study to Public and Private Charity' 49; 'Setting the Poor on Work' 522; *My Windows* I, 213, 216, 217, 160-2

36 Mavor, *My Windows* I, 245, 286, 178; II, 213; 'Labour and Politics in England' 515-16, 510, 503, 509; *Applied Economics* 201, 443; 'The Intelligentsia and the Revolution' 306; *The Russian Revolution* 437

37 Mavor, 'The Relation of Economic Study to Public and Private Charity' 53; 'Labour and Politics in England' 500; 'The New Crusade' 537; 'Setting the Poor on Work' 522; *My Windows* I, 217; *Applied Economics* 415-16, 427, 263, 264

38 Mavor, 'The New Crusade' 533, 527, 526; *My Windows* I, 217; II, 234, 158; 'Setting the Poor on Work' 524

39 Mavor, *My Windows* II, 116; 'The Relation of Economic Study to Public and Private Charity' 59

40 Mavor, *My Windows* I 258; II 181-2, 401; *Government Telephones* II; Mavor Papers, Francis Hankin to James Mavor, 20 Feb. 1919

CHAPTER EIGHT
CONCLUSION: CONVICTION IN AN AGE OF TRANSITION

1 These fears are evident in W.B. Munroe, 'The Church and the Social Crisis,' *UM* VIII 2 (1909) and Pelham Edgar, 'A Confession of Faith and a Protest,' *UM* VIII 2 (1909).

2 See Northrop Frye, 'Conclusion,' in Klinck, *Literary History of Canada* 840 (1st ed., 1965).

3 Among those lamenting the demise of individualism were Max Aitken, *My Early Life* (Fredericton 1965) 12, 46; R.J. Manion, *Life is an Adventure* (Toronto 1936) 18; W.C. Good, *Farmer Citizen* (Toronto 1958) 58.

4 Many late Victorians recalled such reading: Good, *Farmer Citizen* 59-60; Pelham Edgar, *Across My Path* 17; Stephen Leacock, *The Boy I Left Behind Me* (New York 1946) 81. See also Claude T. Bissell, 'Literary Taste in Central Canada during the Late Nineteenth Century,' *CHR* XXXI 3 (1950).

5 The influence of religion and education are noted in E.C. Drury *Farmer Premier* (Toronto 1966) 44; Vincent Massey, *What's Past is Prologue* (Toronto 1963) 5, 27; A.R.M. Lower, *My First Seventy-Five Years* (Toronto 1967) 9, 27, 30.

6 Edgar, 'A Confession of Faith and a Protest' 306

7 See S.F. Wise and R.C. Brown, *Canada Views the United States* (Seattle & London 1967) 98-120. Note also Ruth McKenzie, 'Life in a New Land: Notes on the Immigrant Theme in Canadian Fiction,' *Canadian Literature* 7 (1961).

8 Berger, *The Sense of Power,* especially chapters 6 and 7

9 *Ibid.* 199. Note also W.F. Chipman, 'The Payment of Members,' *UM* X 1 (1911) 18 and F.H. Underhill, 'The University and Politics,' in *In Search of Canadian Liberalism* (Toronto 1960) 269.

10 See, for example, David Levine, *Varieties of Reform Thought* (Madison 1964); David Chalmers, *The Social and Political Ideas of the Muckrakers* (New York 1964); Arthur Mann, *Yankee Reformers in an Urban Age* (Cambridge, Mass. 1954); Richard Hofstadter, *The Age of Reform* (New York 1955).

11 See Olivar Asselin, *A Quebec View of Canadian Nationalism* (Montreal 1909). See also Joseph Levitt, 'Henri Bourassa and Modern Industrial Society, 1900-1914,' *CHR* L 1 (1969) 44-8 and Ramsay Cook, *Canada and the French-Canadian Question* (Toronto 1966) 94-6.

12 Bernard Semmel, *Imperialism and Social Reform* (New York 1968) chapter 5

13 C.L. Burton, *A Sense of Urgency* (Toronto 1952) 42

14 Stephen Leacock, 'The Apology of a Professor' 185-6. A popular statement of this view is found in Martin J. Griffen, 'Dying Speeches and Confessions of the Nineteenth Century,' *CM* XVI 4 (1901).

15 Northrop Frye hints at this debate in his 'Conclusion,' in Klinck, *A Literary History of Canada.* See also Veysey, *The Rise of the American University* 59, 143, for comments on the American debate and Alice Chandler, *A Dream of Order* 146, for the British aspect.

16 Donald Creighton, 'John A. Macdonald,' *Our Living Tradition,* First Series (Toronto 1957) 52

17 L.R. Furst, *Romanticism in Perspective* (London 1969) 27, 28, 44

18 S.P. Lamprecht, *Our Philosophical Tradition* (New York 1955) 351-2; Emile Brehier, *The History of Philosophy: The Nineteenth Century: Period of Systems, 1800-1850,* trans. by Wade Baskin (Chicago 1968) 97-100

19 Frederick Copleston, *A History of Philosophy* VIII, 52-71; Crane Brinton, *English Political Thought in the 19th Century* 90-4

20 Samuel E. Stumpf, *Philosophy: History and Problems* (New York 1971) 307, 327-33, and C.H. Perelman, *An Historical Introduction to Philosophical Thinking,* trans. by Kenneth A. Brown (New York 1965) 178

21 Sir Henry Jones and John Henry Muirhead, *The Life and Philosophy of Edward Caird* (Glasgow 1921) 22, 126-7

22 Morton White, *The Age of Analysis* (New York 1955) 16

23 Jones and Muirhead, *Caird* 252; Watson, 'Edward Caird as a Teacher and Thinker' 304

24 Jones and Muirhead, *Caird* 277-8, 317-27; John Watson, 'The Idealism of Edward Caird,' *The Philosophical Review* XVIII 3 (1909) 260

25 Cappon, 'Edward Caird: A Reminiscence' 266

26 Watson, 'Edward Caird as a Teacher and Thinker' 305, 311. Cf. Goudge, 'A Century of Philosophy in English Canada' 538-9.

27 John A. Irving, 'The Development of Philosophy in Central Canada from 1850 to 1900' 261-3, 277-80

28 *Ibid.* 285

29 *Supra,* ch. 6, p 000

30 Mavor Papers, Patrick Geddes to Mavor, 10 Oct. 1903

31 Mavor, 'The Relation of Economic Study to Public and Private Charity' 40-4; 'The New Crusade' 532; *My Windows* I, 244, 239-40; II, 110

32 Stumpf, *Philosophy* 347, 354; Leszek Kolakowski, *The Alienation of Reason: A History of Positivist Thought,* trans. by Norbert Guterman (Garden City, NY 1968) 50-63, 99-100; Simon, *European Positivism,* ch. 8

33 L.L. Bernard and Jessie Bernard, *Origin of American Sociology: The Social Science Movement in the United States* (New York 1965) 158-9

34 See H. Stuart Hughes, *Consciousness and Society* 15-16.

35 Pfautz, *Charles Booth* 6

36 See, for example, Daniel M. Gordon, 'The Functions of a Modern University,' *QQ* x 4 (1903).

37 A similar contrast of idealist and empiricist opinion on the Empire existed between Stephen Leacock and John S. Ewart. See Alan Bowker, ed., introduction, *The Social Criticism of Stephen Leacock: The Unsolved Riddle of Social Justice and Other Essays* xxiii.

38 *A Quebec View of Canadian Nationalism* 27, 30; *Grain Growers' Guide,* 6 Mar. 1912; W.C. Good, 'Tariffs, Bounties and the Farmer,' *UM* VII 3 (1908) 429

39 *Grain Growers' Guide,* 21 Feb. 1912; E.A. Partridge, *War on Poverty* (Winnipeg 1926) 84, 89, 96, 114

40 F.H. Underhill, 'Some Reflections on the Liberal Tradition in Canada,' *In Search of Canadian Liberalism* (Toronto 1961) 8

41 Hughes, *Consciousness and Society* 405

42 J. Lee Thompson and John H. Thompson reach a similar conclusion regarding Ralph Connor's decline in popularity during the 1920s. See 'Ralph Connor and the Canadian Identity,' *QQ* LXXIX 2 (1972).

43 Cited in F.W. Watt, 'Climate of Unrest,' *Canadian Literature* 12 (1962) 17-19

44 See, for example: Queen's University Department of Political Economy, 'Financial Problems of the Federal System,' *QQ* XL 4 (1934); Norman Rogers, 'The Constitutional Impasse,' *QQ* XLI 4 (1935); B.K. Sandwell, 'Sovereignty in Canada,' *QQ* XXXIX 2 (1932); F.R. Scott, 'The Royal Commission on Dominion-Provincial Relations,' *UTQ* VII 2 (1938).

45 Alexander Brady, 'The State and Economic Life in Canada,' *UTQ* II 4 (1933) 422; G.F. Drummond, 'Economic Adaptations,' *UTQ* I 4 (1933) 422.

46 E.F. Scott, 'The Effect of the War on Literature and Learning,' *QQ* XXVII 2 (1919) 150; W.R. Taylor, 'Freedom and Contemporary Thought,' *UTQ* x 4 (1939-40) 398. Cf. W.A. Mackintosh, 'O.D. Skelton,' *Our Living Tradition,* Fifth Series (Toronto 1965) 62.

47 Sir Edward Beatty, 'Freedom and the Universities,' *QQ* XLIV 4 (1937-8) 470; F.H. Knight, 'Social Science and the Political Trend,' *UTQ* III 4 (1934) 426; R.O. MacFarlane, 'Provinces versus Dominion,' *QQ* XLII 2 (1935) 214; Sir Josiah Stamp, 'Democracy and Economic Affairs,' *UTQ* II 4 (1933) 407

Bibliography

INTRODUCTORY NOTE

Included in the section 'Primary Sources – Published' are a number of books and articles by persons other than the six individuals studied. They were selected for inclusion from a large number of sources on the basis of relevance to the main themes of this study. Among the most useful periodical sources are the following: *Canadian Club Addresses* (Montreal, Ottawa, and Toronto); *Canadian Forum; Canadian Magazine; Dalhousie Review; Empire Club Speeches* (Toronto); *McGill University Magazine; Royal Society of Canada, Proceedings and Transactions* (Series III); *Queen's Quarterly; Queen's Review; University Magazine; University of Toronto Monthly; University of Toronto Quarterly; The Week.*

No personal papers are available for James Cappon. Though such material existed at the time of his death, it appears that it was destroyed by his close friend, W.E. McNeill. Numerous letters from Cappon are found in the papers of the following individuals: W.L. Grant, Sir Sandford Fleming, and Sir J.S. Willison. According to the late Mrs Hume Wrong, Maurice Hutton's daughter, none of her father's papers are extant. A scattering of his letters is located in the papers of the following individuals: Sir Robert Falconer, Sir William Peterson, and James Mavor.

PRIMARY SOURCES

Unpublished

Personal Papers: Public and University Repositories
Dalhousie University Archives, Halifax. Archibald McKellar MacMechan Papers
McGill University Archives, Montreal. Sir William Peterson Papers
Public Archives of Canada, Ottawa. Sir Robert L. Borden Papers

– Sir Arthur Currie Papers
– John W. Dafoe Papers
– Sir Sandford Fleming Papers
– Governor-General Lord Grey of Howick Papers
– George M. Grant Papers
– William L. Grant Papers
– William Lyon Mackenzie King Papers
– Sir Wilfrid Laurier Papers
– Sir George Parkin Papers
– Adam Shortt Papers
– Sir Clifford Sifton Papers
– Sir John S. Willison Papers
Queen's University Archives, Kingston. George H. Clarke Papers
– Daniel M. Gordon Papers
– Lorne Pierce Papers
– Bernard K. Sandwell Papers
– Adam Shortt Papers
University of Saskatchewan Archives, Saskatoon. Adam Shortt Papers
University of Toronto Archives, Toronto. Sir Robert A. Falconer Papers
– James Louden Papers
– James Mavor Papers
– Sir Daniel Wilson Papers
– George M. Wrong Papers
Victoria College Library, Toronto. Pelham Edgar Papers

Personal Papers: Private Repositories
Sir Andrew Macphail Papers. Privately held by Mrs Dorothy Lindsay, Montreal

Miscellaneous Manuscript Sources
Queen's University Archives, Kingston. Kingston Historical Society
    Minute Book
– *Queen's Quarterly* treasurers' accounts, 1893-1902 and secretarial notes
– Saturday Club correspondence and minutes
– John Watson, 'The Relation of Philosophy to Science' Inaugural lecture,
    Queen's University, 1872
– John Watson, 'Education and Life' Address at Queen's University, 1873
– Queen's University *Report of the Principal* session 1911-12
– Queen's University *Report of the Principal, Deans, and Treasurer* session
    1915-16

– R. Bruce Taylor, *Memoirs* bound photocopy of a typed manuscript
McGill University Archives. McGill scrapbooks, nos 2, 3, 6, 7, 8, 9

Published

Books, Pamphlets and Reports
Aberdeen, Lady Ishbel *The Canadian Journal of Lady Aberdeen, 1893-1898*
    Edited by J.T. Saywell. Toronto: Champlain Society 1960
A Group of Classics Graduates *Honours Classics in the University of Toronto*
    Toronto: University of Toronto Press 1929
Aitken, Max *My Early Life* Fredericton: Brunswick Press 1965
Arnold, Matthew *Culture and Anarchy and Friendship's Garland* New York:
    Macmillan Co. 1906
Asselin, Olivar *A Quebec View of Canadian Nationalism* Montreal: Guertin
    Printing Co. 1909
Booth, Charles *Life and Labour of the People in London* Vol. xvii. London:
    Macmillan Co. 1903
Borden, Robert L. *Memories* Toronto: Macmillan Co. 1938
Burton, C.L. *A Sense of Urgency: Memoirs of a Canadian Merchant* Toronto:
    Clarke, Irwin & Co. 1952
Cappon, James *Bliss Carman* Toronto: Ryerson Press 1930
– *Britain's Title in South Africa* London: Macmillan Co. 1901
– *The Principle of Sectarianism in the Constitution of Canada* Privately printed
    pamphlet. Kingston 1905
– *Roberts and the Influence of His Times* Toronto: William Briggs 1905
– *What Classical Education Means* Privately printed pamphlet. Kingston nd
– *What the Present War Means* Privately printed pamphlet. Kingston 1914
Cartwright, Sir Richard *Reminiscences* Toronto: William Briggs 1912
Colquhoun, A.V.H. *Press, Politics and People* Toronto: Macmillan Co. 1935
Drury, E.C. *Farmer Premier* Toronto: McClelland & Stewart 1966
Edgar, Pelham *Across My Path* Toronto: Ryerson Press 1952
Geddes, Patrick and Gilbert Slater *The Making of the Future: Ideas at War*
    London: Williams & Norgate 1917
Good, W.C. *Farmer Citizen* Toronto: Ryerson Press 1958
Gordon, C.W. *Postscript to Adventure: The Autobiography of Ralph Connor*
    New York: Farrar & Rinehart 1938
Grant, W.L. and C.F. Hamilton *Principal Grant* Toronto: Morang & Co. 1904
Haultain, Arnold *Of Walks and Walking Tours: An Attempt to Find a Philosophy
    and a Creed* London 1917
Hémon, Louis *Maria Chapdelaine* Translated by Andrew Macphail. London &

New York: John Lane; Montreal: A.T. Chapman; Toronto: Oxford University Press 1921

Hutton, Maurice *All the Rivers Run into the Sea* London: Hodder & Stoughton, nd [1928]

– *Many Minds* London: Hodder & Stoughton nd [1927]

– *Reflections of a Professor of Greek* Pamphlet. Ottawa: University of Women's Club of Ottawa 1929

– *The Greek Point of View* London: Hodder & Stoughton, nd [1925]

Kropotkin, Peter Aleksieevich *Memoirs of a Revolutionist* Boston: Houghton Mifflin Co. 1899

Leacock, Stephen *Economic Prosperity within the British Empire* Toronto: Macmillan Co. 1933

– *The Boy I Left behind Me* New York: Doubleday & Co. 1946

Logan, J.D. *Dalhousie University and Canadian Literature* Privately printed pamphlet. Halifax 1922

Lower, A.R.M. *My First Seventy-Five Years* Toronto: Macmillan Co. 1967

MacMechan, Archibald McKellar *Headwaters of Canadian Literature* Toronto: McClelland & Stewart 1924

– *Late Harvest* Toronto: Ryerson Press 1934

– *Life of a Little College, and Other Papers* Boston & New York: Houghton Mifflin Co. 1914

– *Old Province Tales* Toronto: McClelland & Stewart 1924

– *Sagas of the Sea* New York: E.P. Dutton & Co.; London & Toronto: G.M. Dent 1924

– *Tales of the Sea* Edited by Thomas Raddall. Toronto: McClelland & Stewart 1947

– *The Book of Ultima Thule* Toronto: McClelland & Stewart 1927

– *The Memorial Tower* Privately printed pamphlet. Halifax 1922

– *The Porter of Bagdad and Other Fantasies* Toronto: George N. Morang 1901

– *There Go the Ships* Toronto: McClelland & Stewart 1928

– *The Winning of Popular Government: A Chronicle of the Union of 1841* Toronto: Glasgow, Brook & Co. 1916

Macnaughton, John *Essays and Addresses* Kingston: Queen's University 1946

Macphail, Sir Andrew *Essays in Fallacy* New York & London: Longmans, Green & Co. 1910

– *Essays in Politics* London: Longmans, Green & Co. 1909

– *Essays in Puritanism* Boston & New York: Houghton Mifflin & Co. 1905

– *Official History of the Canadian Forces in the Great War, 1914-19: The Medical Services* Ottawa: King's Printer 1925

– *The Bible in Scotland* London: John Murray 1931

– *The Book of Sorrows* London: Oxford University Press 1916

- *The Land, a Play of Character* Montreal: University Magazine 1914
- *The Master's Wife* Montreal: Jeffrey Macphail & Dorothy Lindsay 1939
- *The Vine of Sibmah: A Relation of the Puritans* London & New York: Macmillan Co. 1906
- *Three Persons* London: John Murray 1929

Manion, R.J. *Life is an Adventure* Toronto: Ryerson Press 1936

Massey, Vincent *What's Past is Prologue* Toronto: Macmillan of Canada 1963

Mavor, James *An Economic History of Russia* 2 vols. London & Toronto: G.M. Dent & Sons 1914
- *Applied Economics: A Practical Exposition of the Science of Business with Illustrations from Actual Experience* New York: Alexander Hamilton Institute 1914
- ed. *Book of the Victorian Era Ball* Toronto 1898
- *Government Telephones: The Experience of Manitoba, Canada* New York: Moffat, Yard & Co. 1916
- *My Windows on the Street of the World* 2 vols. London & Toronto: J.M. Dent & Sons, nd [1923]
- *Niagara in Politics: A Critical Account of the Ontario Hydro-Electric Commission* New York: E.P. Dutton & Co. 1925
- et al. *Report on Labour Colonies* Glasgow: The Association for Improving the Condition of the People 1892
- *Report to the Board of Trade on the North-West of Canada, with Special Reference to Wheat Production for Export* British Parliamentary Papers, Cd. 2628. London 1905
- *The Russian Revolution* London: George Allen & Unwin Ltd 1928

Mill, John Stuart *Mill's Ethical Writings* Edited by J.B. Schneewind. New York: Collier Books 1965

Munro, William B. *Forty Years On, 1896-1936: A Historical Record of Arts '96 at Queen's University* np, nd

Nicholson, James Shield *A Project of Empire* London: Macmillan Co. 1909
- *Historical Progress and Ideal Socialism* London: Adam & Charles Black 1894
- *Principles of Political Economy* Vol. I. New York: Macmillan Co. 1894

Partridge, E.A. *War on Poverty* Winnipeg: Wallingford Publishers 1926

Ross, Sir George *Getting into Parliament and After* Toronto: William Briggs 1913

Shortt, Adam *Canada and Chamberlainism* Pamphlet, reprint from the *London Daily Chronicle* London: Liberal Publication Department 1905
- and A.G. Doughty, eds *Canada and Its Provinces: A History of the Canadian People and Their Institutions* 23 vols. Toronto: Glasgow, Brook & Co. 1914-17
- *Early Records on Ontario* Kingston 1900
- *Imperial Preferential Trade from a Canadian Point of View* Toronto: Morang and Co. 1904

– *Life of the Settler in Western Canada before the War of 1812* Bulletin of the Departments of History and Political and Economic Science in Queen's University. Kingston 1914

– *Lord Sydenham* Toronto: G.N. Morang & Co. 1908

– *Report of the Commission Appointed to Investigate the Economic Conditions and Operations of the British Columbia Electric Railway Company and Subsidiary Companies* Victoria: King's Printer 1918

Smith, Goldwin *A Selection from Goldwin Smith's Correspondence, 1846-1910* Edited by T.A. Haultain. Toronto: McClelland & Goodchild, nd

– *Reminiscences* Edited by A.T. Haultain. New York: Macmillan Co. 1910

Thomson, Sir William *Popular Lectures and Addresses* 3 vols. London: Macmillan Co. 1889

– and P.G. Tait *Elements of Natural Philosophy* Oxford: Clarendon Press 1873

Tolstoi, Leo *Last Diaries* Translated by Lydia Weston-Kesich. Edited by Leon Stillman. New York: G.P. Putnam & Sons 1960

Watson, John *Comte, Mill and Spencer* New York: Macmillan Co. 1895

Wickett, S. Morley *Political Economy at Canadian Universities* Appendix to the Report of the Ontario Bureau of Industries, 1897. Toronto: Ontario Department of Agriculture 1899

Willison, Sir John A. *Reminiscences, Political and Personal* Toronto: McClelland & Stewart 1919

Articles

Beatty, Sir Edward 'Freedom and the Universities' *Queen's Quarterly* XLIV 4 (1937-8)

– 'Inaugural Address as a Chancellor of Queen's University' *Queen's Quarterly* XXVII 1 (1919)

Bell, F. McKelvey 'Social Maladies' *Queen's Quarterly* XVI 1 (1908)

Brady, Alexander 'The State and Economic Life in Canada' *University of Toronto Quarterly* II 4 (1933)

Brown, W.J. 'Immigration and Agriculture' *University Magazine* XIII 1 (1914)

Campbell, F.J. 'Relation of Our Educational System to Practical Life' *Queen's Quarterly* X 2 (1902)

Cappon, James 'A School of Idealism: Meditateo Laici' *Philosophical Essays Presented to John Watson* Kingston: Queen's University 1922

– 'Bliss Carman's Beginnings' *Queen's Quarterly* XXXVI 4 (1929)

– 'Canada's Relation to the Empire' *Queen's Quarterly* XIX 2 (1911)

– 'Current Events' *Queen's Quarterly* I 4 (1893). Also in the following: VII 2 (1899); X 3 (1903); X 4 (1903); XI 1 (1903); XI 3 (1904); XI 4 (1904); XII 2 (1904); XII 3 (1905); XII 4 (1905); XIII 3 (1905); XIV i (1906);

xiv 3 (1907); xiv 4 (1907); xv 3 (1908); xv 4 (1908); xvi 4 (1909);
xviii 3 (1911); xix 3 (1912); xix 4 (1912); xx 3 (1913); xxi 2 (1913);
xxxiii 2 (1915); xxxiii 3 (1916); xxiv 3 (1917); xxv 1 (1917);
xxv 3 (1917); xxvi 3 (1919)
- 'Democracy and Monarchy in the Modern State' *Queen's Quarterly*
xxiv 1 (1916)
- 'Edward Caird: A Reminiscence' *Queen's Quarterly* xvi 3 (1909)
- 'Facts and Comments' *Queen's Quarterly* xii 2 (1905)
- 'In Memoriam' *Queen's Quarterly* xxv 2 (1917)
- 'Is Ontario to Abandon Classical Education?' *Queen's Quarterly* xii 2 (1904)
- 'Literature for the Young: Notes on the High School Reader' *Queen's Quarterly* i 1 (1893)
- 'Modern Universities and the Training of the Clergy' *Standards of Ministerial Education* Privately published pamphlet, np, nd
- 'Notes on Our Art Collection' *Queen's Quarterly* xii 3 (1905)
- 'Roberts and the Influence of His Time' *Canadian Magazine* xxiv (1904-5)
- 'Some Considerations on Queen's Position' *Queen's Quarterly* xvii 2 (1909)
- 'The Great American Democracy' *Queen's Quarterly* xi 3 (1904)
- 'The Scandinavian Nations and the War' i *Queen's Quarterly* xxiv 3 (1917)
- 'The Scandinavian Nations and the War' ii *University Magazine* xvi 3 (1917)
- 'The Situation in Queen's' *Queen's Quarterly* xvii 3 (1910)
Cochrane, C.N. 'Head of Department Retires: Professor W.S. Milner Leaves Department of Greek and Roman History' *University of Toronto Monthly* xxix 8 (1929)
Cody, H.J., Malcolm Wallace, W.R. Taylor, Katherine Wales 'In Memoriam, Sir Robert Falconer, kcmg' *University of Toronto Quarterly* xiii 2 (1944)
Coleman, H.T.J. 'The Teacher and the New Age' *Queen's Quarterly* xxv 4 (1918)
- 'Training for the New Citizenship' *Queen's Quarterly* xxxiii 1 (1919)
'Comments on Current Events: The College Professor in the Public Service' *Queen's Journal* xxxvi 1 (1908)
Cooper, J.A. 'Canada's Progress in the Victorian Era' *Canadian Magazine* ix 2 (1897)
Cox, Mrs C.O. 'Play for the People' *University Magazine* vii 4 (1908)
Cox, John 'Commercial Education' *Canadian Magazine* xviii 5 (1902)
'C.W.C.' 'The Religious Unrest' *Queen's Quarterly* xxxiv 4 (1926)
Dale, J.A. 'On Some Definitions of Poetry' *University Magazine* viii 2 (1909)
- 'Teacher and Community' *Canadian Magazine* lxii 6 (1924)
Drummond, G.F. 'Economic Adaptations' *University of Toronto Quarterly* i 4 (1933)

Dupuis, F.N. 'The Conservative and Liberal in Education' *Queen's Quarterly* IX 2 & 3 (1901-2)

Edgar, Pelham 'Confession of Faith and a Protest' *University Magazine* VIII 2 (1909)

Falconer, Sir Robert A. 'From College to University' *University of Toronto Quarterly* IV 4 and V 1 (1935)

– 'Glimpses of the University at Work from 1907 until the First World War' *University of Toronto Quarterly* XI 2 & 4 (1942)

– 'The Individuality of the Canadian People' *University of Toronto Monthly* X 8 (1910)

Flammer, E. 'Relativity and Gravitation' *Queen's Quarterly* XXVIII 3 & 4 (1920)

Gibson, J.M. 'The Foreign Born' *Queen's Quarterly* XXV 4 (1920)

Gordon, D.M. 'The Functions of a Modern University' *Queen's Quarterly* X 4 (1903)

Grant, W.L. 'Reminiscences' *Queen's Quarterly* XXV 2 (1917)

– 'The Education of the Working Man' *Queen's Quarterly* XXVII 2 (1919)

– 'The Present Intellectual Status of Canada' *Queen's Quarterly* XXIX 1 (1921)

Grey, F.W. 'Education and Nationality' *University Magazine* XII 2 (1913)

– 'The Race Question' *University Magazine* VII 2 (1908)

Griffin, Martin J. 'Dying Speeches and Confessions of the Nineteenth Century' *Canadian Magazine* XVI 4 (1901)

Hamilton, C.F. 'Militarism' *University Magazine* IX 4 (1910)

Haultain, Arnold 'A Search for an Ideal' *Canadian Magazine* XXII 5 (1904)

Hutton, Maurice 'A Canadian in Paris' *Addresses Delivered before the Canadian Club of Toronto, 1910-11* Toronto: Warwick Bros. & Rutter 1915

– 'Address at the Annual Reception of the Students of the First Year on October 2, 1906' *University of Toronto Monthly* VII 1 (1906)

– 'Address at the Annual Reception of the Students of the First Year on October 2, 1905' *University of Toronto Monthly* VI 1 (1905)

– 'Address of Welcome' *Proceedings of the Sixty-Fourth Annual Convention of the Ontario Educational Association* Toronto 1925

– 'Address to the Incoming Students of the First Year on October 3, 1907' *University of Toronto Monthly* VIII 2 (1907)

– 'Address to the Senate of the University of Saskatchewan' *University of Toronto Monthly* VIII 6 (1908)

– 'Address to the University College Literary Society' *University of Toronto Monthly* XI 1 (1910)

– 'Address to the Women Graduates of the Normal School, Toronto' *University of Toronto Monthly* IX 3 (1909)

- 'All Men are Either Platonists or Aristotelians' *University Magazine* VIII 3 (1909)
- 'A Traveller's Notes in Greece' *University Magazine* X 4 (1911)
- 'Classical Golf' *University of Toronto Monthly* XXIV 7 (1924)
- 'Freshmen, Yesterday and To-Day' *University of Toronto Monthly* XXII 2 (1921)
- 'Gollicana Quaedam' *University of Toronto Monthly* X 5 & 6 (1910)
- 'Hellenism' *University of Toronto Monthly* II 7 (1902)
- 'In Memoriam, John Fletcher, MA, LLD' *University of Toronto Monthly* XVIII 2 (1918)
- 'In Paris' *University Magazine* X 1 (1911)
- 'In the House of one Simon a Tanner.' *University Magazine* XIII 2 (1914)
- 'John Macnaughton' *University of Toronto Monthly* XXVI 4 (1925)
- 'Kipling' *University Magazine* XXVIII 4 (1918)
- 'Language Study – The Classics' *University of Toronto Monthly* XIX (June 1919)
- 'Militarism and Anti-Militarism' *University Magazine* XII 2 (1913)
- 'Nathanael Burwash' *University of Toronto Monthly* XVIII 7 (1918)
- 'On Schoolmasters' *Queen's Quarterly* XIV 2 (1906)
- 'On Taking Orders' *University of Toronto Monthly* XXXI 6 (1931)
- 'Plato and Poetry' *University Magazine* VII 1 (1908)
- 'Plato's Watchdog' *University Magazine* VII 4 (1908)
- 'Principal Hutton is Guest of Honour' *University of Toronto Monthly* XXVIII 8 (1928)
- 'Review of the Past Session' *University of Toronto Monthly* VII 9 (1907)
- 'Signs of the Times' *Proceedings of the Sixty-Fourth Annual Convention of the Ontario Educational Association* Toronto 1925
- 'Speech at Graduating Class Dinner' *University of Toronto Monthly* XI 7 (1910)
- 'Speech at the Arts Dinner, 1909' *University of Toronto Monthly* IX 6 (1909)
- 'Speech at University College Dinner' *University of Toronto Monthly* XI 3 (1910)
- 'The Arts Colleges: University College' *The University of Toronto and Its Colleges, 1832-1906* Toronto: University of Toronto Library 1906
- 'The British and the German Mind' *University Magazine* XIV 3 (1915)
- 'The Canadian National Character' *Empire Club Speeches 1903-04* Toronto: William Briggs 1904
- 'The Changes of Forty Years' *University of Toronto Monthly* XXII 8 (1922)
- 'The Dream of Greek Letters' *Canadian Magazine* XVII 1 (1901)

- 'The Dublin Insurrection' *University Magazine* xvi 2 (1917)
- 'The Folly of the Wise' *Proceedings of the Canadian Club of Toronto, 1922-23* Toronto: Warwick Bros & Rutter 1923
- 'The League of Nations and Its Relation to the Public Schools' *Proceedings of the Sixty-Fifth Annual Convention of the Ontario Educational Association* Toronto 1926
- 'The Necessity of Religion' *Dalhousie Review* viii 3 (1928-9)
- 'The New Minister of Education' *University of Toronto Monthly* xviii 9 (1918)
- 'The Objects of the Canadian Defence League' *Addresses Delivered before the Canadian Clubs of Montreal, 1912-13* Montreal, nd
- 'The Philosophy of Our Political Parties' *University Magazine* viii 4 (1909)
- 'The Plight of University College' *University of Toronto Monthly* xxii 5 (1922)
- 'The Politics of Greece since 1914' *University Magazine* xviii 2 (1919)
- 'The Position of Greece in Relation to the War' *Addresses Delivered before the Canadian Club of Ottawa, 1915-16* Ottawa: Dodson-Merrill 1915
- 'The Quincentennial of St Andrew's University' *University of Toronto Monthly* xii 1 (1911)
- 'The Recent History of Greece' *University Magazine* xviii 1 (1919)
- 'The Retirement of Dr Burwash' *University of Toronto Monthly* xiv 1 (1914)
- 'The Rhodes Scholarships Symposium' *University of Toronto Monthly* xxx 1 (1902)
- 'The University Dinner to Dr Hutton' *University of Toronto Monthly* xxix 5 (1929)
- 'The Wisdom of the Vulgar' *Proceedings of the Canadian Club of Toronto, 1921-22* Toronto: Warwick Bros & Rutter 1923
- 'To the Alumni Leaving for the Front' *University of Toronto Monthly* xv 6 (1915)
- 'To the Members of the COTC' *University of Toronto Monthly* xvi 3 (1915)
- 'University Students in Toronto and Oxford' *University of Toronto Monthly* vii 8 (1907)
- 'What the New Administration Building Means to University College' *University of Toronto Monthly* xxiii 4 (1923)

Jordan, W.G. 'The Return to Traditionalism' *Queen's Quarterly* xxix 4 (1922)
Knight, A.P. 'Family Stock: An Address to Young People' *Queen's Quarterly* xiv 2 (1908)
Knight, F.H. 'Social Science and the Political Trend' *University of Toronto Quarterly* iii 4 (1934)
Leacock, Stephen 'Greater Canada: An Appeal' *University Magazine* vi 2 (1907)

- 'Literature and Education in America' *University Magazine* VIII 1 (1909)
- 'The Apology of a Professor' *University Magazine* IX 2 (1910)
- 'The Devil and the Deep Sea' *University Magazine* IX 4 (1910)

Leathe, Sonia 'Votes for Women' *University Magazine* XIII 1 (1914)

Loes, J.M. 'Education and Good Manners' *The Week* V 44 (1888)

McBride, W.D. 'What of the West' *University Magazine* VIII 2 (1909)

MacFarlane, R.O. 'Provinces versus Dominion' *Queen's Quarterly* XLII 2 (1935)

MacLean, J.S. 'Social Amelioration and the University Settlement' *Canadian Magazine* VIII 6 (1897)

MacMechan, Archibald McKellar 'Ab Urbe Condita' *Dalhousie Review* VII 2 (1927)
- 'A Canadian Krahwinkel' *The Week* V 28 (1888)
- 'A Canadian of the Mutiny' *Canadian Magazine* XIV 5 (1900)
- 'Afoot in Ultima Thule' *Dalhousie Review* III 2 (1923)
- 'Alfred Tennyson, Artist' *University Magazine* VII 2 (1908)
- 'Alice in Wonderland' *University Magazine* VII 3 (1908)
- 'A Professor of the English Language and Literature' *The Week* V 52 (1888)
- 'Athenian Days' *Queen's Quarterly* XI 1 (1903)
- 'Book and Beaver' *Montreal Standard* weekly column, March 1906-September 1907
- 'Canada as a Vassal State' *Canadian Historical Review* I 4 (1920)
- 'Canada at War' *The Nation* CL (January 1916)
- 'Canadian Literature: The Beginnings' *Essays and Studies by Members of the English Association* XII Oxford: Clarendon Press 1926
- 'Canada's Diamond Jubilee' *Christian Science Monitor* 1 July 1927
- 'Canada's Future' *Canadian Magazine* March 1917
- 'Carlyle's Prentice Hand' *Citizen* November 1897
- 'Changing Halifax' *Canadian Magazine* XXVII 5 (1906)
- 'Clamming' *Introducing Essays* Edited by S.A. Leonard. Chicago: Scott, Foreman & Co. 1933
- 'Dalhousie College' *The Varsity* 19 November 1902
- 'Declaring Our Independence' *The Canadian Courier* 2 December 1916
- 'De Mille, the Man and Writer' *Canadian Magazine* XXVII 5 (1906)
- 'Evangeline and the Real Acadians' *Atlantic Monthly* XCIX (February 1907)
- 'Frederick Henry Sykes' *University of Toronto Monthly* XVIII 7 (1918)
- 'George Paxton Young: An Acknowledgement of Debt' *University of Toronto Monthly* VII 4 & 6 (1907)
- 'Halifax in Books' *Acadiensis* VI (1906)
- 'Halifax in Trade' *Canadian Geographic Journal* III 3 (1931)
- 'Halifax Letter' *Canadian Forum* IX 100 (1929)

- 'Heartha' *The Week* v 53 (1888)
- 'History to be Read' *Yale Review* x 1 (1920)
- 'How a "Seminary" is Conducted at Johns Hopkins' *The Week* v 23 (1888)
- 'Impressions of a Train-Flight across Canada' Halifax *Chronicle* 28 April 1928
- 'In a Fighting Submarine' *Canadian Courier* 24 March 1917
- 'In Memory of Scott' *Dalhousie Review* I 3 (1921)
- introduction, Thomas Carlyle, *On Heroes, Hero-Worship and the Heroic in History* Edited by Archibald MacMechan. Boston: Atheneum Press 1901
- introduction, Thomas Carlyle, *Sartor Resartus* Edited by Archibald Mac-Mechan. Boston: Atheneum Press 1897
- introduction, *Select Poems of Alfred Tennyson* Edited by Archibald Mac-Mechan. Boston & London: D.C. Heath & Co. 1907
- 'Journalism: Another View' *University of Toronto Monthly* III 4 (1903)
- 'Life on a Cattle Ship' *The Week* VII 16 October 1890
- 'Memories of James Seth' *Dalhousie Review* IV 4 (1924)
- 'Mrs Lilly Sweetwich's Coffee' *The Week* v 38 (1888)
- 'Nova Scotia: General History 1775-1886' *Canada and Its Provinces* Vol. XIII. Edited by Adam Shortt and A.G. Doughty. Toronto: Glasgow, Brook & Co. 1914-17
- 'Nova Scotia: Political History 1867-1912' *Canada and Its Provinces* Vol. XIII. Edited by Adam Shortt and A.G. Doughty. Toronto: Glasgow, Brook & Co. 1914-17
- 'Of Girls in a Canadian College' *Atlantic Monthly* XCIX (February 1907)
- 'Old Lovers' *Dalhousie Review* VI 1 (1926)
- 'Oxford for a Day' *Canadian Magazine* XXXIX 4 (1912)
- 'Painted Music' *Dalhousie Review* v 3 (1925)
- 'Picton Boys Sixty Years Ago' Picton *Gazette* (28 December 1930)
- 'Principal Falconer of Toronto University' *Canadian Magazine* XXXV 3 (1910)
- 'Red Snow on Grand Pré' *Dalhousie Review* x 1 & 2 (1930)
- 'Reminiscences of Toronto University – Professor George Paxton Young' *The Presbyterian* New Series VIII 19 (1906)
- 'Reminiscences of Toronto University – The Convocation Hall' *The Presbyterian* New Series VIII 18 (1906)
- 'Storia de Christo' *Dalhousie Review* II 2 (1922)
- 'The Best Sea Story Ever Written' *Queen's Quarterly* VII 2 (1899)
- 'The Canadian Achievement' *Proceedings and Transactions of the Royal Society of Canada* Series III, XX (1926)
- 'The Coasts of Ultima Thule' *Dalhousie Review* VI 3 (1926)
- 'The Dean's Window' Montreal *Standard* weekly column, September 1907-August 1933

- 'The Great Ship' *Dalhousie Review* VIII 2 (1928)
- 'The Literature of Nova Scotia' *Canadian Magazine* XXV 6 (1905)
- 'The Malvern Festival of 1932' *Dalhousie Review* XIII 2 (1933)
- 'The Maritime Provinces to Confederation' *Encyclopedia Americana* New York: Scientific American 1911
- 'The National Vices' *The Nation* CIII (July 1916)
- 'The Nova Scotia-ness of Nova Scotia' *Canadian Magazine* XXV 2 (1905)
- 'The Rise of Samuel Cunard' *Dalhousie Review* IX 2 (1929)
- 'The Strength and Splendour of England's War' Halifax *Chronicle* (17 July 1911)
- 'The Vanity of Travel' *University Magazine* XI 2 (1912)
- 'Thoreau' *Cambridge History of American Literature* Vol. II. New York: G.P. Putnam & Sons 1918
Macphail, Andrew 'A History of the Idea of Evolution' *Dalhousie Review* V 1 (1925)
- 'An address on the Sources of Modern Medicine' *Canadian Medical Association Journal* XXVIII 3 (1933)
- 'An Ambulance in Rest' *University Magazine* XVI 3 (1917)
- 'An Obverse View of Education' *University Magazine* IX 2 (1910)
- 'Article Nineteen' *University Magazine* XVIII 3 (1919)
- 'Art in Democracy' *Dalhousie Review* IV 2 (1924)
- 'As Others See Us' *University Magazine* IX 2 (1910)
- 'A Voice from the East' *University Magazine* IX 4 (1910)
- 'British Diplomacy and Canada' *University Magazine* VIII 2 (1909)
- 'Canadian Writers and American Politics' *University Magazine* IX 1 (1910)
- 'Certain Varieties of the Apples of Sodom' *University Magazine* X 1 (1911)
- 'Confiscatory Legislation' *University Magazine* X 2 (1911)
- 'Consequences and Penalties' *University Magazine* XIII 2 (1914)
- 'Conservative-Liberal-Socialist' *University of Toronto Quarterly* III 3 (1933-4)
- 'Design' *Queen's Quarterly* XLIV 1 (1937)
- 'Evolution and Life' *Annals of Medical History* New Series I 5 (1929)
- 'Family and Society' *Quarterly Review* CCLXVIII 532 (1917)
- 'Greek Medicine' *Queen's Quarterly* XLIII 1 (1936)
- 'Hindenburg' *Queen's Quarterly* XLI 4 (1934)
- 'History of Prince Edward Island' *Canada and Its Provinces* Vol. XIII. Edited by Adam Shortt and A.G. Doughty. Toronto: Glasgow, Brook & Co. 1914-17
- 'I Believe, This is My Credo, My Philosophy of Life' Montreal *Herald* (10 December 1934)
- 'In This Our Necessity' *University Magazine* XVI 4 (1917)
- 'John Knox in the Church of England' *University Magazine* VI 1 (1907)

- 'John McCrae: An Essay in Character' John McCrae, *In Flanders Fields and Other Poems* Toronto: William Briggs 1919
- 'Lessons Proper' *University Magazine* XIV 1 (1915)
- 'Loyalty – to What?' *University Magazine* VI 2 (1907)
- 'New Lamps for Old' *University Magazine* VIII 1 (1908)
- 'On Certain Aspects of Feminism' *University Magazine* XIII 1 (1914)
- 'Oxford and Working-Class Education' *University Magazine* IX 1 (1910)
- 'Patriotism and Politics' *University Magazine* XIII 1 (1914)
- 'Prince Edward Island' *Proceedings of the Canadian Club of Toronto, 1911-12* Toronto: Warwick Bros & Rutter 1912
- 'Protection and Politics' *University Magazine* VII 2 (1908)
- 'Robert E. Lee' *Queen's Quarterly* XLV 1 (1938)
- 'Sir Arthur Currie' *Queen's Quarterly* XLI 1 (1934)
- 'Sir Gilbert Parker: An Appraisal' *Proceedings and Transactions of the Royal Society of Canada* Series III, XXXIII (1939)
- 'Sir Sandford Fleming' *Queen's Quarterly* XXXVI 2 (1929)
- 'Sir William Dawson' *McGill University Magazine* V 1 (1905)
- 'The Atlantic Provinces in the Dominion: Introduction' *Canada and Its Provinces* Vol. XIII. Edited by Adam Shortt and A.G. Doughty. Toronto: Glasgow, Brook & Co. 1914-17
- 'The Attainment of Consideration' *British Medical Journal* 15 November 1902
- 'The Burden of the Stuarts' *Quarterly Review* CCLIV 504 (1930)
- 'The Cleansing of the Slate' *University Magazine* X 2 (1911)
- 'The Conservative' *University Magazine* XVIII 4 (1919)
- 'The Cost of Living' *University Magazine* XI 4 (1912)
- 'The Day of Wrath' *University Magazine* XIII 3 (1914)
- 'The Dominion and the Provinces' *University Magazine* XII 4 (1912)
- 'The Dominion and the Spirit' *University Magazine* VII 1 (1908)
- 'The Freedom of England' *Quarterly Review* CCLV 505 (1930)
- 'The Graduate' *Queen's Quarterly* XXXIX 3 (1932)
- 'The Hand or the Book' *Dalhousie Review* VI 2 (1926)
- 'The Healing of a Wound' *Canadian Medical Association Journal* XXX 6 (1934)
- 'The Hill of Error' *University Magazine* XII 4 (1913)
- 'The Immigrant' *University Magazine* XIX 2 (1920)
- 'The Last Rising' *Queen's Quarterly* XXXVII 2 (1930)
- 'The Navy and Politics' *University Magazine* XII 2 (1913)
- 'The New Theology' *University Magazine* IX 4 (1910)
- 'The Nine Prophets' *University Magazine* VIII 3 (1909)
- 'The Old College' *Saturday Night* LIII 28 (1938)

- 'The Old School' *Saturday Night* LIII 9 (1938)
- 'The Patience of England' *University Magazine* VI 3 (1907)
- 'The Peace and Its Consequences' *University Magazine* XIX 2 (1920)
- 'The Reading of History' *Canadian Medical Association Journal* XXIX 6 (1933)
- 'The Sonnets' *University Magazine* XVIII 3 (1919)
- 'The Tariff Commission' *University Magazine* XI 1 (1912)
- 'The Women of Moscow' *Saturday Night* L 43 (1935)
- 'Two Sonnets' *University Magazine* XIII 3 (1914)
- 'Unto the Church' *University Magazine* XII 2 (1913)
- 'Val Cartier Camp' *University Magazine* XIII 3 (1914)
- 'What Canada Can Do' *University Magazine* VI 4 (1907)
- 'Why the Conservatives Failed' *University Magazine* VII 4 (1908)
- 'Why the Liberals Failed' *University Magazine* X 4 (1911)
- 'Women in Democracy' *University Magazine* XIX 1 (1920)

Magrath, C.A. 'The Civil Service' *University Magazine* XII 2 (1913)

Mavor, James 'Agricultural Development in the North-West of Canada, 1905 until 1909' *Report of the Seventy-Ninth Meeting of the British Association for the Advancement of Science, 1904* London: John Murray 1910
- 'Count Leo N. Tolstoy, 1899-1910' *Canadian Forum* I, 10, 11, 12 (1921) & II, 13 (1920)
- 'Economic Survey' *Oxford Survey of the British Empire* Edited by H.J. Herbertson and O.J.R. Howarth. Oxford: Clarendon Press 1914
- 'Finance and Taxation' *Canada and Its Provinces* Vol. XVII. Edited by Adam Shortt and A.G. Doughty. Toronto: Glasgow, Brook, and Co. 1914-17
- 'General Sketch of the Economical Resources, Trade and Population' *Handbook of Canada* Toronto: British Association for the Advancement of Science 1897
- 'Goldwin Smith' *Maclean's Magazine* XXXIV 5 (1921)
- 'Labour and Politics in England' *Political Science Quarterly* X 3 (1895)
- 'Notes on an Expedition to the Estuary of the Mackenzie River' *University of Toronto Monthly* VII 7 (1907)
- 'Portrait of a Lady' *Canadian Forum* I 4 (1921)
- 'Recent Financial Movements in the United States' *Economic Journal* XIV (June 1904)
- 'Setting the Poor on Work' *Nineteenth Century* XXXIV, no. CC (1893)
- 'The Art of the United States' *Canadian Forum* I 5 (1921)
- 'The Awakening of China' *University of Toronto Monthly* VIII 8 (1908)
- 'The Economic Results of the Specialist Production and Marketing of Wheat' *Political Science Quarterly* XXVI 4 (1911)

- 'The English Railway Rates Question' *Quarterly Journal of Economics* VIII 3 & 4 (1894)
- 'The Eskimo of the Mackenzie River District' *University of Toronto Monthly* XII 2 (1911)
- 'The "Intelligentsia" and the Revolution' *University Magazine* XII 2 (1913)
- 'The New Crusade' *Universal Review* VIII (Sept.-Dec. 1890)
- 'The Portrait of Dr Witt van der Smissen' *University of Toronto Monthly* XIV 8 (1914)
- 'The Relation of Economic Study to Public and Private Charity' *Annals of the American Academy of Political and Social Science* IV (July 1893)
- 'The Russo-Japanese War' *Empire Club Speeches 1903-04* Toronto: William Briggs 1904
- 'The Shakespeare Playhouse' *University of Toronto Monthly* VI 3 (1906)
- 'The Situation in the Far East' *Addresses Delivered before the Canadian Club of Ottawa, 1910* Ottawa: Mortimer Press 1911
- 'Two Portraits of Dr James Loudon' *University of Toronto Monthly* XII 1 (1911)
- 'Van Horne and His Sense of Humour' *Maclean's Magazine* XXXVI 22 (1923)
Munro, William B. 'The Church and the Social Crisis' *University Magazine* VIII 2 (1909)
Parkin, George R. 'Victoria and the Victorian Age' *Canadian Magazine* XVI 5 (1901)
Peterson, Sir William 'The Earliest Universities and the Latest' *McGill University Magazine* V 1 (1905)
- 'True Imperialism' *McGill University Magazine* IX 4 (1910)
- 'University Interests' *McGill University Magazine* I 1 (1901)
Scott, E.F. 'The Effects of the War on Literature and Learning' *Queen's Quarterly* XXVII 2 (1919)
Scott, Walter 'The Place of Classics in Education' *McGill University Magazine* V 1 (1905)
Selby, C.W. 'Worry — The Disease of the Age' *Canadian Magazine* XXIX 2 (1907)
Shortt, Adam 'Aims of the Political Science Association' *Proceedings of the Canadian Political Science Association* 1 (1913)
- 'A Personality in Journalism' *Canadian Magazine* XXIX 6 (1907)
- 'Britain's Treatment of Canada' *Addresses Delivered before the Canadian Club of Toronto, 1913-14* Toronto: Warwick Bros & Rutter 1914
- 'Canada and Mr Chamberlain' *Canadian Magazine* XXII 2 (1903)
- 'Canada's Industrial and Economic Growth' *Addresses Delivered before the Canadian Club of Toronto, 1927-28* Toronto: Warwick Bros & Rutter 1928

- 'Commerce, Tariffs and Transportation' *Encyclopedia Americana* Edited by F.C. Beach. New York: Scientific American 1911
- 'Co-operation' *Queen's Quarterly* v 2 (1897)
- 'Current Events' *Queen's Quarterly* I 2 (1893). Also in the following: I 3 (1894); II 1 (1894); VI 1 (1898); VI 2 (1898); VI 3 (1899); VI 4 (1899); IX 2 (1901); IX 3 (1902); IX 4 (1902); X 1 (1902); X 2 (1902); X 3 (1903); X 4 (1903); XI 2 (1903); XII 1 (1904); XI 3 (1905); XIII 1 (1905); XIII 2 (1905)
- 'Early Economic Effects of the European War upon Canada' *Preliminary Economic Studies of the War* Edited by David Kinley. New York: Oxford University Press 1918
- 'Economic Effect of the War of 1812 on Upper Canada' Ontario Historical Society *Papers and Proceedings* Vol. x. Toronto 1913
- 'Financing after the War Industry' *Monetary Times Annual* (January 1919)
- 'Founders of Canadian Banking' *Journal of the Canadian Bankers' Association* XXIX (1921) to XXXII (1924)
- 'History of Canadian Currency' *Journal of the Canadian Bankers' Association* v (1897) to XII (1905)
- 'In Defence of Millionaires' *Canadian Magazine* XIII 6 (1899)
- 'Labour and Capital and the Cost of Living' *Industrial Canada* (February 1910)
- 'Legislation and Morality' *Queen's Quarterly* VIII 4 (1901)
- 'Money and Banks' *Addresses Delivered before the Canadian Club of Ottawa, 1912-13* Ottawa: Mortimer Press 1913
- 'Municipal Government in Ontario: An Historical Sketch' *University of Toronto Studies* II 2 (1897)
- 'Municipal Taxation in Relation to Speculative Land Values' *Annals of the American Academy of Political and Social Science* LVIII (1915)
- 'Personality as a Social Factor' *Clarkson Bulletin* VI 3 (1909)
- 'Phases of Democracy since the War' *Empire Club Speeches, 1926* Toronto: Hunter Rose 1927
- 'Preferential Trade between Britain and Canada' American Economic Association *Papers and Proceedings of the Seventeenth Annual Meeting* (December 1904)
- 'Principal Grant' *Queen's Quarterly* X 1 (1901)
- 'Railroad Construction and National Prosperity: An Historic Parallel' *Proceedings and Transactions of the Royal Society of Canada* Series III, VIII (1914)
- 'Random Recollections of Queen's' *Queen's Quarterly* I, XXVII 4 (1920) and II, XXVIII 2 (1920)

- 'Recent Phases of Socialism' *Queen's Quarterly* v 1 (1897)
- 'Reflections on the University Monopoly' *Queen's Quarterly* VIII 3 (1901)
- 'Should We Revise the Constitution of Queen's?' *Queen's Quarterly* VIII 2 (1900)
- 'Social Evolution According to Mr Kidd' *Queen's Quarterly* II 4 (1895)
- 'Some Aspects of the Imperial Problem' *Canadian Magazine* XVIII 4 (1902)
- 'Some Aspects of the Social Life of Canada' *Canadian Magazine* XI 1 (1898)
- 'Some Observations on the Great North-West' *Queen's Quarterly* II 3 (1895) and III 1 (1895)
- 'Some New Books in Political Science' *Queen's Quarterly* I 3 (1894)
- 'Taxation of Corporation' *Addresses Delivered before the Canadian Club of Toronto, 1905-06* Toronto: Warwick Bros & Rutter 1906
- 'The Basis of Economic Value' *Queen's Quarterly* II 1 (1894)
- 'The Canadian Civil Service' *Addresses Delivered before the Canadian Club of Toronto, 1908-09* Toronto: Warwick Bros & Rutter 1909
- 'The Colonial Conference and Its Functions' *Queen's Quarterly* XIV 4 (1907)
- 'The Educational Value from a National Point of View of the Canadian Archives' Dominion Educational Association *Minutes of Proceedings, 1907* Toronto 1907
- 'The Economic Effects of the War upon Canada' *Proceedings and Transactions of the Royal Society of Canada* Series III, X (1916)
- 'The Incorporation of Trade Unions' *Canadian Magazine* XX 4 (1903)
- 'The Nature and Sphere of Political Science' *Queen's Quarterly* I 2 (1893)
- 'The Nicaragua Canal and the Clayton-Buliver Treaty' *Canadian Magazine* XII 5 (1899)
- 'The Relation between the Legislative and Executive Branches of the Canadian Government' *American Political Science Review* VII 2 (1913)
- 'The Significance for Canadian History of the Work of the Board of Historical Publications' *Proceedings and Transactions of the Royal Society of Canada* Series III, XIII (1919)
- 'The Significance of Locarno' *Dalhousie Review* v 4 (1925)
- 'The Social and Economic Significance of the Movement from the Country to the City' *Addresses Delivered before the Canadian Club of Montreal, 1912-13* Montreal, nd

Shortt, Elizabeth 'The Women's Medical College' *Queen's Review* III 3, 4, & 5 (1929)

Spicer, Anne H. 'The Settlement Spirit' *University Magazine* XII 2 (1913)

Squair, John 'The Admission of Women to the University of Toronto' *University of Toronto Monthly* XXIV 5 (1924)

Stamp, Sir Josiah 'Democracy and Economic Affairs' *University of Toronto Quarterly* II 4 (1933)

Stevenson, Lionel 'Canadian Poetry and the New Universe' *Queen's Quarterly* XXXIII 2 (1925)

Taylor, R.B. 'Academic Freedom' *Queen's Quarterly* XXX 1 (1919)

— 'Inaugural Address' *Queen's Quarterly* XXXIII 1 (1919)

Taylor, W.R. 'Freedom and Contemporary Thought' *University of Toronto Quarterly* X 4 (1939-40)

Trant, William 'The Treatment of Criminals' *University Magazine* VII 4 (1908)

Wallace, M.M. and A.S.P. Woodhouse 'In Memoriam: William John Alexander' *University of Toronto Monthly* XIV 1 (1944)

Watson, John 'Democracy and the Universities' *Queen's Quarterly* XXXIII 3 (1926)

— 'The Idealism of Edward Caird' *Philosophical Review* XVIII 2 & 3 (1909)

— 'Thirty Years in the History of Queen's University' *Queen's Quarterly* X 2 (1902)

'Westerner, A' 'Imperialism, Nationalism or a Third Alternative' *University Magazine* IX 3 (1910)

'Workers' Educational Association' *University of Toronto Monthly* XXIV 4 (1924)

Wrong, George M. 'Canadian Nationalism and the Imperial Tie' *University of Toronto Monthly* X 4 (1910)

Miscellaneous Newspaper and Periodical Articles

Canadian Medical Association Journal Article on Sir Andrew Macphail by 'H.E.M.' XXXIV 5 (1939)

— Obituary for Sir Andrew Macphail XXXIV 5 (1939)

Grain Growers' Guide Article on Adam Shortt (6 March 1912)

— Article on Sir Andrew Macphail (21 February 1912)

Halifax *Herald* Obituary for Archibald MacMechan (8 August 1933)

Journal of the Canadian Bankers' Association Obituary for Adam Shortt XXXVIII 3 (1931)

— Obituary for James Mavor XXXIII 2 (1926)

Montreal *Gazette* Obituary for Sir Andrew Macphail (24 September 1938)

Montreal *Star* Obituary for Sir Andrew Macphail (24 September 1938)

Queen's Review Obituary for Adam Shortt V (1931)

— Obituary for James Cappon XIII 7 (1939)

Queen's University Journal 'A Queen's Professor in Toronto' Reprint from *Saturday Night* XXV 11 (1898)

Saturday Night Obituary for Sir Andrew Macphail LII 48 (1938)
The Presbyterian 'The Late John MacMechan' (January 1903)
Toronto *Daily Mail and Empire* Article on Sir Andrew Macphail (25 February 1932)
Toronto *Daily Star* Obituary for James Mavor (2 November 1925)
– Obituary for Maurice Hutton (6 April 1940)
Toronto *Globe* Obituary for Maurice Hutton (6 April 1940)
University of Toronto Monthly Article on James Mavor's retirement XXIV 1 (1924)

SECONDARY SOURCES

Books
Alexander, Ian W. *Bergson: Philosophy of Reflection* London: Bowes & Bowes, nd
Allen, Frederick Lewis *Only Yesterday* New York: Harper and Bros 1931
– *The Big Change, 1900-1950* New York: Bantam Books 1962
Allen, Richard *The Social Passion: Religion and Social Reform in Canada, 1914-1928* Toronto: University of Toronto Press 1971
Allot, Kenneth *Matthew Arnold* London: Longmans, Green & Co. 1955
Ashley, Anne *William Ashley: A Life* London: P.S. King & Son 1932
Arnot, R. Page *William Morris* London: Lawrence & Wishart 1964
Berger, Carl *The Sense of Power: Studies in the Ideas of Canadian Imperialism, 1867-1914* Toronto: University of Toronto Press 1970
Bernard, L.L. and Jessie Bernard *Origins of American Sociology: The Social Science Movement in the United States* New York: Russell & Russell 1965
Boller, Paul F. *American Thought in Transition: The Impact of Evolutionary Naturalism, 1865-1900* Chicago: Rand McNally & Co. 1969
Bowker, Alan, ed. *The Social Criticism of Stephen Leacock: The Unsolved Riddle of Social Justice and Other Essays* Toronto: University of Toronto Press 1973
Brehier, Emile *The History of Philosophy: The Nineteenth Century: Period of Systems, 1850-1900* Translated by Wade Baskin. Chicago: University of Chicago Press 1968
Brinton, Crane *English Political Thought in the Nineteenth Century* New York: Harper & Row 1965 [1933]
– *The Political Ideas of the English Romanticists* New Yorker: Harper & Row 1962 [1926]
Brooke, Michael A. *Le Play: Engineer and Social Scientist* London: Longman 1970
Buckley, Jerome H. *The Victorian Temper* Cambridge: Harvard University Press 1951

Calvin, D.D. *Queen's University at Kingston, 1841-1948* Kingston: Queen's University 1941

Caponigri, A. Robert *A History of Western Philosophy: Philosophy from the Romantic Age to the Age of Positivism* Notre Dame: University of Notre Dame Press 1971

Chalmers, David *The Social and Political Ideas of the Muckrakers* New York: Citadel Press 1964

Chandler, Alice *A Dream of Order: The Medieval Ideal in Nineteenth-Century English Literature* Lincoln: University of Nebraska Press 1970

Chapman, Raymond *The Victorian Debate: English Literature and Society, 1832-1901* London: Weidenfeld and Nicolson 1968

Chapple, J.A.V. *Documentary and Imaginative Literature, 1880-1920* London: Blandford Press 1970

Clark, S.D. *The Canadian Manufacturers' Association* Toronto: University of Toronto Press 1939

Cobban, Alfred *Edmund Burke and the Revolt against the Eighteenth Century* New York: Macmillan Co. 1929

Cook, Ramsay *Canada and the French-Canadian Question* Toronto: Macmillan Co. 1966

Copleston, Frederick *A History of Philosophy* Vol. VIII London: Burns and Oates 1966

Coutts, James *A History of the University of Glasgow* Glasgow: James Maclehose & Sons 1909

Crowther, J.G. *British Scientists of the Nineteenth Century* London: Routledge and Kegan Paul Ltd. 1935

Crysdale, Stewart *The Industrial Struggle and Protestant Ethics in Canada* Toronto: Ryerson Press 1961

Dewar, David *Queen's Profiles* Kingston: Queen's University 1951

Diamond, Sigmund *The Reputation of American Businessmen* New York: Harper & Row 1966

Ellery, John B. *John Stuart Mill* New York: Twayne Publishers 1964

Eshleman, Lloyd W. *A Victorian Rebel: The Life of William Morris* New York: Charles Scribner's Sons 1940

Ferns, H.S. and B. Ostry *The Age of Mackenzie King: The Rise of the Leader* London: Heinemann 1955

Fetherstonhaugh, Robert C. *McGill University at War* Montreal: McGill University 1947

Frye, Northrop, ed. *Romanticism Reconsidered* New York: Columbia University Press 1963

Furst, Lilian R. *Romanticism in Perspective* London: Macmillan Co. 1969

Gallagher, Idella J. *Morality in Evolution: The Moral Philosophy of Henri Berg-son* The Hague: Martinus Nijhoff 1970

Glazier, J. Bruce *William Morris and the Early Days of the Socialist Movement* London: Longmans, Green & Co. 1921

Gleckner, Robert F. and Gerald E. Enscoe, eds *Romanticism: Points of View* 2nd ed. Englewood Cliffs, NJ: Prentice-Hall 1970

Goldman, Eric *Rendez-Vous with Destiny* New York: A.A. Knopf 1952

Gordon, Wilhelmina *Daniel M. Gordon: His Life* Toronto: Ryerson Press 1941

Grant, George *Lament for a Nation* Toronto: McClelland & Stewart 1965

Grant, W.L. and C.F. Hamilton *Principal Grant* Toronto: Morang & Co. 1904

Griese, William F. *Sainte-Beuve: A Literary Portrait* Madison: University of Wisconsin Studies in Language and Literature, no. 31, 1931

Hamburger, Joseph *Intellectuals in Politics: John Stuart Mill and the Philosophic Radicals* New Haven and London: Yale University Press 1965

Heller, Otto *Prophets of Dissent* New York: A.A. Knopf 1918

Henderson, Philip *William Morris* London: Longmans, Green & Co. 1952

– *William Morris: His Life, Work and Friends* London: Thames and Hudson 1967

Herbertson, Dorothy *The Life of Frederic Le Play* Ledbury, Herefordshire: Le Play House 1950

Himmelfarb, Gertrude *Victorian Minds* New York: Harper & Row 1970 [1952]

Hodgetts, J.E., William McCloskey, Reginald Whitaker, and V. Seymour Wilson *The Biography of an Institution: The Civil Service Commission of Canada, 1908-1967* Montreal: McGill-Queen's University Press 1972

Hofstadter, Richard *Anti-Intellectualism in American Life* New York: Vintage Books 1963

– *Social Darwinism in American Thought* 1st rev. ed. Boston: Beacon Press 1967

– *The Age of Reform* New York: Vintage Books 1955

Hogben, John *Richard Holt Hutton of the Spectator* Edinburgh: Oliver & Boyd 1899

Hole, William *Quasi Cursores: Portraits of the High Officers and Professors of the University of Edinburgh at Its Tercentenary Festival* Edinburgh: T & A Constable 1884

Hollis, Christopher *G.K. Chesterton* London: Longmans, Green & Co. 1950

– *The Mind of Chesterton* London: Hollis & Carter 1970

Horowitz, Gad *Canadian Labour in Politics* Toronto: University of Toronto Press 1968

Houghton, Walter *The Victorian Frame of Mind, 1830-1870* New Haven & London: Yale University Press 1957

Hughes, H. Stuart *Consciousness and Society: The Reconstruction of European Social Thought, 1890-1930* New York: Vintage Books 1961

Hulse, James N. *Revolutionists in London: A Study of Five Unorthodox Socialists* Oxford: Clarendon Press 1970

Hynes, Samuel *The Edwardian Turn of Mind* Princeton: Princeton University Press 1968

Ideas and Beliefs of the Victorians New York: E.P. Dutton & Co. 1966

Jaher, Frederic C. *Doubters and Dissenters: Cataclysmic Thought in America, 1885-1918* New York: Free Press of Glencoe 1964

Jones, Sir Henry and John Henry Muirhead *The Life and Philosophy of Edward Caird* Glasgow: Maclehose, Jackson & Co. 1921

Kennedy, D.R. *The Knights of Labour in Canada* London: University of Western Ontario 1956

King, Agnes Gardner *Kelvin the Man* London: Houghton & Stoddard 1925

Kolakowski, Leszek *The Alienation of Reason: A History of Positivist Thought* Translated by Norbert Guterman. Garden City NY: Doubleday & Co. 1968

Lamprecht, Sterling P. *Our Philosophical Traditions* New York: Appleton-Century Crofts 1955

Lasch, Christopher *The New Radicalism in America, 1889-1963: The Intellectual as a Social Type* New York: A.A. Knopf 1965

Lester, John A. *Journey through Despair, 1880-1914: Transformation in British Literary Culture* Princeton University Press 1968

Levine, Daniel *Varieties of Reform Thought* Madison: Wisconsin Historical Society 1964

Levine, Richard A., ed. *Background to Victorian Literature* San Francisco: Chandler Publishing Co. 1967

Logan, Harold A. *Trade Unions in Canada* Toronto: Macmillan Co. 1948

McCloskey, Robert G. *American Conservatism in the Age of Enterprise, 1865-1910* New York: Harper & Row 1964

Macdonald, D.K.C. *Faraday, Maxwell, and Kelvin* Garden City, NY: Doubleday Co. 1964

Macmillan, Cyrus *McGill and Its Story, 1821-1921* Toronto: Oxford University Press 1921

Mairet, Philip *Pioneer of Sociology: The Life and Letters of Patrick Geddes* London: Lund Humphries 1957

Mann, Arthur *Yankee Reformers in an Urban Age* Cambridge: Harvard University Press 1954

Marpell, William H. *Man Made Morals: Four Philosophies that Shaped America* Garden City, NY: Doubleday & Co. 1968

Marx, Leo *The Machine in the Garden: Technology and the Pastoral Ideal in America* New York: Oxford University Press 1964

May, Henry F. *The End of American Innocence: A Study of the First Years of Our Own Time, 1912-1917* New York: A.A. Knopf 1959

Morgan, H.J., ed. *Canadian Men and Women of the Time* 2nd ed. Toronto: William Briggs 1912

Morris, Lloyd *Postscript to Yesterday: American Life and Thought, 1896-1946* New York: Random House 1947

Morton, W.L., ed. *The Shield of Achilles: Aspects of Canada in the Victorian Age* Toronto: McClelland & Stewart 1968

Mowry, George *The California Progressives* Los Angeles: University of California Press 1951

Murray, David *Memories of the Old College of Glasgow* Glasgow: Jackson, Wylie and Co. 1927

Nash, Roderick *The Nervous Generation: American Thought, 1917-1930* Chicago: Rand McNally & Co. 1970

Nicolson, Harold *Sainte-Beuve* Garden City, NY: Doubleday & Co., nd

Noble, David *The Progressive Mind, 1890-1917* Chicago: Rand McNally & Co. 1970

O'Connor, Michael J.L. *Origins of Academic Economics in the United States* New York: Columbia University Press 1944

Parker, C.W., ed. *Who's Who and Why* Toronto: International Press 1914

Parkin, Charles *The Moral Basis of Burke's Political Thought* Cambridge: Cambridge University Press 1956

Peckham, Morse *Victorian Revolutionaries: Speculations on Some Heroes of a Culture Crisis* New York: George Braziller 1970

Perelman, C.H. *An Introduction to Philosophical Thinking* Translated by Kenneth A. Brown. New York: Random House 1965

Pfautz, Harold W., ed. *Charles Booth* Chicago: University of Chicago Press 1967

Queen's University: A Centenary Volume, 1841-1941 Toronto: Ryerson Press 1941

Reeves, James *A Short History of English Poetry, 1340-1940* New York: E.P. Dutton & Co. 1964

Robin, Martin *Radical Politics and Canadian Labour, 1880-1930* Kingston: Queen's University 1968

Rokeache, Milton *Beliefs, Attitudes, and Values: A Theory of Organization and Change* San Francisco 1969

Rolland, Romain *Tolstoi* Translated by Bernard Miall. New York: Garland Publishing Co. 1972 [1911]

Sabine, George H. *A History of Political Theory* 3rd ed. New York: Holt Rinehart & Winston 1961

Schenk, H.G. *The Mind of the European Romantics* London: Constable 1966

Semmel, Bernard *Imperialism and Social Reform: English Social-Imperial Thought, 1895-1914* London: George Allen & Unwin 1960

Simon, W.H. *European Positivism in the Nineteenth Century* Ithaca: Cornell University Press 1963

Splane, Richard B. *Social Welfare in Ontario, 1791-1893: A Study of Public Welfare Administration* Toronto: University of Toronto Press 1965

Stumpf, Samuel Enoch *Philosophy: History and Problems* New York: McGraw-Hill Co. 1971

Sussman, Herbert L. *Victorians and the Machine: The Literary Response to Technology* Cambridge: Harvard University Press 1968

Thornton, A.P. *The Imperial Idea and Its Enemies* Garden City, NY: Doubleday & Co. 1968

Turner, A. Logan, ed. *History of the University of Edinburgh, 1883-1933* Edinburgh: Oliver & Boyd 1933

Underhill, Frank H. *In Search of Canadian Liberalism* Toronto: Macmillan Co. of Canada 1961

– *The Image of Confederation* Toronto: Canadian Broadcasting Corp. 1964

Utley, T.E. *Edmund Burke* London: Longmans, Green & Co. 1957

Veysey, Laurence R. *The Emergence of the American University* Chicago and London: University of Chicago Press 1965

Wallace, Elisabeth *Goldwin Smith: Victorian Liberal* Toronto: University of Toronto Press 1957

Wallace, R.C. *Some Great Men of Queen's* Toronto: Ryerson Press 1941

Wallace, W.S. *A History of the University of Toronto, 1827-1927* Toronto: University of Toronto Press 1927

Watson, George *The English Ideology: Studies in the Language of Victorian Politics* London: Allen Lane 1973

White, Lucia and Morton White *The Intellectual versus the City, from Thomas Jefferson to Frank Lloyd Wright* Cambridge: Harvard University Press 1962

White, Morton *Social Thought in America: The Revolt against Formalism* Boston: Beacon Press 1957

– *The Age of Analysis* New York: Mentor Books 1955

Wiebe, Robert A. *The Search for Order* New York: Hill and Wang 1967

Wiley, Basil *Nineteenth Century Studies: Coleridge to Matthew Arnold* London: Chatto and Windus 1949

Wilkins, Burleigh Taylor *The Problem of Burke's Political Philosophy* Oxford: Clarendon Press 1967

Wills, Gerry *Chesterton: Man and Mask* New York: Sheed and Ward 1961

Wilson, R. Jackson *In Quest of Community: Social Philosophy in the United States, 1860-1920* New York: John Wiley and Sons 1968

Wise, S.F. and R.C. Brown *Canada Views the United States* Seattle: University of Washington Press 1967

Woodcock, George and Ivan Avakumović *The Anarchist Prince: A Biographical Study of Peter Kropotkin* New York: Schocken Books 1971

Articles

Allen, Richard 'The Social Gospel and the Reform Tradition in Canada, 1890-1928' *Canadian Historical Review* XLIX 4 (1968)

Bennet, C.L. 'Dr Archibald MacMechan' *The Alumni News, Dalhousie University* XIX 3 (1962)

Berger, Carl 'Race and Liberty: The Historical Ideas of John George Bourinot' *Canadian Historical Association Annual Report* (1965)

– 'The True North Strong and Free' *Nationalism in Canada* Edited by Peter Russell. Toronto: McGraw-Hill Co. 1966

Bissell, Claude T. 'Literary Taste in Central Canada during the Late Nineteenth Century' *Canadian Historical Review* XXXI 3 (1950)

Bliss, Michael 'The Methodist Church and World War I' *Canadian Historical Review* XLIX 3 (1968)

– 'The Protective Impulse: An Approach to the Social History of Oliver Mowat's Ontario' *Oliver Mowat's Ontario* Edited by Donald Swainson. Toronto: Macmillan Co. of Canada 1972

Careless, J.M.S. 'Mid-Victorian Liberalism in Central Canadian Newspapers' *Canadian Historical Review* XXXI 3 (1950)

Church, Alfred J. 'Richard Holt Hutton' *Memories of Men and Books* London: Smith, Elder & Co. 1908

Cole, Douglas 'Canada's "Nationalist" Imperialists' *Journal of Canadian Studies* V 3 (1970)

– 'John S. Ewart and Canadian Nationalism' *Canadian Historical Association Annual Report* (1969)

Collard, E.A. 'Voice from the Past' *McGill News* LIII 5 (November 1972)

Cook, Ramsay 'John W. Dafoe: Conservative Progressive' *Canadian Historical Association Annual Report* (1961)

– 'Stephen Leacock and the Age of Plutocracy' *Character and Circumstance* Edited by John S. Moir. Toronto: Macmillan Co. of Canada 1970

Creighton, Donald G. 'John A. Macdonald' *Our Living Tradition* First Series. Edited by Claude Bissell. Toronto: University of Toronto Press 1957

Donnelly, M.S. 'J.W. Dafoe' *Our Living Tradition* Fourth Series. Edited by R.L. McDougall. Toronto: University of Toronto Press 1962

Eayrs, James 'The Round Table Movement in Canada, 1909-1920' *Canadian Historical Review* XXXVIII 3 (1957)

Edgar, Pelham 'James Mavor' *Proceedings and Transactions of the Royal Society of Canada* Series III, XX (1926)

— 'Sir Andrew Macphail, 1864-1938' *Proceedings and Transactions of the Royal Society of Canada* Series III, XXXIII (1938)

— 'Sir Andrew Macphail' *Queen's Quarterly* LIV 1 (1947)

Eggleston, Wilfrid 'The Dream of "Geordie" Grant' *Queen's Quarterly* LX 4 (1954)

Falconer, Sir Robert A. 'Maurice Hutton' *Proceedings and Transactions of the Royal Society of Canada* Series III, XXXIV (1940)

Frye, Northrop 'Conclusion' *Literary History of Canada.* Carl F. Klinck et al., eds. Toronto: University of Toronto Press 1965

Geddes, Patrick 'A Full Life: James Mavor's' *M & C Apprentices' Magazine* IX 36 (1925)

Goudge, T.A. 'A Century of Philosophy in English-Speaking Canada' *Dalhousie Review* XLVII (1967-8)

Harvey, D.C. 'Archibald McKellar MacMechan' *Proceedings and Transactions of the Royal Society of Canada* Series III, XXVIII (1934)

— 'Notes and Comments' *Canadian Historical Review* XIV 3 (1933)

Haydon, Andrew 'Adam Shortt' *Queen's Quarterly* XXXVIII 1 (1931)

— 'The Makers of Queen's: Adam Shortt, CMG, LLD' *Queen's Review* II 6 (1928)

Horn, Michiel 'Visionaries of the 1930's: The League for Social Reconstruction' *Visions 2020* Edited by Stephen Clarkson. Edmonton: Hurtig 1970

Hutton, Maurice, 'James Mavor' *University of Toronto Monthly* XXVI 3 (1925)

Irving, John A. 'The Achievement of George Sidney Brett, (1879-1944)' *University of Toronto Quarterly* XIV 4 (1945)

— 'The Development of Philosophy in Central Canada from 1850 to 1900' *Canadian Historical Review* XXXI 3 (1950)

Jordan, G.H.S. 'Popular Literature and Imperial Sentiment' *Canadian Historical Association Annual Report* (1967)

Keys, D.R. 'Principal Maurice Hutton' *University of Toronto Monthly* XXVIII 9 (1928)

Leacock, Stephen 'Andrew Macphail' *Queen's Quarterly* XLV 4 (1938)

LeRoy, Gaylord C. 'Richard Holt Hutton' *Publications of the Modern Language Association* LVI 3 (1941)

Levitt, Joseph 'Henri Bourassa and Modern Industrial Society' *Canadian Historical Review* L 1 (1969)

Loewenburg, Bert 'The Controversey over Evolution in New England, 1859-73' *New England Quarterly* VIII 2 (1935)

Lovejoy, Arthur O. 'The Meaning of Romanticism for the Historian of Ideas' *Journal of the History of Ideas* II 3 (1941)

Lower, A.R.M. 'Adam Shortt, Founder' *Historic Kingston* Kingston Historical Society. No. 17 (1968)

McKenzie, Ruth 'Life in a New Land: Notes on the Immigrant Theme in Canadian Fiction' *Canadian Literature* 7 (1961)

Mackerness, E.D. 'Richard Holt Hutton and the Victorian Lay Sermon' *Dalhousie Review* XXXVII 3 (1957)

Mackintosh, W.A. 'Adam Shortt' *Some Great Men of Queen's* Edited by R.C. Wallace. Toronto: Ryerson Press 1941

— 'Adam Shortt, 1859-1931' *Canadian Journal of Economics and Political Science* IV 2 (1938)

— 'O.D. Skelton' *Our Living Tradition* Fifth Series. Edited by R.L. McDougall. Toronto: University of Toronto Press 1965

Maclear, J.F. ' "The Heart of New England Rent": The Mystical Element in Early Puritan History' *Mississippi Valley Historical Review* XLII 4 (1956)

MacMechan, Archibald 'Andrew Macphail' *The Warner Library: The World's Best Literature* Vol. XVII. Edited by J.W. Cunliffe and A.H. Thorndike. New York: Warner Library Co. 1917

McNeill, W.E. 'James Cappon' *Some Great Men of Queen's* Edited by R.C. Wallace. Toronto: Ryerson Press 1940

— 'James Cappon, 1854-1939' *Proceedings and Transactions of the Royal Society of Canada* Series III, XXXIV (1940)

— 'John Watson' *Proceedings and Transactions of the Royal Society of Canada* Series III, XXXIII (1939)

Magney, W.H. 'The Methodist Church and the National Gospel' *The Bulletin* Committee on Archives of the United Church of Canada. No. XX (1968)

Martin, C.F. 'Andrew Macphail' *Canadian Medical Association Journal* XXXIV 5 (1938)

Neatby, H. Blair 'Politics: The Opiate of the 1930's' *Canadian Forum* L 591, 592 (1970)

Neill, R.F. 'Adam Shortt: A Bibliographical Comment' *Journal of Canadian Studies* II 1 (1967)

Ostry, Bernard 'Conservatives, Liberals, and Labour in the 1880's' *Canadian Journal of Economics and Political Science* XXVII 2 (1961)

Pacey, Desmond 'Sir Charles G.D. Roberts' *Our Living Tradition* Fourth Series. Edited by R.L. McDougall. Toronto: University of Toronto Press 1965

Page, R.J.D. 'Canada and the Imperial Idea in the Boer War Year's *Journal of Canadian Studies* V 1 (1970)

— 'Carl Berger and the Intellectual Origins of Canadian Imperial Thought, 1867-1914' *Journal of Canadian Studies* V 3 (1970)

Penfield, Wilder 'Sir William Osler' *Our Living Tradition* Fifth Series. Edited by R.L. McDougall. Toronto: University of Toronto Press 1965

Persons, Stow 'The Cyclical Theory of History in Eighteenth Century America' *American Quarterly* VI (Summer 1954)

Pierce, Lorne 'The Makers of Queen's: James Cappon, MA, LLD, FRSC' *Queen's Review* III 6 (1929)

Quigley, Carroll 'The Round Table Group in Canada, 1908-1938' *Canadian Historical Review* XLIII 3 (1962)

Reade, R.C. 'Professor Hutton and the Greek View of Life' *University of Toronto Monthly* XXVI 5 (1925)

Ross, Malcolm 'Goldwin Smith' *Our Living Tradition* First Series. Edited by Claude Bissell. Toronto: University of Toronto Press 1957

Sedgewick, G.G. 'A.M.' *Dalhousie Review* XIII 4 (1933)

Sherman, Richard B. 'The Status Revolution and Massachusetts Progressive Leadership' *Political Science Quarterly* LXXVIII (March 1963)

Shortt, S.E.D. 'Social Change and Political Crisis in Rural Ontario: The Patrons of Industry, 1889-1896' *Oliver Mowat's Ontario* Edited by Donald Swainson. Toronto: Macmillan Co. of Canada 1972

Skelton, O.D. 'Adam Shortt' *Proceedings and Transactions of the Royal Society of Canada* Series III, XXV (1931)

Smith, Allan 'Metaphor and Nationality in North America' *Canadian Historical Review* LI 3 (1970)

Stevenson, J.A. 'Sir Andrew Macphail' *Canadian Defence Quarterly* XVI 2 (1939)

Sutherland, Ronald 'The Body-Odour of Race' *Canadian Literature* 37 (1968)

Taylor, K.W. 'The Founding of the Canadian Political Science Association' *Canadian Journal of Economics and Political Science* XXXIII 4 (1967)

Thomas, Clara 'Happily Ever After: Canadian Women in Fiction and Fact' *Canadian Literature* 34 (1967)

Thompson, J. Lee and John H. Thompson, 'Ralph Connor and the Canadian Identity' *Queen's Quarterly* LXXIX 2 (1972)

Wade, Mason 'Olivar Asselin' *Our Living Tradition* Fifth Series. Edited by R.L. McDougall. Toronto: University of Toronto Press 1965

Wallace, Elisabeth 'Goldwin Smith and Social Reform' *Canadian Historical Review* XXIX 4 1948

Wallace, Malcolm 'Principal Maurice Hutton' *University of Toronto Monthly* XL 7 (1940)

Wallace, W.S. 'The Life and Work of George M. Wrong' *Canadian Historical Review* XXIX 3 (1948)

Watt, F.W. 'Climate of Unrest' *Canadian Literature* 12 (1962)

– 'Critic or Entertainer? Stephen Leacock and the Growth of Materialism'
   Canadian Literature 5 (1960)
– 'Peter McArthur and the Agrarian Myth' *Queen's Quarterly* LXVII 2 (1960)
– 'The National Policy, the Workingman and Proletarian Ideas in Victorian
   Canada' *Canadian Historical Review* XL 1 (1959)
– 'The Theme of "Canada's Century" ' *Dalhousie Review* XXXVIII 2 (1958)
Whittaker, Herbert 'Dora Mavor Moore: Zeal and Achievement Earn Tribute for
   Toronto Theatre's Great Lady' Toronto *Globe and Mail* (20 November 1971)
Ziffren, Abbie 'Biography of Patrick Geddes' *Patrick Geddes: Spokesman for
   Man and Environment* Edited by Marshall Stalley. New Brunswick, NJ:
   Rutgers University Press 1972

Index